Criminal Justice in New York

THIRD EDITION

ELLEN G. COHN
Florida International University

Upper Saddle River, New Jersey 07458

Executive Editor: Frank Mortimer, Jr.
Assistant Editor: Sara Holle
Production Editor: Barbara Cappuccio
Director of Manufacturing and Production: Bruce Johnson
Managing Editor: Mary Carnis
Manufacturing Buyer: Cathleen Petersen
Creative Director: Cheryl Asherman
Cover Design Coordinator: Miguel Ortiz
Cover Design: Denise Brown
Cover Image: Day Williams/Photo Researchers, Inc.

Copyright © 2005 by Pearson Education, Inc., Upper Saddle River, New Jersey, 07458.
Pearson Prentice Hall. All rights reserved. Printed in the United States of America. This publication is protected by Copyright and permission should be obtained from the publisher prior to any prohibited reproduction, storage in a retrieval system, or transmission in any form or by any means, electronic, mechanical, photocopying, recording, or likewise. For information regarding permission(s), write to: Rights and Permissions Department.

Pearson Prentice Hall™ is a trademark of Pearson Education, Inc.
Pearson® is a registered trademark of Pearson plc
Prentice Hall® is a registered trademark of Pearson Education, Inc.

Pearson Education LTD.
Pearson Education Singapore, Pte. Ltd
Pearson Education, Canada, Ltd
Pearson Education–Japan
Pearson Education Australia PTY, Limited
Pearson Education North Asia Ltd
Pearson Educaçion de Mexico, S.A. de C.V.
Pearson Education Malaysia, Pte. Ltd

10 9 8 7 6 5 4 3 2
ISBN 0-13-114026-4

CONTENTS

Preface		vi
Chapter 1	**The State of New York**	1
	The History of New York	1
	New York Today	6
	Notes	7
Chapter 2	**Introduction to New York Criminal Law**	9
	The Structure of the Government	9
	The New York State Penal Law	11
	The Definition and Classification of Crime	13
	Defenses to a Criminal Charge	16
	Sources of Information for Legal Research	24
	Notes	26
Chapter 3	**Index Crimes**	29
	Introduction	29
	Criminal Homicide	29
	Forcible Rape	39
	Robbery	44
	Aggravated Assault	47
	Burglary	54
	Larceny-Theft	56
	Motor Vehicle Theft	60
	Arson	61
	Hate Crimes	65
	Notes	67
Chapter 4	**The Police in New York**	71
	Introduction	71
	Local Policing	72
	County Policing	75
	State Policing	79
	Police Training	84
	Notes	85
Chapter 5	**The Court System in New York**	87
	United States Federal Courts	87
	The History of the New York Unified Court System	87
	The Structure of the New York Unified Court System	89
	The New York State Court of Appeals	89

	The New York State Supreme Court	93
	Trial Courts in New York	95
	Other Court Agencies and Commissions	98
	New York Criminal Court Procedures	100
	Notes	112

Chapter 6   **Sentencing in New York**   115
- Introduction   115
- The Sentencing Reform Act of 1995   115
- Jenna's Law   116
- Types of Sentences   117
- When Sentencing Occurs   117
- Restitution, Reparation, and Fines   118
- Concurrent Versus Consecutive Sentences   120
- Sentences of Incarceration   121
- The Rights of the Victim During Sentencing   124
- Notes   128

Chapter 7   **Capital Punishment in New York**   129
- The History of Capital Punishment in New York   129
- Capital Punishment in New York Today   131
- New York's Death Row   134
- Legal Procedures Relating to Executions in New York   135
- Notes   136

Chapter 8   **Corrections in New York**   139
- Introduction   139
- Prisons in New York   139
- Jails in New York   147
- Parole in New York   149
- Probation in New York   152
- Notes   156

Chapter 9   **The Juvenile Justice System in New York**   159
- Introduction   159
- New York Family Court   161
- Sentencing of Juvenile Offenders   165
- The New York City Department of Juvenile Justice   165
- The New York City Department of Probation   168
- Notes   169

Chapter 10   **Drugs and Crime in New York**   171
- Introduction   171
- The Availability of Drugs in New York   171
- The DEA in New York   172
- New York State Office of Alcoholism and Substance Abuse Services   172

	New York City Bureau of Alcoholism and Substance Abuse Services	174
	Drug Courts in New York	174
	Notes	177
Appendix	**Web Sites of Interest**	179

PREFACE

This supplementary text will provide you with specific information on the New York criminal law and the New York criminal justice system. Throughout the text, you will find quotations which have been taken verbatim from legal documents, such as the New York Penal Law and the New York Constitution. Any misspellings or other irregularities are reproduced exactly as they appear in the original documents.

I hope that you enjoy this supplement and find it both interesting and informative. If you have any questions, comments, or suggestions, please feel free to contact me via email.

Ellen G. Cohn, Ph.D.
cohne@fiu.edu

CHAPTER 1

THE STATE OF NEW YORK

New York is located in the Middle Atlantic region of the United States. It is bordered on the north by Ontario and Quebec, on the northwest and west by Lake Ontario and Lake Erie, on the west and south by Pennsylvania, on the east by Connecticut, Massachusetts, and Vermont, and on the south by New Jersey and the Atlantic Ocean. The capital city, New York City, is the largest city in the United States. However, despite being home to such a large urban center, much of the state is still rural in nature. The state fruit is the apple, the state bird is the bluebird, the state flower is the rose, and the state tree is the sugar maple. New York's nickname is the "Empire State."

THE HISTORY OF NEW YORK

The Early History of the Region

New York was originally occupied by a variety of Native American tribes, including two of the largest and most powerful groups. The Algonquian group included the Delaware, Mahican, Montauk, Munsee, and Wappinger tribes. The Iroquois Confederacy or Five Nations group included Cayuga, Mohawk, Oneida, Onondaga, and Seneca tribes. Both groups lived off the land, hunting, fishing, and farming.

The first European to reach New York was probably the Italian explorer Giovanni da Verrazzano. Verrazzano, who was employed by King Francis I of France to explore the northern sections of America, is believed to have sailed into New York and to have reached the Hudson River in approximately 1524. However, he did not explore the area.

In 1609, the English explorer Henry Hudson, who was employed by the Dutch to search for a Northwest Passage to the Orient, sailed up what was later named the Hudson River. Although his search was unsuccessful, he claimed a large territory for the Netherlands. This area, which included most of present-day New York, New Jersey, Delaware, and part of Connecticut, was later named "New Netherland." In the same year, France also established a claim to New York when French explorer Samuel de Champlain discovered what is now Lake Champlain.

European Colonization

After Hudson's voyage, the Dutch sent settlers to the Hudson River Valley and established trading posts and settlements. They developed a profitable fur trade with the Indians living in the area. By the early 1600s, the Iroquois had obtained firearms from the Dutch settlers and conquered all the Indian tribes from the St. Lawrence River to Tennessee and from Maine to Michigan. In 1621, a group of Dutch merchants formed the Dutch West India Company and were given all rights to trade in New Netherland for the next 24 years. In 1624, the Company sent 30 families to settle in the region. Upon their arrival, rather than forming one large colony, they split up into groups. One group founded Fort Orange, the first permanent white settlement in the colony. The city that grew up around Fort Orange later became known as Albany. The other families settled in other parts of the colony.

In 1625, the settlement of New Amsterdam (now New York City) was founded on Manhattan Island by a group of Dutch colonists. The following year, the governor of the settlement, Peter Minuit, obtained Manhattan from the Indians in exchange for goods worth 60 Dutch guilders (approximately $24). Dutch colonists continued to arrive in New Netherland and additional settlements were established in the next few years, including Breuckelen (now Brooklyn), Wiltwyck (now Kingston), Rensselaerswyck (now Rensselaer), and Schenectady.

The Dutch West India Company was eager to increase the speed of settlement of the territory of New Netherland. In 1629, the Company organized the "patroon" or landowner system. Under this system, company members received large tracts of land. However, to keep the land, they had to pay to bring over 50 settlers within the next four years. All settlers had to be at least 15 years old. The patroon, who owned the land, controlled the settlers' lives in many ways; he could give or deny the settlers the right to move, to go into business, even to marry. A total of five patroonships were granted. Only one of these, the manor of Amsterdam diamond merchant Kiliaen Van Rensselaer, lasted into the 1700s. Van Rensselaer's patroonship included much of Columbia, Rensselaer, and Albany counties. Van Rensselaer leased his land to tenant farmers; this tenant system lasted until the mid-1800s when a series of tenant revolts ended the system. The patroon system failed for several reasons. Very few settlers were willing to give up their personal freedom permanently, even in exchange for passage to the new colony. In addition, the company had other settlement policies which undermined the patroon system. For example, the company offered free land in New Netherland to settlers paying their own passage. Eventually, in an attempt to attract more settlers, the company even paid their passage over.

Meanwhile, English colonists from the colonies of Connecticut and Massachusetts had settled on the area of Long Island. At first, the English and Dutch settlers cooperated. Eventually, however, King Charles II of England determined to seize the area for England and gave James, Duke of York, a charter for the territory. In 1664, an English fleet of warships was sent to seize New Amsterdam. They arrived in the harbor of New Amsterdam and the Dutch governor, Peter Stuyvesant, surrendered the settlement without a fight. In 1667, the Dutch signed the Treaty of Breda, formally ceding the entire colony of New Netherland to England. The settlement was renamed New York, after the Duke of York who later became King James II of England.

In 1669, the French developed a renewed interest in the northern part of New York, when the French explorer Rene-Robert Cavelier, Sieur de la Salle, entered the Niagara region of the state. In 1731, a French fortress was constructed at Crown Point on Lake Champlain and the French prepared to take permanent possession of the northern area of New York.

The French and Indian Wars

Between 1689 and 1763, the region was involved in a series of four wars fought between England and France for domination of the colonies in North America. In the United States today, these wars are collectively known as the French and Indian Wars. At this time, England's colonies were located along the Atlantic coast while the French settlements were primarily found further north, along the shores of the Great Lakes and the St. Lawrence River, as well as in the Mississippi River Valley. Both the French and the English traded with the Indians for furs. While England laid claim to all the territory inland of its own colonies, the French also claimed much of this land. The two countries each attempted to control the fur trade as well as the fishing grounds off the coast of Newfoundland. Both also claimed the land between the Appalachian Mountains and the Mississippi River.

As both countries had an interest in New York, battles were fought at forts throughout the colony, including Crown Point, Fort Niagara, and Fort Ticonderoga. The Algonquian Indians provided aid to the French while the Iroquois Indians sided with the English. As a result of these wars, frontier settlement was delayed and previously settled areas did not grow and expand as quickly as expected.

The first of the four wars, which ran from 1689 to 1697, was known as King William's War, after King William III of England. The war began when the English and their Indian allies raided French settlements near Montreal. The French settlers and their Indian allies fought back against New York and the New England colonies. Eventually, the war ended in 1697 with the signing of the Treaty of Ryswick, which returned to England and France all the American land they had lost during the war.

The second war, Queen Anne's War, which ran from 1702 to 1713, was named after Queen Anne of Britain. This war, which began when the French and their Indian supporters raided English settlements in New England, took place primarily in New England, South Carolina, and Florida. As much of Florida was Spanish territory, Spain also became involved in this war. The signing of the Treaty of Utrecht in 1713 ended this war. As a result of the treaty, France turned Newfoundland, the mainland Nova Scotia region of Acadia, and the French territory around Hudson Bay over to Britain. However, as the treaty did not clearly define the boundaries of the land France ceded to Britain, more fighting soon broke out.

King George's War, which was named for King George II of Britain, ran from 1744 to 1748. This was an outgrowth of the War of the Austrian Succession; fighting began in North America when the French attempted to regain possession of Nova Scotia. The war ended with the signing of the Treaty of Aix-la-Chapelle, which returned to France and Britain the territory each had lost during this war.

Finally, the French and Indian War ran from 1754 to 1763. In Europe and Canada, this conflict was known as the Seven Years' War. After the end of King George's War, France and Britain continued to expand their settlements and clash over possession of land. When the Iroquois Indians began to allow British settlement in the Ohio River Valley, the French, fearful of losing the fur trade in the Ohio region, attempted to strengthen their claim to the area by building a chain of forts at the eastern end of the valley, along the Allegheny River in Pennsylvania. However, Virginia, a British colony, also claimed this land and demanded the French abandon the forts and return to Canada. In 1754, the first battle of the war broke out when the French defeated colonial troops, led by then-Major George Washington. The Albany Congress, including representatives of seven British colonies, met in Albany, New York, to plan additional military action against the French. In the first years of this war, the French had several important military successes against the British and colonial soldiers, including the capture of Britain's Fort Oswego in 1756 and the destruction of Fort William Henry in 1757. However, in 1758 the tide turned and the British began to dominate the war. In 1759, the French were severely damaged by the fall of Quebec; in 1760, British troops captured Montreal. The war ended with the signing of the Treaty of Paris in 1763. As a result of this treaty, England gained almost all of France's territorial possessions

New York During and After the American Revolution

New York was of course greatly involved in the Revolutionary War. While it is not known how many New Yorkers were Loyalists (who did not oppose British rule of the colonies), over 30,000 people left the state during and after the Revolutionary War. Almost one-third of the battles fought in the American Revolution took place in New York. The First and Second Battles of Freeman's Farm, which were fought in New York in 1777, were a key turning point in the war as they led to a British surrender at Saratoga.

The first provincial congress of New York met in White Plains, N.Y., on July 9, 1777. In addition to approving the Declaration of Independence, the congress also organized an independent government. In 1778, New York adopted its first state constitution and the first legislature met in Kingston, New York. The state's first governor, George Clinton, was elected that year as well.

After the end of the war, New York supported the Articles of Confederation, fearing a strong national government. Only one New York delegate to the Constitutional Convention, Alexander Hamilton, signed the final draft of the U.S. Constitution in 1787. In 1788, a New York convention was elected to consider the ratification of the U.S. Constitution. Although supporters of the Constitution were in the minority, they were led by Alexander Hamilton and John Jay, two major statesmen. New Hampshire's ratification of the Constitution in June of that year also had a significant impact; the state faced isolation if it did not join the Union. New York became the eleventh state to enter the union, ratifying the United States Constitution on July 26, 1788. Between 1785 and 1790, New York City served as the temporary capital of the United States. George Washington's inauguration as the first President of the United States took place in Federal Hall in New York City on April 30, 1789.

Between 1777 and 1797, temporary state capitals existed in Kingston, Poughkeepsie, and New York City. In 1797, Albany was named the permanent capital of the state of New York.

New York During the 19th Century

Much of the fighting in the War of 1812 between the United States and Great Britain took place in the frontier regions of New York, along the Canadian border. After the end of the war, many new settlers began to settle the northern and western regions of the state. By 1820, New York had a population of over 1,370,000, making it the most populous state in the country. It held that position until the 1960s, at which time California's population passed that of New York.

Between 1820 and 1860, waves of European immigrants arrived in the United States. Most of them entered the country in New York City and many stayed there. By 1860, New York City was the largest city in the United States and nearly 50 percent of its population were foreign-born immigrants.

In 1825, the 363-mile Erie Canal, which crossed New York from Buffalo on Lake Erie to Troy and Albany on the Hudson River, was completed, providing a key link in an all-water route between Buffalo and New York City. Products from New York factories were shipped on the canal to the western frontier, while western farmers shipped their produce to the east coast. New York's first railroad, the Mohawk and Hudson line, began operation between Albany and Schenectady in 1831. Railroads were soon constructed throughout the state, providing jobs and increasing the state's population. By 1850, New York, by then known as the Empire State, led the country in population, manufacturing, and commerce.

During the early 1800s, the state began to adopt more democratic practices. In 1821, a new law gave all white men the right to vote; earlier laws required property ownership for voter eligibility. However, the property requirement applied to blacks until 1874. The anti-rent movement, beginning in 1839, resulted in wealthy landowners breaking up their estates into smaller independent farms. In 1846, a new state constitution required that all major state officials be elected by the voters.

During the Civil War, New York fought against slavery and provided more soldiers, supplies, and money to the Union cause than any other state. During the First Battle of Bull Run, fought in 1861, one-third of the casualties were from New York. However, not all New Yorkers were in favor of the war. New York City Mayor Fernando Wood wanted the state to remain neutral so that it could maintain commercial ties with both northern and southern states. Many poor immigrants, fearing that free blacks would compete with them for jobs, also opposed the anti-slavery policies. The draft riots in July 1863 were an objection to the policy of drafting men into the Union Army. As a result of the riots, approximately 1,000 people were killed or injured and over $1.5 million worth of property was destroyed.

In the latter part of the 19th century, manufacturing continued to develop and increase in New York, attracting immigrants from all over Europe, particularly Russia, Italy, Poland, and other countries in eastern and southern Europe. Between 1890 and 1920, the state population increased from 6 million to 10.4 million. Prior to the Civil War, New York City had a population of 1.2 million; by 1910 it had grown to almost 5 million. Between 1914 and 1918, large numbers of blacks moved from the southern states to New York; most settled in New York City.

New York During the 20th Century

By the turn of the century, New York was recognized as the industrial and financial center of the United States, as well as a leading cultural center. In 1901, Buffalo was the site of a Pan-American Exposition, which was meant to promote unity and understanding between North and South America. Theodore Roosevelt, who served as state governor from 1899 to 1900, was elected Vice President of the United States in 1901. Six months later, after the assassination of President William McKinley at the Pan-American Exposition, Roosevelt became President.

New York was severely impacted by the Great Depression as unemployment became a serious problem. During the early part of the Depression, between 1929 and 1932, Franklin D. Roosevelt served as state governor. After he was elected President, he was succeeded as governor by Herbert H. Lehman. Much of the social legislation which both Roosevelt and Lehman supported as governors attacked the depression and later served as a model for federal "New Deal" laws endorsed by Roosevelt during his tenure as President.

During and after World War II, New York became an important center of the United States' defense industry, producing war materials during World War II, the Korean War, and the Vietnam War. In 1946, New York City was selected to be the site of the permanent home of the United Nations. Two world's fairs were held in New York; one in 1939/1940 and the other in 1964/1965. The State University of New York was established in 1948.

In 1971, the Attica Prison Riots resulted in the deaths of 41 people. It was the worst prison riot in United States history.

The state continued to grow in population over the next few decades. Between 1950 and 1970, the population of New York increased to over 18 million. However, during the 1970s, the closing of a number of manufacturing plants led to the loss of approximately 600,000 jobs, forcing many people out of the state. New York City and other major cities in the state were particularly affected; many residents began to move to the outlying suburbs. The urban population became increasingly black and Puerto Rican. During the 1970s, Governor Hugh Carey, a Democrat, was forced to request emergency federal and state aid to prevent New York City from going bankrupt. Governor Carey's administration also focused on the issue of crime in New York. In 1978, he sponsored a new law increasing penalties for many violent crimes and allowing older juveniles accused of serious crimes to be tried in adult court.

Recently, the growth of service industries and electronics manufacturing has greatly improved the state's economy and increased its attractiveness to immigrants. Currently, New York is second only to California in the number of new immigrants arriving each year.

On September 11, 2001, New York was significantly impacted by the most spectacular and devastating terrorist attack in U.S. history. Two passenger jets were hijacked and deliberately crashed into the Twin Towers at New York City's World Trade Center. Both buildings collapsed, killing approximately 3,000 people and covering the area with debris. Two other planes were hijacked the same morning; one crashed into the Pentagon while the other crashed in Pennsylvania.

NEW YORK TODAY

Today, New York is considered the commercial and financial leader of the United States and New York City's Wall Street is often called the financial center of the world. In addition to financial institutions, insurance companies, and real estate companies, important sources of income include services, trade, manufacturing, and agriculture. Leading industries in New York include printing and publishing, and the production of electronic devices and components, photographic equipment, chemicals, industrial machinery, textiles, and clothing.

Among the key social challenges New York currently faces are the need to improve social services and housing for the poor and mentally disabled, providing better education for an increasingly large number of minority students, reducing drug abuse in the state, and improving methods of handling the state's growing prison population.

Currently, New York is the third most populous state in the country, after California and Texas. The 2000 census[1] reported a total population of 18,976,457, an increase of 5.5 percent over the 1990 census figure. New York City, with a population of over 8 million in 2000, is not only the largest city in the state but also the largest in the United States and one of the largest cities in the world. Other cities in New York with a population of over 100,000 include Buffalo, Rochester, Yonkers, and Syracuse. The population of Albany, the capital of New York, was 95,658 in 2000.

New York is one of the most densely populated states in the United States, with 402 persons per square mile in 2000. According to the 2000 census,[2] approximately 68 percent of the state's population are white and 16 percent are black; the rest of the population includes Asians, Pacific Islanders, and Native Americans. Approximately 15 percent of the population are reported as being of Hispanic origin, although they may be of any race. Most of the population lives in urban areas.

New York has a total area of 53,989 square miles, including 1,888 square miles of inland water, 976 square miles of coastal water, and 3,901 square miles of the portion of the Great Lakes over which the state has jurisdiction. It is the twenty-seventh largest state in area. New York has two United States Senators and 31 Representatives, for a total of 33 electoral votes, more than any other state except California. The current state constitution was adopted in 1894.

NOTES

1. U.S. Census Bureau (http://www.census.gov)
2. *Ibid.*

CHAPTER 2

INTRODUCTION TO NEW YORK CRIMINAL LAW

THE STRUCTURE OF THE GOVERNMENT

New York State law is found in the State Constitution and in the New York State Penal Code. Both have been frequently modified, amended, and altered over the past century.

The first **New York State Constitution**[1] was ratified in 1777; the present constitution was adopted in 1894. It has been amended more than 180 times since then. The New York State Constitution is the primary law of the state, although it is of course subordinate to the United States Constitution. No criminal law or constitutional amendment enacted in New York may conflict with or violate any individual rights which are guaranteed by the U.S. Constitution, the Bill of Rights, any other Constitutional Amendments, or any federal laws. If any part of the New York State Constitution or legal code is found to be in conflict with the U.S. Constitution or federal statutes, the New York enactment is unconstitutional and must be changed.

There are two ways in which the New York State Constitution may be **amended**, as described in Article XIX of the State Constitution. First, a new amendment may be proposed in the New York State Legislature. The amendment must then be approved by a majority of the members of each of the two legislative houses (the Senate and the Assembly). If this occurs, the proposed amendment is referred to the next regular legislative session that is convened after the next general election of the Assembly. The proposal must then be approved by a majority of both houses of this legislature as well. In other words, the proposal must be approved by a majority of both legislative houses of two successive, separately elected legislatures. The proposal must then be approved and ratified by a majority of the voters at a general election. It will then become a part of the state constitution on the first day of January following the general election.

The second way to amend the Constitution is by a **constitutional convention**. A proposal to call for a constitutional convention must be approved by both a majority of the members of the legislature and a majority of the voters in the state. Delegates are elected to the convention to develop and propose constitutional amendments. Proposed amendments must first be approved by a majority of the elected delegates to the convention. The proposal is then placed before the state electorate (the voters) and, if ratified by a majority of the voters at a general election, will then go into effect on the first day of January following the election. The most recent constitutional convention was held in 1967.

Like most states, New York has three branches of government: executive, legislative, and judicial.

The Executive Branch

Article IV of the New York State Constitution discusses Florida's **executive branch**. Many of the executive officers of New York, including the governor, are elected to a four-year term. Although some states (e.g., California) limit the number of times the governor may be re-elected, in New York, the governor may serve an unlimited number of terms. The lieutenant-governor, comptroller, and attorney general are elected by the voters at the same general election as the governor and serve the same term. The secretary of state is not elected by the voters but is appointed by the governor with the approval of the New York State Senate.

To be elected to the office of either governor or lieutenant-governor of New York, a candidate must be a citizen of the United States, at least 30 years of age, and a state resident for a minimum of five years immediately preceding election to office.[2] Candidates for comptroller and attorney general must also meet these requirements.[3]

Among the powers and duties of the state governor is the "power to grant reprieves, commutations and pardons after conviction, for all offenses except treason and cases of impeachment, upon such conditions and with such restrictions and limitations, as he or she may think proper, subject to such regulations as may be provided by law..."[4]

On November 8, 1994, George E. Pataki became the fifty-third governor of New York State. He was re-elected to a second term in 1998 and to a third term in 2002. Governor Pataki is a Republican-Conservative.

The Legislative Branch

The **State Legislature** is discussed in Article III of the New York State Constitution and is the lawmaking branch of the state government. The Legislature is made up of two houses: a **Senate** and an **Assembly**. Each member of the legislature represents one Senatorial or Assembly district. Currently, the Senate has 62 members and the Assembly has 150 members. Members of the Legislature are elected to two-year terms and there is no limit to the number of times they may be re-elected. The Legislature meets annually on the first Wednesday after the first Monday in January. In addition, a special session of the Legislature may be called by the governor or by a petition signed by two-thirds of the Legislature. There are no time limits on either regular or special legislative sessions.

To serve as a member of the New York State Legislature, a candidate must be a United States citizen and a state resident for at least five years. In most cases, the candidate must have been a resident of the Assembly or Senate district for the twelve months immediately preceding election. Members of the Legislature who are elected to the U.S. Congress or appointed to any state or federal civil or military office (with a small number of exceptions) must resign their seats in the Legislature.

The Judicial Branch

The judicial branch of the government, which is discussed in Article VI of the New York State Constitution, contains the various New York courts. The state is divided into twelve judicial districts, each of which elects a number of **Supreme Court** judges to fourteen-year terms. It is important to understand that in New York, the Supreme Court is not the highest court in the state.

The state is also divided into four judicial departments, each of which has an **appellate division** of the Supreme Court. These appellate divisions hear appeals from the Supreme Court and from other trial courts within their jurisdictions. Supreme Court justices of these appellate divisions are appointed by the state governor Two of the four divisions have at least seven justices each; the other two divisions each have five justices.

The highest court in the state is the **New York Court of Appeals**. It is composed of seven justices, including one chief justice and six associate justices, each of whom is appointed by the governor to a fourteen-year term. The Court of Appeals only hears cases from the appellate divisions of the Supreme Court.

Each county in the state, except those counties making up New York City, has a **county court**. These county courts hear both civil and criminal cases. All state counties also have **family courts** to handle domestic matters. New York city has separate civil and criminal courts. In addition, throughout the state, there is a variety of town justices, city court judges, and village courts. The New York State court system is discussed in more detail in Chapter 5.

Passing a Law in New York

In New York a bill, or proposed law, may be introduced into either the Senate or the Assembly.[5] After the bill is introduced into one of the legislative houses, it is referred to a Standing Committee for study and debate. For example, bills which affect criminal law usually go to the Codes Committee. The committee may reject the bill, amend the bill, or send it to the full house for review and consideration. When the bill is placed before the full legislative house of origin, it is debated on, may be amended, and eventually goes to a floor vote. Passage of a bill requires a majority vote from the members of the legislative house. After the bill is passed by one legislative house, it must go through the same procedure in the other house. If amendments are made, both houses must agree to the changes. After both legislative houses have passed identical bills, the bill goes to the state governor, who may choose either to veto the bill or to sign it into law.[6]

THE NEW YORK STATE PENAL LAW

There are several sources of criminal law in New York. These include:

1. Federal and state constitutions
2. Substantive criminal law
3. Case law

Together, the New York State Constitution and the U.S. Constitution provide the basic framework for criminal law, first by focusing on individual rights and on the limitations placed on government power and second by requiring the establishment of a judicial system. However, neither the federal nor the state constitution significantly emphasizes the creation or definition of crimes.

The statutory law in New York is found in the **New York Consolidated Laws**.[7] The primary source of substantive criminal law in New York is the **New York State Penal Law**, which is frequently amended. Amendments to the Penal Law may be proposed by individual legislators, by lobbying organizations, or by various groups such as the Law Revision Commission. These amendments must then go through the process discussed above (see "Passing a Law in New York") before becoming a part of the Penal Law.

The New York State Penal Law is the basic criminal code for the state of New York. It was originally based on the English **common law**, which is essentially judge-made law, or laws based on judicial decisions. The common law became the law of the original thirteen colonies and eventually evolved into the law of individual states as they entered the union. Because of this, New York state courts may use the common law to analyze and interpret the penal law of the state. The New York State legal system is based entirely on written law, so that all crimes are defined by statute. However, because the meanings of statutes are not always clear, or may have multiple interpretations, the meaning of the terms in the state statutes may be determined or clarified by common law. Much of the current Penal Law was also influenced by the Model Penal Code.

The first New York Penal Code was originally enacted in 1881. Prior to this time, although there was no one single set of criminal statutes, there were a number of separate statutes which defined criminal liability for various offenses. The Penal Code was reorganized in 1909; at that time it was renamed the "Penal Law." In 1961, the state legislature appointed a commission to revise the Penal Law. The new Penal Law, which was enacted in 1965 and which took effect in September 1967, is the current penal law of the state.

Case law consists of appellate court decisions or opinions which interpret the meaning of the law. Effectively, case law is made by judges when they hand down decisions in court. Because of the principle of *stare decisis*, or precedent, a decision made by a judge in one court will be followed by later judges in the state until the same court reverses its decision or until the decision is overturned by a higher court.

The courts have a significant amount of power in New York because of Article 5 of the Penal Law (Pen.L.), which states that:

> The general rule that a penal statute is to be strictly construed does not apply to this chapter, but the provisions herein must be construed according to the fair import of their terms to promote justice and effect the objects of the law.

Essentially, this statute states that the Penal Law must be flexible because it is not possible to write laws that cover every possible situation. Some judges are "strict constructionists," preferring to follow the strict letter of the law as closely as possible, while others are more flexible and hold that Article 5 allows them to also consider the spirit or intent of the law.

The statutory law includes two different types of laws, substantive and procedural. **Substantive criminal law** includes definitions of specific crimes and identifies the punishments associated with each criminal act. Article 125 of the Penal Law, which defines criminal homicide and outlines the legal punishments which may be imposed by the court, is an example of substantive criminal law. **Procedural law**, on the other hand, focuses on the methods that are used to enforce substantive criminal law. In other words, procedural law outlines the rules that the state must follow when dealing with crimes and criminals. These include the procedures that must be used to investigate crimes, arrest suspects, and carry out formal prosecution. The protection against double jeopardy is an example of procedural law.[8]

THE DEFINITION AND CLASSIFICATION OF CRIME

In New York, Pen.L. §10.00(1) defines an **offense** as:

> conduct for which a sentence to a term of imprisonment or to a fine is provided by any law of this state or by any law, local law or ordinance of a political subdivision of this state, or by any order, rule or regulation of any governmental instrumentality authorized by law to adopt the same.

This definition basically means that an offender has violated a state law of some type. An offender can be a person, corporation, association, or government agency.[9]

There are several categories of offenses, which are differentiated by their relative levels of seriousness. The most serious type of offense is a **crime**, which is defined as "a misdemeanor or a felony."[10] In New York, the difference between a misdemeanor and a felony is not determined by the offense itself, or the action committed by the offender, but by the possible punishment that is prescribed by the Penal Law. **Felonies** are the most serious offenses in New York. The Penal Law defines a felony as "an offense for which a sentence to a term of imprisonment in excess of one year may be imposed."[11] Capital offenses, crimes for which the offender may be sentenced to death, are also felonies. Felonies are classified into five categories, which are used in the determination of the sentence.[12]

- A **Class A felony** is the most serious category. Examples of Class A felonies include second degree murder, first degree kidnapping, and first degree arson. Murder in the first degree is also a Class A felony. There are a few specified exceptions, but in most cases, every offender convicted of a Class A felony must be sentenced to a term of imprisonment. If the offender has been convicted of murder in the first degree, s/he will generally receive either a sentence of death or a sentence of life imprisonment without parole. For purposes of sentencing, Class A felonies are subdivided into Class A-I and Class A-II felonies.

- **Class B violent felony offenses** include attempts to commit the above Class A felonies, as well as second degree kidnapping; second degree arson; first degree manslaughter; first degree rape; first degree sodomy; first degree aggravated sexual abuse; first degree sexual conduct against a child; first degree assault; first degree burglary; first degree robbery; first degree criminal possession of a dangerous weapon; first degree criminal use of a firearm; aggravated assault against a peace officer; first degree gang assault; and first degree intimidation of a victim or witness.

- **Class C violent felony offenses** include attempts to commit any Class B felony as well as second degree aggravated sexual abuse; assault on a peace officer, police officer, firefighter, or emergency medical services professional; second degree burglary; second degree robbery; second degree criminal possession of a weapon; second degree criminal use of a firearm; and first degree criminal sale of a firearm.

- **Class D violent felony offenses** include attempts to commit any Class C felony as well as second degree assault; first degree sexual abuse; second degree sexual conduct against a child; third degree aggravated sexual abuse; third degree criminal possession of a weapon; second degree criminal sale of a firearm; criminal sale of a firearm with the aid of a minor; and second degree intimidation of a victim or witness.

- **Class E violent felony offenses** include attempts to commit any felony offense that involves third degree criminal possession of a weapon.

A **misdemeanor** is defined in §10(4) as:

> an offense, other than a "traffic infraction," for which a sentence to a term of imprisonment in excess of fifteen days may be imposed, but for which a sentence to a term of imprisonment in excess of one year cannot be imposed.

Therefore, even if the Penal Law does not specifically identify a crime as a misdemeanor or a felony, the classification can easily be inferred from the prescribed sentence. Misdemeanors are classified into three categories:

- **Class A misdemeanors**

- **Class B misdemeanors**

- **Unclassified misdemeanors**[13]

The New York Criminal Procedure Law (CPL) defines **petty offenses** as violations or traffic infractions.[14] While these acts are offenses, they are not crimes. Therefore, individuals who are convicted of petty offenses do not have a "criminal record." A **traffic infraction** is defined as any offense that is so defined by the New York Vehicle and Traffic Law,[15] while a **violation** is any offense other than a traffic infraction, for which the maximum sentence is imprisonment for fifteen days.[16]

The Penal Law also recognizes acts that are known as **anticipatory offenses**, or inchoate offenses. These are actions that take place prior to the commission of an actual substantive offense, but which are effectively steps taken in preparation for committing the actual crime. It is possible to be found guilty of an anticipatory offense even if the underlying substantive crime that the offenders intended to commit was never actually completed. There are four main types of anticipatory offenses recognized by the Penal Law in New York. **Criminal solicitation**, which is discussed in Article 100 of the Penal Law, occurs when the offender asks, commands, or in some other way attempts to cause another person to commit a crime.[17] The level of seriousness of criminal solicitation depends on the type of crime solicited and the age of both the solicitor and the person being solicited. Criminal solicitation in the fifth degree is merely a violation, while criminal solicitation in the first degree is a Class C felony. The offense of **conspiracy** occurs when an individual agrees with another person to engage in a crime or cause a crime to occur. As with criminal solicitation, the seriousness of the offense depends on the nature of the underlying intended crime and the age of the participants. In addition, it is not enough to merely talk about committing a crime; the law requires that some overt act be committed to further the progress of the conspiracy.[18] The third type of anticipatory offense is that of **attempt**, which is discussed in Article 110 of the Penal Law. This crime is defined as:

> A person is guilty of an attempt to commit a crime when, with intent to commit a crime, he engages in conduct which tends to effect the commission of such crime.[19]

The level of seriousness of this offense depends entirely upon the nature of the crime attempted. In most cases, the charge is one level down from that of the crime that was attempted. Thus, if the offender attempts to commit a Class B felony, s/he would be charged with Class C felony attempt. Finally, **criminal facilitation**, which is discussed in Article 115 of the Penal Law, involves providing aid and assistance to someone who intends to commit a crime. The offender must know that the individual being assisted intends to commit a crime. The seriousness of the offense depends upon both the nature of the intended crime and the age of the participants. Unlike other anticipatory offenses, for an individual to be found guilty of criminal facilitation, the intended crime must actually be committed. However, it is still possible for an offender to be found guilty of criminal facilitation even if the individual who was facilitated or assisted is acquitted of the criminal act.

The Criminal Act (*Actus Reus*) and Intent (*Mens Rea*)

There are several elements which are necessary for an individual to be considered criminally liable for his or her behavior. According to Pen.L. §15.10,

> The minimal requirement for criminal liability is the performance by a person of conduct which includes a voluntary act or the omission to perform an act which he is physically capable of performing. If such conduct is all that is required for commission of a particular offense, or if an offense or some material element thereof does not require a culpable mental state on the part of the actor, such offense is one of "strict liability." If a culpable mental state on the part of the actor is required with respect to every material element of an offense, such offense is one of "mental culpability."

Essentially, a crime requires two key components: ***actus reus*** (a criminal act) and ***mens rea*** (a guilty mind).

Most criminal acts are deliberate and voluntary on the part of the offender. However, the act necessary to make up a crime will vary with each crime. Verbal actions, or words, can be a sufficient action in, for example, the crime of perjury. Merely possessing something may be a sufficient act if the crime is one that involves illegal possession of goods (for example, possession of illegal drugs).

It is clear from Pen.L. §15.10 that the criminal act may also consist of some form of passive participation or omission or failure to act. An **omission** occurs when someone who has a legal duty to act fails to perform an action that is required by law. For example, a security guard who deliberately looks the other way while company property is stolen is a passive participant and is guilty of failure or omission to act. Similarly, a parent or other legal caretaker who fails to adequately feed and shelter an infant, resulting in the death of the child, has committed a crime by his or her failure to act. Corporations may also be held criminally liable for omissions.[20]

Failing to act is only a crime of omission when an individual has a legal duty to act in that situation. For example, consider the case of a swimmer at a local public pool who develops a cramp while in deep water. The lifeguard who is on duty at the pool has a legal duty to act and, if s/he fails to go to the swimmer's assistance, would be guilty of a crime of omission. However, the other swimmers in the pool have only a moral duty to aid the distressed swimmer and if they fail to provide assistance would not be guilty of any crime. In addition, the omission or failure to act must also be voluntary for this statute to apply.

Mens rea involves the offender's mental state at the time of the criminal action. Pen.L. §15.10 states that, in addition to the act or omission, a **culpable mental state** may also be required. A culpable mental state means that the crime is committed intentionally, knowingly, recklessly, or with criminal negligence. A crime is committed **intentionally** when the offender consciously desires the outcome.[21] The offender does not have to declare intent to be convicted of a crime; the intent may be inferred by the actions of the offender. Intent is basically a state of mind and circumstantial evidence is sufficient to prove intent. The key point is that the offender must want to achieve the outcome of his or her actions (the crime). A crime is committed **knowingly** when the offender is aware that his or her conduct violates the law. However, the offender does not need to be aware that his or her conduct will cause a certain outcome defined by an offense.[22] A crime is committed **recklessly** when the offender is aware of the risk of his or her actions and consciously disregards that risk. The statute specifically states that if an individual is intoxicated voluntarily, s/he may not claim a lack of awareness of risk due solely to that intoxication.[23] Finally, **criminal negligence** occurs when the offender fails to perceive a risk that would be perceived by any reasonable person. This definition requires that the court determine whether the behavior that caused the injury or death involved substantial risk and whether the offender's failure to perceive that risk deviated from the perception of a reasonable person under the same circumstances.[24]

Pen.L. §15.10 specifically mentions **strict liability offenses**. These are offenses for which a culpable mental state, or *mens rea*, does not have to be shown. In these situations, the offender may be punished without any proof of criminal intent. Strict liability crimes are rare. In most cases, even if the specific statute does not list a required culpable mental state, it will usually be interpreted as requiring one. Most statutes do specifically set out the required mental culpability in the section.

DEFENSES TO A CRIMINAL CHARGE

There are a wide variety of defenses to a criminal charge, many of which are specifically mentioned in the New York Penal Law. The Penal Law recognizes two basic types of defenses: ordinary and affirmative. The main difference between them is where the burden of proof is placed.

When a **traditional** or **ordinary defense** is raised at a trial, the burden of proof is on the prosecution to disprove the defense beyond a reasonable doubt. When an **affirmative defense** is raised at trial, the burden of proof is on the defendant to establish the defense by a preponderance of the evidence.[25] If a defense is not specifically identified as an affirmative defense, it is considered to be an ordinary defense.

The majority of defenses in the New York Penal Law are affirmative defenses, primarily those falling in the excuse category. This does not mean that the presumption of innocence does not exist in New York; a defendant presenting an affirmative defense is not required to prove his or her innocence. Essentially, the defendant is claiming that s/he did commit the offense but that s/he has an excuse that negates criminal liability. The defendant is required by the court to show why this conduct should be excused in this case. The prosecution still has the responsibility of proving all the elements of the offense.

Alibi

An individual who uses the defense of an **alibi** essentially is claiming that s/he was at another place when the crime was committed and thus could not have committed the crime. For an alibi defense to be effective, it must cover the entire time period when the defendant's presence was necessary to commit the crime. Alibi is not specifically classified as a defense by the Penal Law but it is generally considered to be an ordinary statutory defense.[26]

CPL §250.20(1) discusses the rules that must be followed if the defendant plans to offer evidence of an alibi in his/her defense. It states that:

> At any time, not more than twenty days after arraignment, the people may serve upon the defendant or his counsel, and file a copy thereof with the court, a demand that if the defendant intends to offer a trial defense that at the time of the commission of the crime charged he was at some place or places other than the scene of the crime, and to call witnesses in support of such defense, he must, within eight days of service of such demand, serve upon the people, and file a copy thereof with the court, a "notice of alibi," reciting
> (a) the place or places where the defendant claims to have been at the time in question, and
> (b) the names, the residential addresses, the places of employment and the addresses thereof of every such alibi witness upon whom he intends to rely.
> For good cause shown, the court may extend the period for service of the notice.

Justifications

A defendant who uses a **justification** defense admits to the commission of the criminal act but also claims that it was necessary to commit the act in order to avoid some greater evil or harm. Article 35, which is arguably one of the most complicated articles in the New York Penal Law, discusses the issue of the defense of justification. Justification is an ordinary defense.

Probably the most well-known justification defense is that of **self-defense**, in which the defendant claims that the use of force against the victim was justifiable because it was the only way the defendant could ensure his or her own safety. In addition, the defendant may also claim that force was used in the **defense of others** or in the **defense of home and property**.

The issue of the use of physical force in self defense or in the defense of others is discussed in Pen.L. §35.10(6), which states that:

> A person may ... use physical force upon another person in defense of himself or a third person, or in defense of premises, or in order to prevent larceny of or criminal mischief to property, or in order to effect an arrest or prevent an escape from custody...

Even if an individual is justified in using physical force, he or she may only use the degree of force that the individual reasonably believes to be necessary in that situation, and may only use force for as long as the individual reasonably believes that the assailant poses a threat.[27]

The Penal Law specifically discusses those situations in which one may actually use physical force in defense of one's self or of another person and places limits on when physical force of any type may be used. Pen.L. §35.15(1) states that:

> A person may, subject to the provisions of subdivision two, use physical force upon another person when and to the extent he reasonably believes such to be necessary to defend himself or a third person from what he reasonably believes to be the use or imminent use of unlawful physical force by such other person, unless:
> (a) The latter's conduct was provoked by the actor himself with intent to cause physical injury to another person; or
> (b) The actor was the initial aggressor; except that in such case his use of physical force is nevertheless justifiable if he has withdrawn from the encounter and effectively communicated such withdrawal to such other person but the latter persists in continuing the incident by the use or threatened imminent use of unlawful physical force; or
> (c) The physical force involved is the product of a combat by agreement not specifically authorized by law.

Deadly physical force is defined as "physical force which, under the circumstances in which it is used, is readily capable of causing death or other serious physical injury."[28] According to Pen.L. 35.15(2), an individual may only use deadly force against another person in three very specific situations:

> A person may not use deadly physical force upon another person under circumstances specified in subdivision one unless:
> (a) He reasonably believes that such other person is using or about to use deadly physical force. Even in such case, however, the actor may not use deadly physical force if he knows that he can with complete safety as to himself and others avoid the necessity of so doing by retreating; except that he is under no duty to retreat if he is:
> (i) in his dwelling and not the initial aggressor; or

> (ii) a police officer or peace officer or a person assisting a police officer or a peace officer at the latter's direction...; or
>
> (b) He reasonably believes that such other person is committing or attempting to commit a kidnapping, forcible rape, forcible sodomy or robbery; or
>
> (c) He reasonably believes that such other person is committing or attempting to commit a burglary, and the circumstances are such that the use of deadly physical force is authorized by subdivision three of section 35.20.

Essentially, in New York, a person may use deadly physical force against another person if:

1. S/he reasonably believes that someone is using or is about to use deadly physical force; and

2. S/he reasonably believes that it is necessary to use deadly physical force in self-defense, or in the defense of a third person; and

3. The amount of force used was reasonable under the circumstances.

Pen.L. §35.20 discusses when an individual is justified in using physical force in the defense of premises. According to the statute, an individual may use physical force to prevent or stop the commission or attempted commission of a crime that involves damage to premises. S/he may use deadly physical force to stop the commission of arson. If an individual is in possession or control of the premises, s/he may use physical force to prevent or stop criminal trespass. In addition, s/he may use deadly force to stop or prevent a burglary.

Probably one of the most well-known cases in New York to use the defense of justification was the landmark case of *People v. Goetz*,[29] which involved Bernard Goetz, the "subway vigilante." This case led to the development of standards, known as **Goetz factors**, which are now used in any case that involves the defense of justification. One key finding of the *Goetz* case was that, if the defendant had a reasonable belief that deadly force was being used or about to be used and/or a reasonable belief that deadly force was necessary for self-defense, the justification defense will not be negated or defeated by the fact that these beliefs were mistaken.

Another justification defense is that of **consent**. This defense claims that the injured person voluntarily consented to the actions that caused the injury and seems to be most commonly used in sex-related offenses, such as rape. Pen.L. §130.05(2) discusses the issue of consent in the context of sex offenses and states that,

> Lack of consent results from:
> (a) Forcible compulsion; or
> (b) Incapacity to consent; or
> (c) Where the offense charged is sexual abuse, any circumstances, in addition to forcible compulsion or incapacity to consent, in which the victim does not expressly or impliedly acquiesce in the actor's conduct; or
> (d) Where the offense charged is rape in the third degree ... or sodomy in the third degree ... in addition to forcible compulsion, circumstances under which, at the time of the act of intercourse or deviate sexual intercourse, the victim clearly

expressed that he or she did not consent to engage in such act, and a reasonable person in the actor's situation would have understood such person's words and acts as an expression of lack of consent to such act under all the circumstances.

The statute makes it clear that coerced consent, obtained through threats of force or violence against the victim or another person, does not constitute a defense of consent. In addition, the law identifies a number of situations in which a person is considered to be incapable of giving consent. These include, among others, individuals who are mentally disabled or mentally incapacitated and individuals who are physically helpless. In addition, individuals under the age of 17 cannot give consent.[30]

Excuses

A defendant using an **excuse** defense is claiming that at the time of the criminal act some circumstance or personal condition creates a situation under which s/he should not be held criminally accountable. Most excuse defenses are considered to be affirmative defenses.

Duress is an affirmative defense in which the defendant states that s/he committed the crime only because s/he was coerced into doing so. This defense is defined in Pen.L. §40.00(1), which states that:

> In any prosecution for an offense, it is an affirmative defense that the defendant engaged in the proscribed conduct because he was coerced to do so by the use or threatened imminent use of unlawful physical force upon him or a third person, which force or threatened force a person of reasonable firmness in his situation would have been unable to resist.

The statute also states that this defense may not be used if the defendant has recklessly or intentionally placed himself or herself in a situation in which it is likely that s/he will be subjected to some type of duress.[31] Essentially, if the defendant commits a crime under some type of threat of *imminent death or great bodily harm*, the intent required is negated and the defendant is not guilty of the offense. The defendant must have been in immediate danger; a fear of future harm is not sufficient to claim duress.

Another defense which falls into this category is that of **infancy**. This defense is discussed in Article 30 of the Penal Law and is considered to be an ordinary defense. Pen.L. §30.00 states that:

1. *Except as provided in subdivision two of this section, a person less than sixteen years old is not criminally responsible for conduct.*
2. *A person thirteen, fourteen or fifteen years of age is criminally responsible for acts constituting murder in the second degree ... provided that the underlying crime for the murder charge is one for which such person is criminally responsible; and a person fourteen or fifteen years of age is criminally responsible for acts constituting the crimes defined in section 135.25 (kidnapping in the first degree); 150.20 (arson in the first degree); subdivisions one and two of section 120.10 (assault in the first degree); 125.20 (manslaughter in the first degree); subdivisions one and two of section 130.35 (rape in the first degree); subdivisions one and two of section 130.50 (sodomy in the first degree); 130.70*

(aggravated sexual abuse); 140.30 (burglary in the first degree); subdivision one of section 140.25 (burglary in the second degree); 150.15 (arson in the second degree); 160.15 (robbery in the first degree); subdivision two of section 160.10 (robbery in the second degree) of this chapter; subdivision four of section 265.02 of this chapter, where such firearm is possessed on school grounds ...; or section 265.03 of this chapter, where such machine gun or such firearm is possessed on school grounds...;or defined in this chapter as an attempt to commit murder in the second degree or kidnapping in the first degree.
3. In any prosecution for an offense, lack of criminal responsibility by reason of infancy, as defined in this section, is a defense.

Thus, in most cases, an individual under the age of sixteen may not be held criminally liable for his or her conduct. However, the statute clearly outlines several specific exceptions. For example, consider the crime of homicide. First, an individual who is between the ages of thirteen and fifteen years of age may be held criminally responsible for and convicted of murder in the second degree. However, a thirteen-year-old offender may not be held to be criminally responsible for the crime of felony murder because s/he cannot be held criminally responsible for the underlying felony. Second, a defendant who is aged fourteen or fifteen may be held criminally responsible for the crimes of first degree manslaughter and attempted murder. S/he may also be held criminally responsible for felony murder if the underlying felony is one for which the defendant can be held criminally responsible. For all other homicide offenses, the defendant must be at least sixteen years of age. The one exception to this is the crime of first degree murder; an individual must be over the age of eighteen to be considered criminally responsible for this crime.

Probably the most well-known and controversial defense in this category is that of **insanity**. Although the term insanity is no longer used by mental health professionals, it is a legal term referring to a defense that is based on the defendant's claim that s/he was mentally ill or mentally incapacitated at the time of the offense. In New York, the insanity defense is defined by statute as:

In any prosecution for an offense, it is an affirmative defense that when the defendant engaged in the proscribed conduct, he lacked criminal responsibility by reason of mental disease or defect. Such lack of criminal responsibility means that at the time of such conduct, as a result of mental disease or defect, he lacked substantial capacity to know or appreciate either:
1. The nature and consequences of such conduct; or
2. That such conduct was wrong.[32]

In New York, insanity is considered to be an affirmative defense. This means that the court presumes that the defendant was sane at the time of the crime and had no mental disease or defect. The burden of proof is on the defense to show that the defendant either did not understand what s/he was doing or that defendant did not know that the behavior was wrong.

A defendant who is found to be insane at the time s/he committed the offense is not considered to be criminally responsible by reason of his/her inability to maintain the culpable mental state. However, the mental disease or defect from which the defendant suffered must be one that is generally accepted in the fields of psychiatry or psychology. For example, in the case of *People v. Wernick*, the insanity defense was based on the claim that the defendant suffered from "neonaticide syndrome." The trial court rejected expert testimony offered in support of this claim and the Court of Appeals upheld the ruling of the trial court, holding that this syndrome was not generally accepted either in the field of psychiatry or psychology.[33]

Another defense that falls into the category of excuse is that of **involuntary intoxication**. Pen.L. §15.25 discusses the issue of intoxication in general, and its effect upon liability. The statute states that:

> Intoxication is not, as such, a defense to a criminal charge; but in any prosecution for an offense, evidence of intoxication of the defendant may be offered by the defendant whenever it is relevant to negative an element of the crime charged.

Thus, if a defendant is charged with a crime that requires intent, the defense of intoxication may be used in an attempt to negate the element of intent. The defense could, for example, claim that the defendant was so intoxicated that s/he was unable to form the required intent. However, even an individual who is intoxicated may be found to have been able to form the required intent to commit the crime in question. In addition, intoxication may not be used as a defense against strict liability crimes that do not require intent, such as criminally negligent homicide, reckless manslaughter, or vehicular homicide, if the offender personally created the risk by becoming intoxicated voluntarily.

The Penal Law does not specifically address the issue of involuntary intoxication as a defense. However, the issue does come up when discussing other topics, such as consent. For example, Pen.L. §130.05(3) states that a mentally incapacitated person is unable to give consent to a sexual act. Pen.L. §130.00(6) defines mentally incapacitated as,

> a person is rendered temporarily incapable of appraising or controlling his conduct owing to the influence of a narcotic or intoxicating substance administered to him without his consent, or to any other act committed upon him without his consent.

Thus, involuntary intoxication may negate the use of consent as a defense against a sex offense in New York.

While in most cases, the old saying that "ignorance of the law is no defense" is true, there are some exceptions. The issue of **mistake of fact** is discussed in Pen.L. §15.20(1). The statute states that a mistake of fact does not relieve the offender of criminal liability. For example, the age of the victim is an element in some crimes, such as sex crimes involving victims or participants who are minors and thus below the age of consent. A mistaken belief that the participant was not a minor is not a defense against such crimes in New York. However, the statute does list three exceptions which may negate criminal liability.

- The mistake of fact negates the culpable mental state that is required for the commission of the crime.

- The statute which defines the crime committed by the offender (or a related statute) specifically allows for a mistake of fact as a defense or exemption.

- The mistake of fact supports a defense of justification.

In addition, Pen.L. §15.20(2) reviews the issue of **mistake of law**. This revolves around the defendant's claim that s/he was unaware that his or her actions violated the law. In most cases, mistake of law is not a defense and does not relieve the offender of criminal liability. However, the statute does provide for one exception: if the defendant's mistaken belief is based on an official statement of the law. Therefore, if an individual's behavior is based on an incorrect interpretation of a statute which was issued by an official agency that has been empowered to interpret that statute, the individual may not be held criminally accountable for his or her behavior. Essentially, the defendant must show that s/he made an effort to learn the true facts of the law and that there was an error in the law as officially publicized.

Procedural Defenses

A **procedural defense** claims that some form of official procedure was not followed or that procedural law was not properly followed during the investigation or the prosecution of the crime. One procedural defense is **entrapment**. Pen.L. §40.05 discusses the issue of entrapment, stating that:

> In any prosecution for an offense, it is an affirmative defense that the defendant engaged in the proscribed conduct because he was induced or encouraged to do so by a public servant, or by a person acting in cooperation with a public servant, seeking to obtain evidence against him for purpose of criminal prosecution, and when the methods used to obtain such evidence were such as to create a substantial risk that the offense would be committed by a person not otherwise disposed to commit it. Inducement or encouragement to commit an offense means active inducement or encouragement. Conduct merely affording a person an opportunity to commit an offense does not constitute entrapment.

Essentially, the defendant is claiming that the behavior of a public servant (usually a law enforcement officer) induced the defendant to commit the illegal act. The statute specifically identifies entrapment as an affirmative defense, so that the burden of proof is on the defense to prove entrapment by a preponderance of the evidence.

The entrapment defense is extremely difficult for the defendant to prove. It is most commonly used when the defendant was ensnared in an undercover police action and the most frequent use relates to the sale of illegal drugs. In general, the defendant will claim that s/he does not regularly sell drugs but made a sale as a favor to the undercover officer. One of the most common ways for the police to prevent the use of this defense is to make two or more purchases of illegal drugs from the same suspect. After the suspect has made multiple sales, the jury is more likely to believe that the undercover officer simply provided the defendant with an opportunity to commit the crime, rather than that the officer induced or encouraged the defendant to engage in a behavior in which s/he would not normally become involved.

Another procedural defense is the **denial of a speedy trial**. CPL §30.20(1) states that, "After a criminal action is commenced, the defendant is entitled to a speedy trial." The time limitations on a speedy trial are reviewed in CPL §30.30. The period of time that may elapse prior to trial varies depending upon the type of crime of which the defendant is accused. However, it generally ranges from 30 days to six months. This time limit may be extended under certain circumstances. Obviously, if the defendant has requested an extension or delay to the start of the trial, s/he may not later claim that his or her right to a speedy trial was denied.

SOURCES OF INFORMATION FOR LEGAL RESEARCH

Legal research involves the study of both statutes and case law from court decisions. Because the law is constantly changing, it is essential that only the most recent references be used. Today, much of the material may be found in electronic format: CD-ROMs and on-line computer databases such as WestLaw and Lexis have significantly streamlined legal research.

Legal Citations

Decisions of state appellate courts and the U.S. Supreme Court are published in books which are generally known as "reports" or "reporters." A sample case citation is: ***People v. Banks*, 76 N.Y.2d 799**. In this particular case, the courts created the defense of transitory or temporary lawful possession, a defense to possessory crimes which does not appear in the Penal Law. *People v. Banks* is the name of the case; all crimes which are heard in New York state courts are prosecuted in the name of "The People of the State of New York" versus the defendant. The first number (76) represents the volume number in which the case is to be found. "N.Y.2d" is an abbreviation for the specific reporter in which the case is to found *(New York Official Reports, 2nd edition)*. The second number (799) is the page number of the first page of the reporter on which the decision is found. Therefore, the above citation, 76 N.Y.2d 799, is found beginning on page 799 of volume 76 of the *New York Official Reports, 2nd edition*.

Statutory citations resemble case citations. A sample statutory citation is: **Pen.L. §35.00**. Pen.L. is an abbreviation for the New York Penal Law and 35.00 refers to the section number of the statute. This particular statute deals with the defense of justification.

Court decisions are found in the following reporters:

- *United States Reports* (US) – contains U.S. Supreme Court decisions
- *Supreme Court Reporter* (S.Ct) – contains U.S. Supreme Court decisions
- *Federal Reporter, 2nd series* (F.2d) – contains decisions from the Federal Court of Appeals
- *Northeastern Reporter, 2nd series* (N.E.2d) – contains decisions from courts in the Northeast region of the United States (including the New York Court of Appeals)
- *New York Reports* (N.Y.) – contains decisions from the New York Court of Appeals
- *New York Appellate Division* (A.D. or App. Div.) – contains decisions from the New York Appellate Division
- *New York Miscellaneous Reports* (Misc.) – contains decisions from the New York Supreme Court and other lower courts

- *New York Supplements* (N.Y.S.) – an unofficial reporter which contains all the opinions published in the *New York Reports, New York Appellate Division Reports,* and *Miscellaneous Reports*

State and federal statutes use the following abbreviations:

- *United States Code* (USC) – contains the federal legal code (including the criminal code)
- *New York State Penal Law* (Pen.L.) – contains the criminal code of the state of New York
- *New York Criminal Procedure Law* (CPL) – contains rules of evidence and matters pertaining to criminal procedure used in New York
- *New York Correction Law* (Cor.L.) – contains laws relating to correctional programs in New York
- *New York Judiciary Law* (Jud.L.) – contains laws relating to the courts, judges, and justices in New York

Shepard's Citations

Shepard's New York Citations, which is available on CD-ROM, contains an analysis of each appellate court decision. Each citation includes a history of the case, other decisions which cite this decision, and any other cases which have modified, overruled, or approved the decision. There are separate analyses for state statutes.

Other Sources of Information

There are a number of other sources of information on New York law. However, it is important to remember that many of these sources are not official legal authorities.

A **legal digest** is a research tool that arranges issues by topic for easy reference. It allows a researcher studying a legal point from one case to easily find other court decisions which were made on similar issues. *West's New York Digest* is one of the most popular legal digests for New York. It indexes New York reported cases by both subject and case name. Another popular digest is the *New York Law Journal Digest-Annotator* which is a subject index of significant lower court cases in the first and second Appellate Division Departments as reported in the *New York Law Journal*. In addition, the New York State Bar Association publishes the *New York Law Digest*, which digests important opinions of the Court of Appeals and the Appellate Divisions. *Abbott's Digest* and *Abbott's Digest 2d* are also available. These digests are not legal authorities.

Black's Law Dictionary is the most popular **legal dictionary** in America today and can be found in any law library. There are also several useful **legal encyclopedias** which discuss New York State law and legal issues. These include *Carmody-Wait Cyclopedia of New York Practice* (an encyclopedia of civil practice and procedural laws) and *New York Jurisprudence* (an encyclopedia of New York substantive law). Legal dictionaries and encyclopedias are not legal authorities.

Law reviews are journals which contain scholarly legal research articles written by lawyers and law students. All the major law schools in New York publish law reviews. Although law review articles are not legal authorities, they are cited in the same way as court cases. For example, **30 BLR 100** would refer to an article beginning on page 100 of volume 30 of the *Buffalo Law Review*, which is published by the Buffalo University School of Law.

The *New York Law Journal*, which is published daily, is the official newspaper for the courts of New York City. It contains court calendars, legal announcements, articles, and summaries or full text of important court decisions from the first and second departments of the Appellate Division. The *Buffalo Law Journal* is a biweekly legal newspaper which includes official notices, court calendars, and articles on legal issues.

McKinney's Consolidated Laws contains the current laws of the state of New York. The laws are annotated with case summaries, references to legal encyclopedias and law review articles, and short articles or practice commentaries which explain specific provisions. *McKinney's Session Laws of New York* is an unofficial publication containing the full text of all laws passed annually by the New York legislature. It also includes supplementary material on New York government and legislative history. Both are published by West Publishing Co. In addition, *West's New York Law Finder*, a one-volume index to New York cases, statutes, court rules, etc., includes West Key numbers for easy reference to other West publications.

Consolidated Laws Service Session Laws, an unofficial publication of the Lawyer's Co-Op, contains the full text of all laws passed annually by the New York legislature.

NOTES

1. The New York State Constitution may be viewed online at http://assembly.state.ny.us/leg/?co=0
2. New York State Constitution, Article IV, §2
3. New York State Constitution, Article V, §1
4. New York State Constitution, Article IV, §4
5. New York State Constitution, Article III, §11
6. New York State Senate home page (http://www.senate.state.ny.us/)
7. The New York State Consolidated Laws may be viewed online at http://www.findlaw.com/11stategov/ny/laws.html
8. CPL §40.20(1)
9. Pen.L. §10.00(7)
10. Pen.L. §10.00(6)
11. Pen.L. §10.00(5)
12. Pen.L. §55.05(1)
13. Pen.L. §55.05(2)
14. CPL §1.20(39)
15. Pen.L. §10.00(2)
16. Pen.L. §10.00(3)
17. Pen.L. §100.00 *et seq.*

18. Pen.L. Article 105
19. Pen.L. §110.00
20. See Pen.L. §20.20(2a)
21. Pen.L. §15.05(1)
22. Pen.L. §15.05(2)
23. Pen.L. §15.05(3)
24. Pen.L. §15.05(4)
25. Pen.L. §25.00
26. *People v. Victor*, 62 N.Y.2d 374, 377, 477 N.Y.S.2d 97, 465 N.E.2d 817 (1984)
27. *People v. Coleccia*, 251 A.D. 2d 5, 6, 674 N.Y.S.2d 10, 11(1st Dep't 1998)
28. Pen.L. §10.00(11)
29. *People v. Goetz*, 68 N.Y.2d 96 (1986)
30. Pen.L. §130.05(3)
31. Pen.L. §40.00(2)
32. Pen.L. §40.15
33. *People v. Wernick*, 89 NY2d 111, 674 NE2d 322, 651 NYS2d 392 (2001)

CHAPTER 3

INDEX CRIMES

INTRODUCTION

The Federal Bureau of Investigation annually publishes the ***Uniform Crime Reports***[1] (UCR), the most widely-used source of official data on crime and criminals in the United States. Much of the UCR deals with **index crimes**, a set of eight serious offenses that the FBI uses as a measure of crime in the United States. They are also known as **Part I Offenses**. Four of them are violent crimes; the other four are property crimes. The eight index crimes measured by the FBI are:

- homicide
- forcible rape
- robbery
- aggravated assault
- burglary
- larceny-theft
- motor-vehicle theft
- arson

However, the definitions used by the FBI in compiling the UCR are not always the same as those found in the New York State Penal Law. This chapter will discuss the definitions of these eight serious crimes as provided by New York state statutes.

All crimes defined in the Penal Law of New York are classified by the seriousness of the crime. For example, first degree manslaughter is a Class B felony. Article 70 of the New York State Penal Law contains mandatory sentencing guidelines for each class of offense. These will be discussed in detail in Chapter 6.

CRIMINAL HOMICIDE

Homicide is the killing of one human being by another. If that killing is illegal, then it is a form of **criminal homicide**. The UCR includes the crimes of murder and nonnegligent manslaughter, which are defined as "the wilful (nonnegligent) killing of one human being by another."[2] New York's homicide statute is found in Article 125 of the Penal Law. To be considered a homicide, a death must meet the conditions outlined in the statute. According to Pen.L. §125.00, homicide is defined as:

> conduct which causes the death of a person or an unborn child with which a female
> has been pregnant for more than twenty-four weeks under circumstances constituting
> murder, manslaughter in the first degree, manslaughter in the second degree,

criminally negligent homicide, abortion in the first degree or self-abortion in the first degree.

Not all homicides are felonies. Self-abortion in the first degree, which is a homicide according to the above definition, is a Class A misdemeanor.[3]

All the homicide offenses discussed in the New York State Penal Law contain two key elements:

- conduct that causes the death of a person (or fetus more than 24 weeks old), and

- the mental culpability of the defendant

Essentially, the first of these elements is the guilty act (*actus reus*) and the second is the guilty mind (*mens rea*).

The specific homicide offense of which a defendant may be convicted depends on his or her level of mental culpability and on the nature of the circumstances surrounding the death (for example, the presence of aggravating factors).

In New York, criminal homicides are divided into two categories:

1. Intentional homicide offenses
   - Murder in the first degree/capital murder[4]
   - Murder in the second degree[5]
   - Manslaughter in the first degree[6]

2. Unintentional homicide offenses
   - Criminally negligent homicide[7]
     - First degree vehicular manslaughter[8]
     - Second degree vehicular manslaughter[9]
   - Second degree manslaughter/reckless homicide[10]

The state also recognizes the crime of felony murder.[11] This is the only form of homicide that does not require a direct relationship between the murderous conduct and the mental state of the defendant. Instead, the intent is based on the intent of the offender to commit one of the felonies listed in the statute.

Criminally Negligent Homicide

Criminally negligent homicide is the lowest level or category of homicide in New York. It is defined in Pen.L. §125.10 as:

> A person is guilty of criminally negligent homicide when, with criminal negligence, he causes the death of another person. Criminally negligent homicide is a class E felony.

To be guilty of this crime, the defendant must create or contribute to the creation of the risk of death. Simply failing to perceive a risk of death that was created by others is not sufficient for a conviction. Death must be reasonably foreseeable under the circumstances to establish criminal negligence. See Chapter 2 for a discussion of the definition of negligence in New York, as found in Pen.L. §15.05.

For example, in the case of *People v. Walden*[12], a woman accidentally shot her husband and then failed to obtain immediate medical attention for him. He died as a result of his injuries and she was found guilty of criminally negligent homicide. On the other hand, in the case of *People v. Boutin*[13], the defendant, while driving a truck on a wet and foggy night at a speed of between 40 and 65 miles per hour, collided with a marked police car. The police car, which was stopped in the right lane of the road behind a disabled tractor trailer, had its emergency lights flashing. The occupants of the police car were killed. The court held that the defendant was not guilty of criminally negligent homicide simply because he failed to see the police car. The court stated that:

> Unless a defendant has engaged in some blameworthy conduct creating or contributing to a substantial and unjustifiable risk of death, he has not committed the crime of criminally negligent homicide; his "nonperception" of a risk, even if death results, is not enough.[14]

In the 1980s the crimes of vehicular manslaughter in the first and second degree were added to the New York State Penal Law as aggravated forms of criminally negligent homicide. These crimes were designed to deal more severely with homicides that were caused by driving while under the influence of alcohol or drugs. To prove either first or second degree vehicular manslaughter, it must be shown not only that the defendant was intoxicated, but also that the intoxication affected his or her capacity to operate the vehicle.

Vehicular Manslaughter in the Second Degree is a Class D felony. According to Pen.L. §125.12, second degree vehicular manslaughter involves criminally negligent homicide in which death is caused by the operation of a vehicle in violation of specified sections of the Vehicle and Traffic Law (V.T.L.) that prohibit driving with a blood alcohol level of 0.10 or greater, driving while intoxicated, and driving while one's ability is impaired by the use of drugs. Basically, to be found guilty of this crime, it must be shown that the defendant acted with criminal negligence, causing death by the operation of a motor vehicle while his or her ability to operate the vehicle was affected by intoxication. Recently the statute was amended to include the operation, while intoxicated, of a snowmobile (added in 1989), an all-terrain vehicle (added in 1990), or a vessel underway (added in 1992).

In addition, there are three situations in which alcohol impairment short of intoxication may be sufficient to lead to a conviction for this offense. These include:

- The operator of a motor vehicle (generally a truck) with a "gross vehicle weight rating of more than eighteen thousand pounds which contains flammable gas, radioactive materials or explosives..."[15]

- The operator of a public vessel who has a blood alcohol level of at least 0.04.[16]

- An individual whose ability to operate a snowmobile is impaired.[17]

Vehicular Manslaughter in the First Degree is a Class C felony. According to Pen.L. §125.13, this crime requires all the elements of second degree vehicular manslaughter as well as the defendant's knowledge that his or her driving license is suspended or revoked following either a past conviction for specified sections of the V.T.L. or the defendant's refusal to submit to a chemical test (e.g., a blood-alcohol test, etc.). The section was recently amended to include suspension or revocation of a driving license issued in another state for conviction of an offense that would be a violation of these specified sections of V.T.L. if committed in New York. This knowledge is the aggravating factor that increases the crime from second to first degree vehicular manslaughter. The burden is placed on the prosecution to prove that the defendant knew of the suspension or revocation of his or her driving privileges and that the defendant knew the reason or the revocation or suspension.

Second Degree Manslaughter

Second degree manslaughter is sometimes known as **reckless homicide**. It is a Class C felony and is defined in Pen.L. §125.15. The statute states that:

> A person is guilty of manslaughter in the second degree when:
> 1. He recklessly causes the death of another person; or
> 2. He commits upon a female an abortional act which causes her death, unless such abortional act is justifiable...; or
> 3. He intentionally causes or aids another person to commit suicide.

The key difference between negligent homicide and second degree manslaughter is the causing of the death recklessly as opposed to negligently. Criminal negligence is based on the negligent failure of the defendant to perceive the risk created by his or her conduct while recklessness requires the defendant's awareness of and conscious disregard of that risk.

Even if the defendant claims that s/he believed the committed act did not create any danger, s/he may be convicted of second degree manslaughter if the belief itself was reckless. For example, in the case of *People v. Gill*[18], a defendant who threw a heavy bucket off a roof, believing that it would land on an empty sidewalk, was found guilty of reckless manslaughter when the bucket struck and killed someone.

The reckless conduct that resulted in the death is not mitigated by the fact that the victim requested or encouraged the offender to engage in the conduct, or in some other way consented to the conduct.

First Degree Manslaughter

First degree manslaughter is a Class B felony, according to Pen.L. §125.20. The Penal Law defines first degree manslaughter as:

> A person is guilty of manslaughter in the first degree when:
> 1. With intent to cause serious physical injury to another person, he causes the death of such person or of a third person; or
> 2. With intent to cause the death of another person, he causes the death of such person or of a third person under circumstances which do not constitute murder because he acts under the influence of extreme emotional disturbance... The fact that homicide was committed under the influence of extreme emotional disturbance constitutes a mitigating circumstance reducing murder to manslaughter in the first degree and need not be proved in any prosecution initiated under this subdivision; or
> 3. He commits upon a female pregnant for more than twenty-four weeks an abortional act which causes her death, unless such abortional act is justifiable...; or
> 4. Being eighteen years old or more and with intent to cause physical injury to a person less than eleven years old, the defendant recklessly engages in conduct which creates a grave risk of serious physical injury to such person and thereby causes the death of such person.

Intent to kill is not a required element of the crime. Although the defendant's actions result in the death of the victim, the prosecution must only show that the defendant had intent to cause serious physical injury to the victim. Obviously, since death is a form of serious physical injury, the intent to kill does establish the intent to seriously injure that is required for this crime. In most cases, guilt is based on some specific definite action of the defendant. Examples of intent to seriously injure the victim might include threats to the victim[19], motive on the part of the defendant[20], and the fact that the attack continued after the victim was incapacitated[21]. It is also possible to convict based on an omission; this is most common in cases of child neglect.

The principle of **transferred intent** also is included in the above statute. Therefore, if the offender intended to injure one victim (A) but accidentally kills a different individual (B), the offender may be found guilty of the intentional murder of B.

Second Degree Murder

Second degree murder, which is defined in Pen.L. §125.25, requires as an element the intent to kill. It is a Class A-I felony, which carries a mandatory life sentence. The statute recognizes four circumstances which constitute second degree murder. The first section of the statute states that;

> A person is guilty of murder in the second degree when (1) with intent to cause the death of another person, he causes the death of such person or of a third person...

The intent required by this statute may include transferred intent. There are two subdivisions of this statute that include various affirmative defenses that may be used by the defendant. These do not negate the defendant's guilt but do allow the defendant to claim the existence of mitigating circumstances that reduce the seriousness of his or her culpability. These include a defense of extreme emotional disturbance and a claim that the conduct consisted of causing or aiding a suicide.

Another type of second degree murder, which is also known as **depraved indifference murder**, occurs when:

> Under circumstances evincing a depraved indifference to human life, he recklessly engages in conduct which creates a grave risk of death to another person, and thereby causes the death of another person...[22]

Essentially, this crime is an aggravated form of reckless homicide, as it requires that the defendant cause the death recklessly. However, this crime contains an additional element in that the reckless act must be performed in a situation that shows a depraved indifference to human life. This element is what distinguishes the crime of second degree murder (a Class A-I felony carrying a mandatory life sentence) from that of second degree manslaughter (a Class C felony). Examples of depraved indifference include behavior that creates a danger to a group of people (e.g., shooting into a crowd, opening the door to the lion's cage in the zoo). The crime may also be committed when the risk of death is to only one individual (e.g., abandoning a seriously injured and/or helpless victim).

The third type of second degree murder is **felony murder**. This is defined as:

> Acting either alone or with one or more other persons, he commits or attempts to commit robbery, burglary, kidnapping, arson, rape in the first degree, sodomy in the first degree, sexual abuse in the first degree, aggravated sexual abuse, escape in the first degree, or escape in the second degree, and, in the course of and in furtherance of such crime or of immediate flight therefrom, he, or another participant, if there be any, causes the death of a person other than one of the participants...[23]

Only murders committed during the commission of the specific crimes listed in this section may lead to a felony murder charge. Therefore, the prosecution must prove the elements necessary for the underlying felony offense to obtain a conviction of felony murder, although the defendant does not have to be separately charged with the underlying felony. However, if the prosecution cannot show beyond a reasonable doubt all the elements of the underlying felony, or an attempt to commit the underlying felony, the prosecution for felony murder is also defeated. The selection of these felonies was based on the belief that they are the most serious and dangerous crimes and that it is therefore acceptable to hold the offender responsible for any deaths that result from these crimes.

The statute does not require that the prosecution show intent to murder. The intent is inferred from the defendant's intent to commit the underlying felony.

For the crime to be felony murder, the killing must occur during the commission of (or attempt to commit) the underlying crime or during the immediate flight from the crime. If the killing occurs first and the underlying crime is committed as an afterthought, rather than having been intended from the start, felony murder has not been committed. Therefore, if an offender murders a victim and then decides to steal the victim's wallet, the offender is not guilty of felony murder.

The statute also requires that the death occur in furtherance of the underlying crime. In the case of *People v. Blake*[24], the defendant and an accomplice planned to steal the victim's purse. The defendant acted as a lookout while the accomplice took the victim into an alleyway. The accomplice then proceed to sexually assault the victim and beat her with a rock until she died. The court held that the defendant was not guilty of felony murder because the killing was not done in furtherance of the planned robbery. Instead, it was committed by the accomplice for a personal and independent reason.

The final type of second degree murder is defined by the statute as:

> Under circumstances evincing a depraved indifference to human life, and being eighteen years old or more the defendant recklessly engages in conduct which creates a grave risk of serious physical injury or death to another person less than eleven years old and thereby causes the death of such person.[25]

Pen.L. §125.25(4) clearly parallels the discussion of depraved indifference murder in Pen.L. §125.25(2). However, there are two key differences between the two sections. First, this section specifies that the defendant must be at least eighteen years of age and the victim must be less than eleven years of age. In addition, the conduct in which the defendant recklessly engages need only created a grave risk of serious physical injury (not death) to the child. Thus, when the victim is under the age of eleven, the level of risk involved in the reckless conduct is reduced.

First Degree Murder

Murder in the first degree is defined in Pen.L. §125.27. There are three key requirements for the crime to be first degree murder:

- the offender must be over the age of 18

- the offender must intentionally kill another person

- at least one of 13 aggravating factors must be present.

The first three of the aggravating factors discussed in the statute focus on the status of the victim:

(i) the intended victim was a police officer... who was at the time of the killing engaged in the course of performing his official duties, and the defendant knew or reasonably should have known that the intended victim was a police officer; or

(ii) the intended victim was a peace officer... who was at the time of the killing engaged in the course of performing his official duties, and the defendant knew or reasonably should have known that the intended victim was such a uniformed court officer, parole officer, probation officer, or employee of the division for youth; or

(iii) the intended victim was an employee of a state correctional institution or was an employee of a local correctional facility... ,who was at the time of the killing engaged in the course of performing his official duties, and the defendant knew or reasonably should have known that the intended victim was an employee of a state correctional institution or a local correctional facility;

According to these first three factors, intentional murder becomes first degree murder if the intended victim is a police officer, a certain type of peace officer, or a state or local correctional employee and that the defendant knew (or reasonably should have known) the victim's status. The statute also requires that the intended victim was involved in performing official duties at the time of the murder. Therefore, the murder of a correctional officer while s/he is off duty and outside the confines of the facility would not necessarily constitute first degree murder.

The fourth factor focuses on the status of the offender, stating that:

(iv) at the time of the commission of the killing, the defendant was confined in a state correctional institution or was otherwise in custody upon a sentence for the term of his natural life, or upon a sentence commuted to one of natural life, or upon a sentence for an indeterminate term the minimum of which was at least fifteen years and the maximum of which was natural life, or at the time of the commission of the killing, the defendant had escaped from such confinement or custody while serving such a sentence and had not yet been returned to such confinement or custody;

This factor elevates intentional murder to first degree murder if the defendant was, at the time of the crime, in custody serving a sentence of life without parole or at least 15 years to life, or had escaped from custody while serving such a sentence. This factor is designed to serve as a deterrent to an offender who is serving a life sentence. This provision does not apply to an offender under sentence of death.

The fifth factor returns to the status of the victim, stating that:

(v) the intended victim was a witness to a crime committed on a prior occasion and the death was caused for the purpose of preventing the intended victim's testimony in any criminal action or proceeding whether or not such action or proceeding had been commenced, or the intended victim had previously testified in a criminal action or proceeding and the killing was committed for the purpose of exacting retribution for such prior testimony, or the intended victim was an immediate family member of a witness to a crime committed on a prior occasion and the killing was committed for the purpose of preventing or influencing the testimony of such witness, or the intended victim was an immediate family member of a witness who had previously testified in a criminal action or proceeding and the killing was committed for the purpose of exacting retribution upon such witness for such prior testimony...;

This factor increases the seriousness of the crime if the intended victim was a witness or an immediate family member of a witness and the victim was killed to prevent or influence testimony or in retribution for prior testimony. Because the statute specifically requires the victim to have witnessed a crime on a prior occasion, it does not include the murder of a potential witness to the immediate crime. Thus, if the offender commits a crime and, during the commission of the crime, kills a witness, this element would not apply.

Factor six focuses on specific circumstances of the commission of the crime as an aggravating factor:

> (vi) the defendant committed the killing or procured commission of the killing pursuant to an agreement with a person other than the intended victim to commit the same for the receipt, or in expectation of the receipt, of anything of pecuniary value from a party to the agreement or from a person other than the intended victim acting at the direction of a party to such agreement;

Essentially, this factor elevates any murder for hire to first degree murder and applies to both the actual killer and the individual who hired the killer.

The next two factors involve murder committed during the commission of another crime:

> (vii) the victim was killed while the defendant was in the course of committing or attempting to commit and in furtherance of robbery, burglary in the first degree or second degree, kidnapping in the first degree, arson in the first degree or second degree, rape in the first degree, sodomy in the first degree, sexual abuse in the first degree, aggravated sexual abuse in the first degree or escape in the first degree, or in the course of and furtherance of immediate flight after committing or attempting to commit any such crime or in the course of and furtherance of immediate flight after attempting to commit the crime of murder in the second degree; provided however, the victim is not a participant in one of the aforementioned crimes and, provided further that, unless the defendant's criminal liability under this subparagraph is based upon the defendant having commanded another person to cause the death of the victim or intended victim pursuant to section 20.00 of this chapter, this subparagraph shall not apply where the defendant's criminal liability is based upon the conduct of another pursuant to section 20.00 of this chapter; or

> (viii) as part of the same criminal transaction, the defendant, with intent to cause serious physical injury to or the death of an additional person or persons, causes the death of an additional person or persons; provided, however, the victim is not a participant in the criminal transaction;

The requirements in factor seven parallel those found in Pen.L. §125.25(3) for second degree felony murder. However, there are several key differences between second degree felony murder and first degree murder under this section. First, while second degree felony murder does not require an intent to kill, in the crime of first degree murder the defendant must intend to kill the victim or another individual. Second, while factor seven applies only to a defendant who was committing or attempting to commit the felony, the second degree felony murder statute also applies to a defendant who was an accomplice of the actual killer. Finally, the crimes listed in factor seven are somewhat more limited than those found in the second degree felony murder statute.

Factor eight requires that the offender must intend to kill at least one victim, intend to kill or seriously injure a second individual, and actually kill at least two people. The purpose of this section is to attempt to deter the offender from killing the second victim: There would be no rational objection to killing a second victim if the penalty for killing two persons was the same as for killing only one. The statute specifically excludes victims who are participants in the crime, so that an offender who kills a victim and then kills an accomplice to the first killing does not fall under this section.

Factor nine focuses on recidivist murderers:

> (ix) prior to committing the killing, the defendant had been convicted of murder..., or had been convicted in another jurisdiction of an offense which, if committed in this state, would constitute a violation...;

Essentially, this applies to a defendant who has been convicted of the crime of first or second degree murder in the past. The prior conviction may have occurred in New York or in some other state.

Factor ten returns to the circumstances of the crime, stating that:

> (x) the defendant acted in an especially cruel and wanton manner pursuant to a course of conduct intended to inflict and inflicting torture upon the victim prior to the victim's death. As used in this subparagraph, "torture" means the intentional and depraved infliction of extreme physical pain; "depraved" means the defendant relished the infliction of extreme physical pain upon the victim evidencing debasement or perversion or that the defendant evidenced a sense of pleasure in the infliction of extreme physical pain;

Essentially, this section applies if the defendant intentionally tortured the victim in some way prior to killing the victim. The statute does not include any type of injury or mistreatment to the body of an unconscious or dead victim because the requirement that extreme physical pain be inflicted would not be met.

Factor eleven returns to the issue of repeat murderers, this time focusing on serial killers:

> (xi) the defendant intentionally caused the death of two or more additional persons within the state in separate criminal transactions within a period of twenty-four months when committed in a similar fashion or pursuant to a common scheme or plan;

The section specifically requires that the victims be killed within the state. If one of the three victims is killed outside of New York, this factor does not apply. The statute is somewhat unclear as to the meaning of "a similar fashion." A broad interpretation of this term might suggest that the requirement would be met if all three victims were killed with the same type of weapon (e.g., all victims were stabbed or all victims were shot). On the other hand, a more narrow interpretation might require that the same method of operation be used in all homicides.

Factor twelve returns to the status of the victim, stating that;

> (xii) the intended victim was a judge... and the defendant killed such victim because such victim was, at the time of the killing, a judge;

This factor elevates intentional murder to first degree murder if the victim is a judge who was killed because of his or her status as a judge. Unlike the first three factors, this section does not require that the victim be engaged in the performance of official duties at the time of the murder. This requirement was deleted because revenge on a judge is more likely to occur outside the courtroom.

Finally, factor thirteen focuses again on the circumstances of the crime, stating that,

> (xiii) the victim was killed in furtherance of an act of terrorism...;

This section was added to the first degree murder statute in 2001.

The statute also requires that, in all of the above situations, the defendant must be "more than eighteen years old at the time of the commission of the crime."[26] It is not really clear from the way the statute is worded whether the defendant must be 19 years old or 18 years and one day old. One lower court has held that a defendant who is at least 18 years and one day old may be tried under this statute.[27]

Like the statute defining second degree murder, this statute also includes various affirmative defenses that may be used by the defendant to plead for mitigating circumstances. These include a defense of extreme emotional disturbance and a claim that the conduct consisted of causing or aiding a suicide.

First degree murder is a Class A-I felony. In 1995, the death penalty was reinstated as a possible sentence for this crime. Capital punishment in New York will be discussed in more detail in Chapter 7.

FORCIBLE RAPE

In the Uniform Crime Reporting Program, **forcible rape** is defined as "the carnal knowledge of a female forcibly and against her will."[28] This originally reflected the prevailing definitions used in many states in the United States, including New York, where sex offenses are discussed in Article 130 of the Penal Law. However, over the past 25 years, the New York State Penal Law relating to sex offenses has been significantly revised. In February, 2001 the Sexual Assault Reform Act came into effect. One of the key provisions of the act was to change the language of Article 130 to be gender neutral. All persons guilty of various sex crimes, and their victims, are now referred to as "he or she." Other changes that have occurred as a result of this Act include:

- raising the age of consent in various sections of Article 130 of the Penal Law

- repealing the law punishing consensual sodomy between consenting adults

- creating two new Class E felonies: rape in the third degree and sodomy in the third degree

- creating a new statute punishing use of date rape drugs

- creating a Class A misdemeanor offense of forcible touching

There have been a number of other recent changes to the New York sex crime laws. First, the marital exemption clauses in statutes prohibiting forcible sexual assaults have been deleted, so that men who rape or sexually abuse their wives may no longer use their marital state as a defense. Because the statutes are gender neutral, the reverse is also true (women who rape or sexually abuse their husbands may not claim marital exemption either). Second, the definition of the "forcible compulsion" necessary to commit rape has been changed. Rather than requiring force sufficient to overcome resistence, the law now accepts express or implied threats that place the victim in fear of immediate physical harm. Thus, it is no longer necessary for the prosecution to produce evidence at trial (bruises, black eyes, broken bones, etc.) that the victim attempted to fight off the attacker before succumbing. Third, the requirement that the elements of force, penetration, and identity must be substantiated also has been abolished so that, as with the prosecution of any other crime, the victim's testimony may be sufficient to prove the defendant guilty of rape. Of course the jury must, as in any case, deal with the issue of the victim's credibility. Finally, the state passed a rape shield law[29] that limits the defense's ability to introduce evidence concerning the rape victim's past sexual conduct. This statute, which only applies to the prosecution of sex crimes, states that:

> Evidence of a victim's sexual conduct shall not be admissible in a prosecution for an offense or an attempt to commit an offense defined in article one hundred thirty of the penal law unless such evidence:
> 1. proves or tends to prove specific instances of the victim's prior sexual conduct with the accused; or
> 2. proves or tends to prove that the victim has been convicted of an offense under section 230.00 of the penal law within three years prior to the sex offense which is the subject of the prosecution; or
> 3. rebuts evidence introduced by the people of the victim's failure to engage in sexual intercourse, deviate sexual intercourse or sexual contact during a given period of time; or
> 4. rebuts evidence introduced by the people which proves or tends to prove that the accused is the cause of pregnancy or disease of the victim, or the source of semen found in the victim; or
> 5. is determined by the court after an offer of proof by the accused outside the hearing of the jury, or such hearing as the court may require, and a statement by the court of its findings of fact essential to its determination, to be relevant and admissible in the interests of justice.

The statute does not prevent the prosecution from admitting into evidence information about any past allegations of rape made by the victim against other defendants, if there is sufficient evidence to show that these prior allegations were false.

According to Pen.L. §130.05, a key element of every sexual offense in Article 130 is that of lack of consent: the sexual act must be committed without the consent of the victim. Pen.L. §130.05(2) states that:

> Lack of consent results from:
> (a) Forcible compulsion; or
> (b) Incapacity to consent; or
> (c) Where the offense charged is sexual abuse, any circumstances, in addition to forcible compulsion or incapacity to consent, in which the victim does not expressly or impliedly acquiesce in the actor's conduct; or
> (d) Where the offense charged is rape in the third degree..., or sodomy in the third degree..., in addition to forcible compulsion, circumstances under which, at the time of the act of intercourse or deviate sexual intercourse, the victim clearly expressed that he or she did not consent to engage in such act, and a reasonable person in the actor's situation would have understood such person's words and acts as an expression of lack of consent to such act under all the circumstances.

Pen.L. §130.05(3) goes on to identify individuals who are considered incapable of consenting to sexual intercourse. These include:

- any individual under the age of seventeen

- any individual who is mentally disabled, mentally incapacitated, or physically helpless

- any individual who is committed to the care and custody of the New York State Department of Corrections, where the offender is an employee of the Department who is not married to the victim

- any individual who is committed to the care and custody of a local correctional facility, where the offender is an employee of the facility who is not married to the victim

- any individual who is in residential care with the Office of Children and Family Services, where the offender is an employee of the Office who is not married to the victim

- any individual who is a client or patient, where the offender is a physical or mental health care provider, and the sexual act occurs during a treatment session, examination, consultation, or interview

Another element of all the rape statutes in this section is that of **sexual intercourse.** According to Pen.L. §130.00(1), some penetration, regardless of how slight, is an essential element of sexual intercourse, which is defined as having "its ordinary meaning." This refers to sexual relations between a male and a female. Because of this, intercourse between two individuals of the same sex does not meet the statutory requirements for this crime. The statutory definition of sexual intercourse does not include a requirement of ejaculation; therefore, the absence of semen will not defeat a charge of rape. However, deviate sexual intercourse, which does not include penetration, does not fulfill the statutory requirements for this crime, although the offender may be guilty of **sodomy in the first degree**.[30]

New York recognizes three degrees of rape. However, unlike most crimes, in which the higher degrees of a crime merely add elements to the basic crime, the higher degrees of rape are significantly different from the lower degrees.

First Degree Rape

According to Pen.L. §130.35, **rape in the first degree** occurs when an individual engages in sexual intercourse with another person under one of the following conditions:

- by forcible compulsion
- when the victim is unable to consent because s/he is physically helpless
- when the victim is less than eleven years old
- when the victim is less than thirteen years old and the offender is at least eighteen years old.

First degree rape is a Class B felony.

Pen.L. §130.00(8) defines **forcible compulsion** as compelling the victim to participate either by the use of physical force or by an express or implied threat of force which places the victim in fear of immediate death or physical injury to himself, herself, or another person, or which places the victim in fear that s/he or another person will immediately be kidnapped. To establish forcible compulsion, the prosecution must also establish the victim's lack of consent.

Physically helpless is defined in Pen.L. §130.00(7) as meaning the victim is unconscious or for some other reason physically unable to communicate his or her unwillingness to participate in sexual intercourse. This includes victims who are unconscious from alcohol or drugs, regardless of whether these substances were consumed voluntarily. The courts have also held that natural uninduced sleep constitutes physical helplessness, so that an individual who is sleeping is incapable of consent. However, victims who are physically incapacitated so that they cannot resist their assailants are not physically helpless under the statute as long as they are able in some way to communicate their lack of consent.

Second Degree Rape

Second degree rape is defined in Pen.L. §130.30:

> A person is guilty of rape in the second degree when:
> 1. being eighteen years old or more, he or she engages in sexual intercourse with another person less than fifteen years old; or
> 2. he or she engages in sexual intercourse with another person who is incapable of consent by reason of being mentally disabled or mentally incapacitated.

The statute also states that an affirmative defense to this crime exists if the defendant was less than four years older than the victim at the time of the sexual act. This crime is a Class D felony.

Third Degree Rape

Third degree rape, which is defined in Pen.L. §130.25, is a Class E felony. According to the statute,

> A person is guilty of rape in the third degree when:
> 1. He or she engages in sexual intercourse with another person to whom the actor is not married who is incapable of consent by reason of some factor other than being less than seventeen years old;
> 2. Being twenty-one years old or more, he or she engages in sexual intercourse with another person less than seventeen years old; or
> 3. He or she engages in sexual intercourse with another person without such person's consent where such lack of consent is by reason of some factor other than incapacity to consent.

Essentially, this crime includes three possible situations. In the first scenario, the defendant has sexual intercourse with a victim who is unable to consent for reasons other than age. The victim may be unable to consent because of being mentally defective, incapacitated, or physically helpless. This includes victims who are under the influence of alcohol or drugs. In addition, the victim might be unable to consent because of his or her status as a prisoner, patient, or client. According to Pen.L. §130.10,

> In any prosecution under this article in which the victim's lack of consent is based solely upon his or her incapacity to consent because he or she was mentally defective, mentally incapacitated or physically helpless, it is an affirmative defense that the defendant, at the time he or she engaged in the conduct constituting the offense, did not know of the facts or conditions responsible for such incapacity to consent.

Therefore, if the defendant was unaware of the victim's mental defect or incapacitation, this may be a defense against the charge of third degree rape.

The second situation involves a defendant who is at least twenty-one years of age and a victim who is less than seventeen years of age. In this situation, the crime is non-consensual solely because the victim is too young to be able to give consent.

The third situation involves a victim who does not consent to the sexual intercourse for some reason other than his or her inability to consent. Thus, in this case, although the victim is legally capable of consenting, s/he chooses not to consent, and the offender engages in sexual intercourse with the victim regardless of this lack of consent. Essentially, this section of the statute legally reinforces the belief that, "No means no!"

For both second and third degree rape, it is not a defense for the actor to claim that s/he did not know the age of the victim or that s/he believed the victim to be above the age of consent that was specified in the statute.

These statutes are gender neutral and apply not only to older males who engage in sexual intercourse with younger females, but also to older females who engage in sexual intercourse with younger males.

ROBBERY

The FBI's Uniform Crime Reporting Program defines **robbery** as "the taking or attempting to take anything of value from the care, custody, or control of a person or persons by force or threat of force or violence and/or by putting the victim in fear."[31] In New York, Pen.L. §160.00 defines **robbery** as:

> Robbery is forcible stealing. A person forcibly steals property and commits robbery when, in the course of committing a larceny, he uses or threatens the immediate use of physical force upon another person for the purpose of:
> 1. Preventing or overcoming resistance to the taking of the property or to the retention thereof immediately after the taking; or
> 2. Compelling the owner of such property or another person to deliver up the property or to engage in other conduct which aids in the commission of the larceny.

This definition identifies three elements that must be proved for an individual to be convicted of the crime of robbery in New York:

1. The defendant must commit a larceny;

2. The defendant must use or threaten to use physical force upon another person; and

3. The defendant's intent is to take or retain the property of another person.

This definition presents robbery as a larceny in which the property is taken from the victim, against the victim's will, using force or the threat of force. Because of the use of force or fear to illegally acquire personal property, New York considers robbery to be both a crime against the person and a crime against property.

Because the element of larceny is a requirement for the crime of robbery, property must be taken for the defendant to be found guilty of robbery. In addition, for the charge of attempted robbery, the intent to take property must be established. However, even if it cannot be shown that the defendant took or intended to take property, s/he may be guilty of assault or some other crime.

The use of force or threatened force is also required for a robbery to occur. This element of using or threatening physical force is what distinguishes robbery from larceny. There is a large amount of case law dealing with the issue of what constitutes force. The force or threat must be directed against a person, not against the property.[32] However, the courts have held that, if the damage to the property would endanger a person, the use or threat of force against that property does constitute the element required for the crime of robbery. In addition, simple bodily contact or touching is not sufficient to constitute the force required for robbery. For example, in *People v. Lumpkin*,[33] the court held that simply taking something from a person's open hand does not constitute force sufficient for a conviction of robbery.

A threat is sufficient to meet the requirement of force if the threat involves the immediate use of physical force upon the victim or another person. The threat may involve a weapon, such as a knife or gun, or may simply involve a threat to hit or punch the victim. The threat does not need to be verbal; threats implied by the defendant's conduct (for example, a case in which a shoplifter lifted his jacket to display a pistol in his waistband[34]) are sufficient to meet the statutory requirement.

New York recognizes three levels of robbery. According to Pen.L. §160.05, **third degree robbery** occurs when the defendant forcibly steals property. This is a Class D felony. Basically, third degree robbery is a forcible larceny and requires only that the three elements of robbery discussed above be established.

Second degree robbery, a Class C felony, is defined in Pen.L. §160.10. The statute states that:

> A person is guilty of robbery in the second degree when he forcibly steals property and when:
> 1. He is aided by another person actually present; or
> 2. In the course of the commission of the crime or of immediate flight therefrom, he or another participant in the crime:
>   (a) Causes physical injury to any person who is not a participant in the crime; or
>   (b) Displays what appears to be a pistol, revolver, rifle, shotgun, machine gun or other firearm; or
> 3. The property consists of a motor vehicle...

In the first two sections of this statute, the crime is elevated from third to second degree robbery by the presence of another person assisting the offender. The statute requires the other person both to be present and to aid the robber in the commission of the crime. Presence alone is not sufficient for a charge of second degree robbery, nor is the assistance of an accomplice who is not actually present at the scene of the crime. In addition, if the defendant or an accomplice physically injures anyone who is not participating in the robbery, the crime is elevated to second degree robbery.

The third section of this statute criminalizes the crime of **carjacking**. Essentially, this section elevates a crime from third to second degree robbery if the property stolen is a motor vehicle. This section, which was added to the Penal Law in 1995, was enacted in response to a series of carjackings that occurred in the state. The stated purpose of this section of the statute is to allow individuals to feel safe in their automobiles by discouraging carjacking.

Finally, Pen.L. §160.15 discusses the crime of **first degree robbery**, which is a Class B felony. The statute states that:

> A person is guilty of robbery in the first degree when he forcibly steals property and when, in the course of the commission of the crime or of immediate flight therefrom, he or another participant in the crime:
> 1. Causes serious physical injury to any person who is not a participant in the crime; or
> 2. Is armed with a deadly weapon; or
> 3. Uses or threatens the immediate use of a dangerous instrument; or
> 4. Displays what appears to be a pistol, revolver, rifle, shotgun, machine gun or other firearm...

According to section 2 of this statute, a robbery is elevated to first degree when the defendant is armed with a deadly weapon. A deadly weapon is any object which is designed primarily for use as a weapon, such as a firearm, a switchblade knife, blackjack, dagger, etc. It does not have to be displayed to, or even seen by, the victim during the robbery. As long as the defendant is carrying the weapon on his or her person at the time, the requirement is met. However, if the defendant steals a deadly weapon during a robbery and immediately flees with it, this does not automatically satisfy the requirement of possession of a deadly weapon.[35] A gun is considered to be a deadly weapon only if it is loaded with live ammunition and operable. The prosecution has the burden of proving this; if they fail, the charge must be reduced.

In addition, under section 3 of this statute, a robbery becomes first degree if the offender uses or threatens to use a dangerous instrument. The term "dangerous instrument" is more general and wide-reaching than the term "deadly weapon." According to Pen.L. §10.00(13), a dangerous instrument is anything that is capable of causing death or serious injury. It may be an ordinary object that is used in such a way as to render it dangerous. An unloaded or non-operable gun that is used as a club may be considered a dangerous instrument, as may a vehicle. The offender must actually possess the dangerous instrument; threats alone are not sufficient. However, if the victim feels the instrument, s/he does not have to actually see it. The case of *People v. Owusa*[36] confirmed that a body part does not constitute a dangerous instrument. In that case, the defendant bit the victim's finger so severely that the nerves were severed. However, the court held that not even the body parts of an individual who has had special training (e.g., in the martial arts or boxing) could be considered to be a dangerous instrument, regardless of the damage that was inflicted by them.

If the offender displays what appears to be a firearm, the crime is either first or second degree robbery. The relevant clauses in the first and second degree robbery statutes are identical.[37] A defendant who, while committing the crime or fleeing from the crime, "displays what appears to be a pistol, revolver, rifle, shotgun, machine gun, or other firearm" may be charged under either section of the robbery statutes. Pen.L. §160.15(4) states that it is an affirmative defense if the firearm is "not a loaded weapon from which a shot, readily capable of producing death or other serious physical injury, could be discharged." If the offender is charged with first degree robbery, the crime will be reduced to second degree robbery if the defense establishes this by a preponderance of the evidence. In most cases, unless it is clear that the weapon used was not loaded and operable, the state will generally charge the defendant with first degree robbery and force him or her to seek a reduction in the charge by proving that the gun was unloaded or inoperable.

AGGRAVATED ASSAULT

There is often some confusion about the actual meaning of **assault**. In some states, such as Illinois and Florida, assault does not actually involve the infliction of an injury upon another person; it is merely an intentional attempt or threat to cause an injury. In these states, when an injury is actually inflicted, a **battery** has occurred. However, in New York, one of the elements of the crime of assault is the infliction of some type of physical injury to another person. An intentional attempt or threat, when no actual injury occurs, is considered an **attempted assault**. There is not crime of battery in New York.

The Uniform Crime Reporting Program also considers assault to involve the actual injury of another person. The UCR focuses specifically on aggravated assault, which it defines as:

> an unlawful attack by one person upon another for the purpose of inflicting severe or aggravated bodily injury. This type of assault is usually accompanied by the use of a weapon or by means likely to produce death or great bodily harm.[38]

The crime of assault is discussed in Article 120 of the New York State Penal Law. In general, two elements are required for the crime of assault in New York:

1. The offender must cause physical injury, serious physical injury, or disfigurement to another person, and

2. The offender must have a specific or particular *mens rea* or intent.

The definition of the term **physical injury** has generated an enormous amount of litigation and has led to the production of much case law on the subject. Pen.L. §10.00(9) defines physical injury as the "impairment of physical condition or substantial pain." Over the years, the courts have held that bumps, bruises, abrasions, and superficial cuts do not constitute sufficient impairment to fit the definition of physical injury under the law.[39] The courts generally consider impairment to be a situation in which, as a result of the assault, the victim had significant difficulty performing basic tasks of living, such as breathing, eating, talking, urinating, seeing clearly, or walking. Permanent scars, fractures, loss of feeling from nerve damage, and damage to teeth may also constitute impairment. The courts have been very strict in requiring proof of physical injury. However, in the absence of an obvious impairment, physical injury may be established by substantial pain. Obviously the level of pain is a subjective issue, but may be determined by the degree and duration of the pain and by the nature of the assault.

Pen.L. §10.00(10) defines **serious physical injury** as a "physical injury which creates a substantial risk of death, or which causes death or serious and protracted disfigurement, protracted impairment of health or protracted loss or impairment of the function of any bodily organ." The creation of a substantial risk of death may be determined by medical testimony. In most cases, unless the testimony is highly conjectural, the testimony of a medical professional that the injuries were serious enough to be life-threatening will suffice to establish serious physical injury. *Serious and protracted disfigurement* generally refers to substantial permanent scars of some type. *Protracted impairment of health* refers to situations such as long-term pain or restricted physical activity as a result of the assault (e.g., as a result of a beating, a victim suffers long-term headaches and facial pain). Finally, *protracted loss or impairment of the function of any bodily organ* includes situations such as sensory impairment (e.g., impaired hearing or vision), lost or broken teeth, serious fractures, loss of mobility, etc. The loss of a fetus has been held by the courts to constitute a serious physical injury to the pregnant mother.[40]

The New York State Penal Law recognizes three degrees of assault. The degree is determined by the seriousness of the injury inflicted upon the victim, the defendant's level of intent or mental culpability, and any additional aggravating factors (e.g., the use of a deadly weapon, the victimization of a police officer or a child, driving under the influence). Thus, the distinction between *physical injury* and *serious physical injury* is significant because causing serious physical injury is generally a felony, while causing physical injury may be a misdemeanor.

Third Degree Assault

Third degree assault is defined in Pen.L. §120.00. This statute states that:

A person is guilty of assault in the third degree when:
1. With intent to cause physical injury to another person, he causes such injury to such person or to a third person; or
2. He recklessly causes physical injury to another person; or
3. With criminal negligence, he causes physical injury to another person by means of a deadly weapon or a dangerous instrument.

One of the key elements of this crime is the culpable mental state of the offender. An assault may be considered third degree if the offender committed the injury intentionally, recklessly, or through criminal negligence.

The second element of this crime is that physical injury must occur. However, if the culpable mental state is criminal negligence, the statute requires that the physical injury be caused by means of a deadly weapon or dangerous instrument. If the crime involves criminal negligence but does not involve the use of a deadly weapon or dangerous instrument, it is not third degree assault.

Another important point about this statute is that it specifically states that, if the assailant intended to cause physical injury to a specific individual but actually injures a third person instead, the action is not excused. In other words, the intent applies to both the intended victim and the actual victim, even if they are not the same person.

Third degree assault is a Class A misdemeanor and would not be considered aggravated assault for the purposes of the UCR.

Second Degree Assault

Second degree assault is considered more serious and is classified as a Class D felony, rather than a misdemeanor. There are a large variety of circumstances that can elevate an assault from a misdemeanor to a felony. According to Pen.L. §120.05,

A person is guilty of assault in the second degree when:
1. With intent to cause serious physical injury to another person, he causes such injury to such person or to a third person; or
2. With intent to cause physical injury to another person, he causes such injury to such person or to a third person by means of a deadly weapon or a dangerous instrument; or
3. With intent to prevent a peace officer, police officer, a fireman..., an emergency medical service paramedic or emergency medical service technician, or medical or related personnel in a hospital emergency department, from performing a lawful duty, by means including releasing or failing to control an animal under circumstances evincing the actor's intent that the animal obstruct the lawful activity of such peace officer, police officer, fireman, paramedic or technician, he causes physical injury to such peace officer, police officer, fireman, paramedic, technician or medical or related personnel in a hospital emergency department; or
4. He recklessly causes serious physical injury to another person by means of a deadly weapon or a dangerous instrument; or
5. For a purpose other than lawful medical or therapeutic treatment, he intentionally causes stupor, unconsciousness or other physical impairment or injury to another person by administering to him, without his consent, a drug, substance or preparation capable of producing the same; or
6. In the course of and in furtherance of the commission or attempted commission of a felony, other than a felony defined in article one hundred thirty which requires corroboration for conviction, or of immediate flight therefrom, he, or another participant if there be any, causes physical injury to a person other than one of the participants; or
7. Having been charged with or convicted of a crime and while confined in a correctional facility ... pursuant to such charge or conviction, with intent to cause physical injury to another person, he causes such injury to such person or to a third person; or
8. Being eighteen years old or more and with intent to cause physical injury to a person less than eleven years old, the defendant recklessly causes serious physical injury to such person; or
9. Being eighteen years old or more and with intent to cause physical injury to a person less than seven years old, the defendant causes such injury to such person; or
10. Acting at a place the person knows, or reasonably should know, is on school grounds and with intent to cause physical injury, he or she:
    (a) causes such injury to an employee of a school or public school district; or
    (b) not being a student of such school or public school district,
    causes physical injury to another, and such other person is a student of such school who is attending or present for educational purposes...
11. With intent to cause physical injury to a train operator, ticket inspector, conductor or bus operator employed by any transit agency, authority or company, public or private, whose operation is authorized by New York state or any of its political subdivisions, he or she causes physical injury to such train operator, ticket inspector, conductor or bus operator while such employee

is performing an assigned duty on, or directly related to, the operation of a train or bus.

Section 1 of the statute is identical to section 1 of the third degree assault statute, except that the level of injury has been increased from *physical injury* to *serious physical injury*. Thus, the seriousness of the assault elevates the crime from a misdemeanor to a felony assault. A further similarity between the two sections is that they both allow for the possibility that the intended and actual victims are different people.

Section 4 of this statute is similar to section 2 of the third degree assault statute, requiring the same mental state, but it also requires a higher level of injury; it also specifies that the means used to commit the assault be a deadly weapon or dangerous instrument.

Most of the other sections of this statute still require only intent to cause physical injury. The crime is elevated from a misdemeanor to a felony assault because of the circumstances surrounding the crime. In section 2 (as well as section 4), the means used to commit the assault (a deadly weapon or dangerous instrument) constitutes an aggravating factor. Similarly, in section 5, the means involves a drug or other substance administered against the victim's will that produces a stupor or unconscious state (including a coma). This section is intended to control the misuse of an anesthetic and is rarely used. In section 3, the victim of the assault (police officers or certain other public servants engaged in performing their duties) increases the seriousness of the offense. In this section, actual intent to injure is not required; the offender need only have the intent to prevent the victim from performing a lawful duty. In section 7, confinement within a correctional facility elevates the assault from a misdemeanor to a felony.

Section 6 of this statute is commonly known as **felony assault** and parallels the crime of felony murder. Felony assault differs from most of the other assault provisions in Article 120 of the Penal Law in that there is no requirement of *mens rea* that relates directly to the injury. According to the courts, "the intent necessary to sustain the conviction for felony assault is inferred from the intent to commit the underlying felony."[41] In addition, because the section includes all participants in the underlying felony, it is possible for a defendant to be convicted of a felony assault committed by an accomplice even if he or she is not physically present at the scene of the assault.[42] Because the actual assault is not actually intended, there is no crime of attempted felony assault.[43] The victim in the crime must not be one of the individuals who is committing or assisting in the commission of the underlying felony.

In 1990, several provisions intended to protect child victims of assault were enacted. One of these was Pen.L. §120.05(8). This section elevates a crime to second degree assault if the offender is an adult (eighteen years of age or over) who has intent to cause physical injury to a child (under the age of eleven) and who recklessly causes serious physical injury to the child. This section requires two separate culpable mental states, both intent and recklessness. It also requires that the injury that is recklessly caused be serious physical injury, although the intent need only be to cause physical injury. The statute primarily targets parents who might intend to injure their child but recklessly disregard the risk of a more serious injury.

In 1996, Pen.L. §120.05(9) was enacted by the legislature to provide additional protection for young victims of assault. This section elevates intentional physical injury from a third degree assault to a second degree assault if the offender is at least eighteen years of age and the victim is less than seven years of age. Unlike section 8, the injury for section 9 does not have to be serious physical injury.

Section 10 was enacted in response to the recent increase in violence on school property. This section of the statute involves two separate possible situations, both of which require that the offender be on school grounds and have intent to cause physical injury to another person. In the first situation, the status of the victim (a school district employee) increases the crime from third to second degree assault. In the second situation, the victim, but not the offender, must be a student of the school at which the assault occurs.

Finally, Section 11 was added to the statute in 2002. The aggravating factor that elevates the crime from third to second degree assault is the occupation and status of the victim: intentionally causing physical injury to an on-duty train or bus operator or other transit employee is a felony.

First Degree Assault

First degree assault is a Class B felony. According to §120.10,

A person is guilty of assault in the first degree when:
1. With intent to cause serious physical injury to another person, he causes such injury to such person or to a third person by means of a deadly weapon or a dangerous instrument; or
2. With intent to disfigure another person seriously and permanently, or to destroy, amputate or disable permanently a member or organ of his body, he causes such injury to such person or to a third person; or
3. Under circumstances evincing a depraved indifference to human life, he recklessly engages in conduct which creates a grave risk of death to another person, and thereby causes serious physical injury to another person; or
4. In the course of and in furtherance of the commission or attempted commission of a felony or of immediate flight therefrom, he, or another participant if there be any, causes serious physical injury to a person other than one of the participants.

Section 1 of this statute is similar to Pen.L. §120.05(2), relating to second degree assault. The only significant difference is that for first degree assault, the required intent must be to cause serious physical injury, rather than physical injury. In both cases, the means must involve the use of a deadly weapon or dangerous instrument. In section 2, the offender's intent to disfigure or disable the victim increases the seriousness of the crime. In these sections of the statute, the intended and actual victims do not have to be the same person.

Section 3 requires a culpable mental state of recklessness, rather than intent, and is, in that respect, similar to Pen.L. §120.00(2), Pen.L. §120.05(4), and Pen.L. §120.05(8). However, here the behavior must be so reckless that it shows a depraved indifference to human life. As with the other crimes involving recklessness, the absence of intent means that there can be no attempt to commit this offense and that intoxication may not be used as a defense. Finally, section 4 is another reference to felony assault. Causing serious physical injury to the victim (as opposed to the physical injury required for second degree assault), elevates the crime from a Class D felony (second degree assault) to a Class B felony (first degree assault). As with second degree felony assault, the intent to injure the victim is inferred from the intent to commit the underlying felony.

Other Types of Assault

There are several other assault offenses which are discussed in Article 120 of the Penal Law. **Vehicular assault in the second degree**, which is a Class E felony defined in Pen.L. §120.03, is an aggravated form of criminally negligent assault. The culpable mental state for this crime is criminal negligence, rather than specific intent. This crime occurs when the defendant, while under the influence of alcohol or drugs, causes serious physical injury through one of the following acts:

- operating a vehicle
- operating a vessel
- operating a vehicle carrying hazardous substances when the serious physical injury is caused by the hazardous substance
- operating a snowmobile
- operating an all terrain vehicle

Vehicular assault in the first degree, which is defined in Pen.L. §120.04, includes all the elements of second degree vehicular assault. In addition, the defendant either knows or has reason to know that his or her license or privilege of obtaining a license is suspended or revoked because of either a past conviction for V&TL §1192(2), (3), or (4), or the defendant's refusal to submit to a chemical test (e.g., a blood-alcohol test).[44] This section is similar to the vehicular manslaughter provisions found in §125.13 and is designed to target repeat offenders. A conviction of first degree vehicular assault actually requires proof of two separate culpable mental states: criminal negligence (as found in the second degree vehicular assault statute) and knowingly (relating to the operation of a motor vehicle with knowledge of a suspended or revoked license). Originally, this section only applied to the revocation or suspension of a New York license. However, in 1996 the statute was amended to include suspension or revocation in another state for an offense that would violate the specified provisions of the Vehicle and Traffic Law if it was committed in New York. This crime is a Class D felony.

In 1996, two new sections of Article 120 were enacted to increase the severity of assaults committed by a group of offenders. Pen.L. §120.06 created the offense of **gang assault in the second degree**, which is a Class C felony. This crime occurs when the following elements are present:

- the offender has intent to cause physical injury to another person

- the offender is aided by at least two others who are present at the scene of the assault

- the offender actually causes serious physical injury to the intended victim or a third person.

Gang assault in the first degree, which is discussed in Pen.L. §120.07 is identical except that the offender must have the intent to cause serious physical injury (rather than physical injury). This elevates the crime to a Class B felony.

There are three sections of Article 120 which specifically deal with assaults upon police officers and other public servants. The first is Pen.L. §120.05(3), which involves second degree assault upon a police officer, peace officer, fireman, etc. This is part of the second degree assault statute discussed above. The second, Pen.L. §120.11, deals with **aggravated assault upon a police office or peace officer**. This crime is a Class B felony and has several elements. The offender must have intent to cause serious physical injury to a person that s/he knows or reasonably should know to be a police officer or peace officer engaged in the course of official duties. In addition, the offender must cause the serious physical injury by means of a deadly weapon or dangerous instrument. This crime is more serious than the second degree assault provision in Pen.L. §120.05(3) because the required level of harm is greater (serious physical harm rather than physical harm). Finally, the third provision, Pen.L. §120.08, was added in 1996 and deals with **assault on a peace officer, police officer, fireman or emergency medical services professional**. This is a Class C felony and requires that the defendant have intent to prevent a public servant from performing a lawful duty and that the defendant cause serious physical injury to that public servant.

In 1990, several provisions were added to Article 120 of the Penal Law as a way of increasing protection for young children under the age of 11 from assault by adults (individuals at least 18 years of age). One of these was Pen.L. §120.05(8), which is part of the second degree assault statute discussed above. The other was Pen.L. §120.12, which deals with **aggravated assault upon a person less than eleven years old**. The key elements of this crime, which is a Class E felony, are:

- The defendant is at least 18 years of age

- The victim is less than 11 years of age

- The defendant commits third degree assault as defined in Pen.L. §120.00

- The defendant is a repeat offender who has been convicted of this crime upon a child victim (under the age of 11) within the past three years

The purpose of this statute was to increase the severity of punishment for recidivist child abusers by elevating third degree assault to a Class E felony if the above elements are present.

In 1996, a third provision, Pen.L. §120.05(9) was added to provide more protection for young victims of assault. This is also is part of the second degree assault statute discussed above. Finally, Pen.L. §120.01 became effective in 1998. This statute focuses on the crime of **reckless assault of a child by a child day care provider**. Essentially, it elevates misdemeanor third degree assault to a Class E felony when the following elements are present:

- The defendant is a child day care provider or the employer of such a provider

- The victim is less than 11 years of age

- The defendant recklessly causes serious physical injury to the child

This crime is considered less serious than second degree assault on a child, as discussed in Pen.L. §120.05(8) because this statute does not require that the offender have any intent to cause physical injury to the victim.

BURGLARY

In common law, the crime of **burglary** was defined as the breaking and entering of a dwelling at night with intent to commit a felony. Today, the definition of burglary includes structures other than a dwelling place, can occur during the daytime as well as at night, and can involve either an intended felony or misdemeanor. The UCR defines burglary as the "unlawful entry of a structure to commit a felony or theft."[45]

In New York, trespass and burglary statutes are found in Article 140 of the Penal Law. **Criminal trespass** occurs when an offender knowingly enters or remains unlawfully on real property. Burglary is criminal trespass for the purpose of committing a crime within a building. It is considered to be more serious than trespass because of the inherent danger that exists when the individual illegally entering or remaining on the property intends to commit a criminal act of some type. Pen.L. §140.00 states that a *building*,

> in addition to its ordinary meaning, includes any structure, vehicle or watercraft used for overnight lodging of persons, or used by persons for carrying on business therein, or used as an elementary or secondary school, or an inclosed motor truck, or an inclosed motor truck trailer. Where a building consists of two or more units separately secured or occupied, each unit shall be deemed both a separate building in itself and a part of the main building.

There are two key elements that are required for a crime to change from criminal trespass to burglary:

- The property involved must be a building as defined by statute

- The offender committing the trespass must intend to commit a crime inside the building at the time he or she unlawfully trespasses

The crime of burglary requires two separate and distinct intents: the intent to enter or remain unlawfully in the building (which establishes the criminal trespass) and the intent, at the time of the trespass, to commit a crime inside the building. Neither intent alone is sufficient to constitute burglary. If the prosecution fails to prove intent to commit a crime, a charge of burglary must be reduced to criminal trespass, even if the defendant did actually commit a crime while in the building. If the prosecution fails to prove intent to trespass, the defendant may be guilty of the intended or attempted crime, but will not be guilty of either criminal trespass or burglary.

To be guilty of burglary under the New York laws, the defendant must first "knowingly enter or remain unlawfully" in a building or dwelling. Entry occurs when any part of the offender's body, no matter how slight, is inside the building.[46] The offender's presence on the roof or just outside a door does not constitute entry. However, reaching an arm through a window or gate is sufficient to establish entry because the offender has essentially broken through the boundaries around the building. Pen.L. §140.00(5) defines *entering or remaining unlawfully* as occurring when the defendant is not licensed or privileged to enter or remain. A defendant who remains unlawfully may have originally entered the premises legally but remains after the termination of this legal right (e.g., a shoplifter who enters a store while it is open to the public but remains in the store after closing hours).[47] Note that the crime requires the offender to *knowingly* enter or remain unlawfully; an offender who enters the premises accidentally or who believes in good faith that he or she has permission to enter or remain cannot be found guilty of burglary, even if the belief is wrong and even if he or she enters or remains with intent to commit a crime. However, if the defendant enters a building thinking it is open to the public and, after discovering that it is closed, still remains in the building, the condition of unlawfully remaining is satisfied.

Burglary also requires that the defendant have the intent to commit a crime inside the building. This may be any felony or misdemeanor other than criminal trespass. Burglary only requires that the offender intend to commit a crime; the prosecution does not need to prove that the defendant actually committed or even attempted to commit the crime to convict. However, if the defendant can prove the entry into the building was for a non-criminal purpose, s/he may not be convicted of burglary, even if s/he did commit a crime on the premises. For example, in the case of *People v. Brown*,[48] the defendant illegally entered a gas station and stole money from the cash register. However, the defendant stated that the only reason he entered the gas station was to find a hose that was missing from the air pump, so that he could inflate a tire with a slow leak. He did not decide to take the money until he saw the unattended register. While the defendant did commit a crime (the theft of the money), he did not commit the crime of burglary because when he entered the premises he did not have any criminal intent.

New York recognizes three levels of burglary. **Third degree burglary**, as defined in Pen.L. §140.20, is a Class D felony. It occurs when the above two elements exist; in other words:

> A person is guilty of burglary in the third degree when he knowingly enters or
> remains unlawfully in a building with intent to commit a crime therein.

The crime is elevated to **second degree burglary**, a Class C felony that is discussed in Pen.L. §140.25, when all the conditions for third degree burglary are met and, in addition, the offender or another participant in the crime:

- is armed with a deadly weapon or with explosives; or
- causes physical injury to any person not a participant in the crime; or
- uses or threatens to use a dangerous instrument; or
- displays what appears to be a pistol, revolver, rifle, shotgun, machine gun, or other firearm.

In addition, the crime is elevated to second degree burglary if the building is a dwelling. Pen.L. §140.00(3) defines a **dwelling** as "a building which is usually occupied by a person lodging therein at night." A home remains a dwelling even if the residents are temporarily absent. In addition, individually occupied units, such as apartments, condominiums, dormitory rooms, and private hospital rooms, have all been held by the courts to be dwellings. However, not every building in which someone occasionally spends the night is a dwelling (e.g., an office containing a bed that is occasionally used by an employee working late is not legally a dwelling).

First degree burglary is a Class B felony and is defined in Pen.L. §140.30. First degree burglary occurs when the building is a dwelling and one of the other four aggravating elements required for second degree burglary is present.

LARCENY-THEFT

The FBI defines **larceny-theft** as:

> the unlawful taking, carrying, leading, or riding away of property from the possession or constructive possession of another. It includes crimes such as shoplifting, pocket-picking, purse-snatching, thefts from motor vehicles, thefts of motor vehicle parts and accessories, bicycle thefts, etc., in which no use of force, violence, or fraud occurs.[49]

In New York, the laws relating to larceny are codified in Article 155 of the Penal Law and are based on the common law origins of the crime. Basically, a larceny is committed when someone steals property. However, the statutory definition of larceny is somewhat more complex. Pen.L. §155.05(1) states that:

> A person steals property and commits larceny when, with intent to deprive another of property or to appropriate the same to himself or to a third person, he wrongfully takes, obtains or withholds such property from an owner thereof.

Therefore, there are three key elements required for the crime of larceny:

1. The offender must take, obtain, or withhold property

2. The property must be taken, obtained, or withheld from an owner of the property

3. The offender must take, obtain, or withhold the property wrongfully and with intent either to deprive another of it or to appropriate it to himself or a third person.

According to Pen.L. §155.00(1), **property** includes:

> any money, personal property, real property, computer data, computer program, thing in action, evidence of debt or contract, or any article, substance or thing of value,

including any gas, steam, water or electricity, which is provided for a charge or compensation.

This definition has been expanded to include items such as drafts, checks, savings account passbooks, food stamp authorization cards, and automobile registration certificates. The addition of the terms "computer data" and "computer program" to the definition of property occurred in 1986, as part of an attempt to deal with the various new forms of crime that involve computers. Thus, illegally taking data that is stored on a computer may constitute a larceny.

For larceny to occur, the property must be in some way obtained by the offender. The courts have held that the element of "taking" is satisfied if the People can show that "the thief exercised dominion and control over the property in a manner, however temporary, in a manner wholly inconsistent with the owner's continued rights..."[50] Under this definition, if a defendant who is being prosecuted for shoplifting was found to be in possession of the stolen item while still in the store, s/he can be found guilty of larceny if there is evidence to show that the defendant concealed the property, acted in an unusual or suspicious way, or attempted to leave the store without paying for the property.[51]

According to Pen.L. §155.00(5), the **owner** of the property is:

> ...any person who has a right to possession thereof superior to that of the taker, obtainer or withholder.
>
> A person who has obtained possession of property by theft or other illegal means shall be deemed to have a right of possession superior to that of a person who takes, obtains or withholds it from him by larcenous means.
>
> A joint or common owner of property shall not be deemed to have a right of possession thereto superior to that of any other joint or common owner thereof.
>
> In the absence of a specific agreement to the contrary, a person in lawful possession of property shall be deemed to have a right of possession superior to that of a person having only a security interest therein, even if legal title lies with the holder of the security interest pursuant to a conditional sale contract or other security agreement.

According to this definition, if two individuals have an equal right to the possession of property, neither can be convicted of stealing that property from the other. Thus, for example, if one owner of a joint bank account withdraws money from the account, s/he cannot be found guilty of theft from the other joint owner of the account.[52] This definition also suggests that an individual who steals stolen property may still be found guilty of theft, even though the property was not stolen from the person who held legal title to it.

The New York State Penal Law defines larceny in Pen.L. §155.05. The first section of this statute, which is quoted above, simply provides that larceny is committed when a person who is acting with the required intent takes, obtains, or withholds property wrongfully. Pen.L. §155.05(2) expands upon this by stating that larceny includes the wrongful taking, obtaining, or withholding of another's property, with the required intent, which is committed in one of the eight ways listed in the statute. The first four forms of larceny are the more traditional types, revolving around the common law. These are outlined in Pen.L. §155.05(2)(a) and include:

- common law larceny by trespassory taking
- common law larceny by trick
- common law larceny by embezzlement
- obtaining property by false pretenses

Larceny by trespassory taking refers to taking property unlawfully from the owner when the owner did not voluntarily give up possession of the property. Therefore, if the owner of the property consents to the taking of the property, the offender has not committed this type of larceny. The next three forms expand upon this to include situations in which property was acquired or withheld unlawfully but without an actual trespassory taking. **Larceny by trick** occurs when the offender obtains possession of property by some type of fraud or misrepresentation. **Larceny by embezzlement** occurs when an offender who has been entrusted with the property of another converts the property to his or her own possession. The element of trust is essential to this crime. Finally, **larceny by false pretenses** occurs when the offender persuades the owner to turn over property by means of falsely representing a material fact. In this situation, the offender obtains title or ownership of the property; in the case of larceny by trick, the offender only obtains possession of the property.

The other four types of larceny, which are listed in Pen.L. §155.05(2), sections b through e, include:

- acquiring lost property
- committing the crime of issuing a bad check
- by false promise
- by extortion

Larceny by acquiring lost property occurs when the offender

> exercises control over property of another which he knows to have been lost or mislaid, or to have been delivered under a mistake as to the identity of the recipient or the nature or amount of the property, without taking reasonable measures to return such property to the owner[53]

Based on this definition, an individual who does not know the property was lost, mislaid, or mistakenly delivered may not be convicted of this type of larceny. However, one lower court in New York has held that if a person finds lost property, locates the rightful owner, and demands a reward that had not previously been offered in exchange for the return of the property, the individual is guilty of this form of larceny.[54]

According to Pen.L. §190.05, the crime of **issuing a bad check** is committed when

> 1. the offender passes a check while knowing that there are insufficient funds to cover it; or

2. the offender passes a check believing or intending that payment will be refused when the check is presented; or

3. payment is refused by the drawee upon presentation.

For this behavior to be a larceny, as discussed in Pen.L. §155.05(2)(c), the offender must obtain some property in return. For example, the courts have ruled that issuing a bad check in payment for a pre-existing debt is not a larceny because in this situation, the victim has not lost or given up anything and the offender has not obtained any property in return for the bad check.[55]

Pen.L. §155.05(2)(d) states that an offender commits **larceny by false promise** when:

> pursuant to a scheme to defraud, he obtains property of another by means of a representation, express or implied, that he or a third person will in the future engage in particular conduct, and when he does not intend to engage in such conduct or, as the case may be, does not believe that the third person intends to engage in such conduct.

The statute states that this crime is committed "pursuant to a scheme to defraud." Essentially, to obtain a conviction of larceny by false promise, it must be shown that the defendant did not intend to engage in the promised conduct or knew that the promise would not be kept. The mere fact that the promise to engage in the conduct was not kept is not alone sufficient to prove this intent.

Finally, **larceny by extortion** is discussed in Pen.L. §155.05(2)(e). The statutory definition of this type of larceny is complex but essentially the crime consists of obtaining property from another person by the use of threats, placing the owner in fear that if the property is not turned over to the offender, the owner will be harmed in some way. Even if the defendant has the right to engage in the conduct used to threaten the victim, it becomes unlawful when it is used to extort money or property. For the crime to occur, the victim must actually give up the property in fear.

New York recognizes five degrees or classes of larceny:

- petit larceny, a Class A misdemeanor[56]
- grand larceny in the fourth degree, a Class E felony[57]
- grand larceny in the third degree, a Class D felony[58]
- grand larceny in the second degree, a Class C felon[59]
- grand larceny in the first degree, a Class B felony[60]

The class of larceny of which the offender is found guilty will depend upon two factors: the amount or type of property taken and the way in which the larceny was committed. The offender does not need to know the value of the stolen property to be convicted of a specific class of larceny

Petit larceny is the lowest level of larceny recognized by the New York State Penal Law. According to Pen.L. §155.25, "a person is guilty of petit larceny when he steals property." All the higher degrees of larceny include the statutory elements required for petit larceny as well as added aggravating factors which increase the seriousness of the crime in some way.

The crime becomes **fourth degree grand larceny** when the value of the property is greater than $1,000, or by stealing a motor vehicle (other than a motorcycle), or a religious item worth over $100. In addition, petit larceny becomes fourth degree larceny if the property, regardless of its value, is obtained by extortion or is taken from the person of another. There are also some specific types of property which, if stolen, elevate the crime to fourth degree larceny regardless of the value of the property. These include secret scientific material, credit or debit cards, firearms, rifles, shotguns, and public records. **Third degree grand larceny** involves stealing property with a value of more than $3,000. **Second degree grand larceny** occurs when the property has a value of more than $50,000 or was obtained by certain types of extortion. Finally, **first degree grand larceny** involves stealing property with a value of more than one million dollars.

It is clear the seriousness of the charge of larceny frequently depends on the actual value of the property that was stolen. Pen.L. §155.20 discusses how the value of property is determined. In most cases, the statute defines value as:

> the market value of the property at the time and place of the crime, or if such cannot be satisfactorily ascertained, the cost of replacement of the property within a reasonable time after the crime.[61]

However, for some items, such as written instruments, the market value may not be easy to determine. Therefore, written instruments such as checks and drafts are generally valued at face value, tickets (for example, theater or airplane tickets) are valued at their purchase price, and other written instruments are valued based on the economic loss suffered by the owner. Pen.L. §155.20(3) also states that when gas, steam, water, or electricity is stolen, they shall be valued at "the value of the property stolen in any consecutive twelve-month period." Finally, that if the value of the property cannot be determined based on this statute, Pen.L. §155.20(4) states that the property value shall be held to be less than $250.

MOTOR VEHICLE THEFT

The UCR considers **motor vehicle theft** to be a separate index crime from larceny-theft. It is defined by the FBI as:

> the theft or attempted theft of a motor vehicle, this offense category includes the stealing of automobiles, trucks, buses, motorcycles, motorscooters, snowmobiles, etc.[62]

While New York does not consider motor vehicle theft to be a separate crime, there are several crimes outlined in the Penal Law which correspond to this index crime. For example, the statutory definition of grand larceny in the fourth degree includes the theft of a motor vehicle (other than a motorcycle) with a value of over $100.[63]

Pen.L. §165.05, which discusses the crime of the **unauthorized use of a vehicle in the third degree**, is also known as the "joyriding" statute. This crime involves the temporary taking and use of a motor vehicle without the consent or permission of the owner. It is not larceny because there is no intent to permanently deprive the owner of the property. This statute has been very controversial because essentially an individual can take a vehicle and deprive the owner of its use, at least temporarily, without being considered to have committed a theft. There are three main ways to commit this crime:

- the offender commits the crime if s/he takes, operates, rides in, or otherwise uses a vehicle while knowing s/he does not have the consent of the owner

- the offender has custody of the vehicle (e.g., the offender is a garage mechanic who has been hired to repair the vehicle) and uses the vehicle without the owner's consent

- the offender borrows or rents the vehicle for a predetermined period of time and then, without the owner's consent, intentionally fails to return the vehicle for a lengthy period of time

Unlike the crime of larceny, the value of the vehicle has no effect on the grade or level of seriousness of the offense.

If the offender commits this crime twice within a ten-year period, the crime is elevated to **unauthorized use of a vehicle in the second degree**.[64] If the offender commits this crime with the intent to use the vehicle in the commission of a felony, s/he is considered to have committed **unauthorized use of a vehicle in the first degree**.[65]

The crime of **carjacking** is defined in Pen.L. §160.10(3) and involve forcibly taking a motor vehicle from another person. While the UCR considers carjacking to be a form of motor vehicle theft, it involves the use of force, violence, assault, or fear, and is considered in New York to be a form of robbery rather than theft. This crime is discussed above under the heading of **Robbery**.

ARSON

Like burglary, the common-law felony crime of **arson** was a crime against a home or dwelling place. While it could occur at any time of day, nighttime arson was considered to be a more serious crime. The UCR defines arson as:

> any willful or malicious burning or attempt to burn, with or without intent to defraud, a dwelling house, public building, motor vehicle or aircraft, personal property of another, etc.[66]

At common law, arson was punishable by death, regardless of whether anyone died as a result of the crime. In New York, prior to the adoption of the 1881 Penal Code, first degree arson was a capital offense that was treated as seriously as murder. There were originally four degrees of arson recognized in New York; the enactment of the Penal Code in 1881 reduced that to three. In 1965, the revised Penal Law included significant changes to the arson statutes. Currently, the statutes outline five levels of arson, and the state recognizes arson against structures other than a home as well as the burning of other types of property.

Article 150 of the Penal Law deals with the crime of arson, making it a crime to damage a building or motor vehicle through the use of a fire or explosion. Damaging a building or motor vehicle by other means is not covered in this article. According to Pen.L. §150.00(1), a building,

> in addition to its ordinary meaning, includes any structure, vehicle or watercraft used for overnight lodging of persons, or used by persons for carrying on business therein. Where a building consists of two or more units separately secured or occupied, each unit shall not be deemed a separate building.

This definition is similar to the definition of property used in the burglary statute.[67] The primary difference is that for the offense of arson, separate units in a building (e.g., apartments in an apartment house) are not treated as separate buildings while for the crime of burglary, they are considered to be separate. This definition does include the "ordinary meaning" of a building, so that essentially any permanent structure which is enclosed by walls and covered by a roof falls within the definition. In addition, motor homes, house trailers, houseboats, and even vans used for business purposes are considered to be buildings under this definition.

A motor vehicle, according to Pen.L. §150.00(2):

> includes every vehicle operated or driven upon a public highway which is propelled by any power other than muscular power, except (a) electrically-driven invalid chairs being operated or driven by an invalid, (b) vehicles which run only upon rails or tracks, and (c) snowmobiles as defined in article forty-seven of the vehicle and traffic law.

The arson statute does not include vehicles that are inoperable, unless they are being repaired at the time of the crime.

In 2001, the arson statutes were amended to include damage through fire or explosion of property other than a building or motor vehicle.

New York recognizes five degrees of arson, all of which require two key elements. First, the prosecution must prove that the defendant set the fire intentionally. Proof that the defendant acted recklessly or carelessly in starting the fire is not sufficient to prove arson. Second, some damage must have been inflicted on the building or motor vehicle, even if the damage is only very slight (such as charring) or was caused by smoke or heat rather than from the fire itself. In addition, for all crimes of arson except fourth degree, the prosecution must also prove that the defendant intended to cause damage.

Fifth degree arson is a Class A misdemeanor. This crime, which is discussed in Pen.L. §150.01, was added to the Penal Law effective November 1, 2001. The statute states that:

> A person is guilty of arson in the fifth degree when he or she intentionally damages property of another without consent of the owner by intentionally starting a fire or causing an explosion.

This is the only type of arson which involves property other than a building or motor vehicle. It requires that the offender have specific intent to start the fire or explosion and to damage the property. This is also the only type of arson which is not a felony offense.

Fourth degree arson, a Class E Felony, is discussed in Pen.L. §150.05. The statute states that:

> A person is guilty of arson in the fourth degree when he recklessly damages a building or motor vehicle by intentionally starting a fire or causing an explosion.[68]

This crime requires that the offender intended to start the fire and that the offender recklessly (rather than intentionally) damaged the property. Because the level of intent is recklessness, voluntary intoxication will not negate the required intent for this crime, although it may serve as defense for higher degrees of arson. The statute includes one affirmative defense to this crime: if it can be shown that "no person other than the defendant had a possessory or proprietary interest in the building or motor vehicle,"[69] the defendant cannot be found guilty of arson in the fourth degree.

Third degree arson is a Class C felony. Pen.L. §150.10(1) states that:

> A person is guilty of arson in the third degree when he intentionally damages a building or motor vehicle by starting a fire or causing an explosion.

Because specific intent is required, a defendant can be convicted of attempted arson in the third degree. However it is necessary to prove that the damage to the building was caused intentionally. The statute provides one affirmative defense to this crime; the defendant must show that:

(a) no person other than the defendant had a possessory or proprietary interest in the building or motor vehicle, or if other persons had such interests, all of them consented to the defendant's conduct, and
(b) the defendant's sole intent was to destroy or damage the building or motor vehicle for a lawful and proper purpose, and
(c) the defendant had no reasonable ground to believe that his conduct might endanger the life or safety of another person or damage another building or motor vehicle.[70]

This defense is more complex than that included as an affirmative defense for fourth degree arson. The first element derives from the common law belief that setting fire to one's own property is not arson. The second element requires that the defendant's intent in setting the fire was lawful and proper. Therefore, if a defendant sets fire to and damages his or her own property for an unlawful purpose, such as insurance fraud, there is no defense against arson. Finally, the defendant must show that he or had no reasonable grounds to believe that other persons might be injured by his or her actions.

Second degree arson is defined in Pen.L. §150.15 as a Class B felony. The statute states that:

> A person is guilty of arson in the second degree when he intentionally damages a building or motor vehicle by starting a fire, and when
> (a) another person who is not a participant in the crime is present in such building or motor vehicle at the time, and
> (b) the defendant knows that fact or the circumstances are such as to render the presence of such a person therein a reasonable possibility.

This situation is considered to be more serious because not only does the defendant have the intent to start a fire and to cause damage, s/he also knows or should know that there is another person present in the building or motor vehicle at the time of the crime. This statute was created in 1971 and specifically applies to arson by fire; there is no mention of damage by explosion in this statute. The key element of this crime is the knowledge that others were present when the fire was started. However, it is not an element of the crime that anyone actually be injured in the fire.

Finally, as a Class A-I felony, **first degree arson** is considered the most serious type of arson. According to Pen.L. §150.20:

> A person is guilty of arson in the first degree when he intentionally damages a building or motor vehicle by causing an explosion or a fire and when
> (a) such explosion or fire is caused by an incendiary device propelled, thrown or placed inside or near such building or motor vehicle; or when such explosion or fire is caused by an explosive; or when such explosion or fire either
>   (i) causes serious physical injury to another person other than a participant, or
>   (ii) the explosion or fire was caused with the expectation or receipt of financial advantage or pecuniary profit by the actor; and when
> (b) another person who is not a participant in the crime is present in such building or motor vehicle at the time; and
> (c) the defendant knows that fact or the circumstances are such as to render the presence of such person therein a reasonable possibility.

Basically, first degree arson requires the following minimum elements:

- The offender intentionally caused damage to a building or motor vehicle by causing a fire or explosion;

- Another person who is not a participant in the crime is present in the building or vehicle; and

- The offender knew or should have known about the presence of that other person.

In addition, for the crime to be first degree arson, at least one of the following four elements also must be present:

- the fire was caused by an explosive
- the fire was caused by an incendiary device
- the fire (regardless of its cause or origin) caused serious physical injury to a non-participant
- the fire was caused for financial gain or profit

Arson is often an extremely difficult crime to prove, because there is frequently little or no direct evidence regarding the origin of the fire; fire usually destroys this type of evidence. The prosecution frequently relies on circumstantial evidence in arson cases. In cases where a charge of arson cannot be proven satisfactorily, other possible charges may include reckless endangerment of property, criminal mischief, and insurance fraud. If a non-participant is injured in the crime, a charge of felony assault may be considered, and if a death results from the crime, the defendant may be charged with felony murder.

HATE CRIMES

Hate or **bias crimes** are not specifically included among the UCR's eight index crimes. However, the FBI began to collect data on this category of crime after President Bush signed the Hate Crimes Statistics Act in 1990. The UCR defines hate or bias crimes as "those offenses motivated in part or singularly by personal prejudice against others because of a diversity—race, sexual orientation, religion, ethnicity/national origin, or disability."[71]

In 2000, the New York State Legislature passed the Hate Crimes Act of 2000, which is found in Article 485 of the Penal Law. The legislature stated that the increasing prevalence of hate crimes in the state is a serious concern because

> Hate crimes do more than threaten the safety and welfare of all citizens. They inflict on victims incalculable physical and emotional damage and tear at the very fabric of free society. Crimes motivated by invidious hatred toward particular groups not only harm individual victims but send a powerful message of intolerance and discrimination to all members of the group to which the victim belongs. Hate crimes can and do intimidate and disrupt entire communities and vitiate the civility that is essential to healthy democratic processes. In a democratic society, citizens cannot be required to approve of the beliefs and practices of others, but must never commit criminal acts on account of them. Current law does not adequately recognize the harm to public order and individual safety that hate crimes cause. Therefore, our laws must be strengthened to provide clear recognition of the gravity of hate crimes and the compelling importance of preventing their recurrence.[72]

The legislature considers a hate crime to be one in which "victims are intentionally selected, in whole or in part, because of their race, color, national origin, ancestry, gender, religion, religious practice, age, disability or sexual orientation."[73]

Pen.L. §485.05 discusses the offense of hate crime, and states that:

1. A person commits a hate crime when he or she commits a specified offense and either:
   (a) intentionally selects the person against whom the offense is committed or intended to be committed in whole or in substantial part because of a belief or perception regarding the race, color, national origin, ancestry, gender, religion, religious practice, age, disability or sexual orientation of a person, regardless of whether the belief or perception is correct, or
   (b) intentionally commits the act or acts constituting the offense in whole or in substantial part because of a belief or perception regarding the race, color, national origin, ancestry, gender, religion, religious practice, age, disability or sexual orientation of a person, regardless of whether the belief or perception is correct.
2. Proof of race, color, national origin, ancestry, gender, religion, religious practice, age, disability or sexual orientation of the defendant, the victim or of both the defendant and the victim does not, by itself, constitute legally sufficient evidence satisfying the people's burden under paragraph (a) or (b) of subdivision one of this section...

Essentially, an offense is considered to be a hate crime when the victim is selected because of his or her status or when that status is the reason the offense is committed. The status of the victim as a member of a protected group is not by itself sufficient for an offense to be considered a hate crime; the motivation for the crime must relate to that status. Therefore, a crime committed against a member of a protected group is not a hate crime if the victim's status as a member of the group was not a factor in the commission of the crime.

Only certain "specified offenses" are included in the statute. These include:

- first, second, and third degree assault
- aggravated assault upon a person less than eleven years old
- first, second, and third degree menacing
- first and second degree reckless endangerment
- first and second degree manslaughter
- second degree murder
- first, second, third, and fourth degree stalking
- first degree rape
- first degree sodomy
- first degree sexual abuse
- first and second degree aggravated sexual abuse
- first and second degree unlawful imprisonment
- first and second degree kidnapping
- first and second degree coercion
- first, second, and third degree criminal trespass
- first, second, and third degree burglary
- first, second, third, and fourth degree criminal mischief

- first, second, third, and fourth degree arson
- petit larceny
- first, second, third, and fourth degree grand larceny
- first, second, and third degree robbery
- first degree harassment
- second degree aggravated harassment
- any attempt or conspiracy to commit any of the specified offenses[73]

According to the New York State Division of Criminal Justice Services, a total of 975 hate crimes were reported to or investigated by police in 2001. This is an increase of 25 percent from the 781 incidents reported in 2000. Of the 975 hate crimes, 74 percent were aggravated harassment and criminal mischief. Approximately 15 percent were aggravated or simple assaults. The remaining 11 percent included a variety of offenses ranging from kidnapping, arson, and robbery, to burglary, larceny, and simple harassment.[74]

The most frequent motivation was the race or color of the victim; approximately 36 percent of hate crimes were motivated by the victim's race or color (including anti-black, anti-Hispanic, anti-white, and anti-other race). Approximately 35 percent were motivated by the victim's religion, primarily anti-Semitism (27 percent). Other motivates included the victim's ethnicity or national origin (15 percent) and the victim's sexual orientation (11.5 percent).[75]

There were 775 individual victims of these hate crime incidents. Of these, 66 percent were male and 27 percent were female (approximately 7 percent were of unknown gender). Approximately 46 percent of the victims were white, 24 percent black, 12 percent Asian, and 18 percent other or unknown. Approximately 5 percent of the victims were of Hispanic ethnicity.[76]

NOTES

1. Recent issues of the *Uniform Crime Reports* may be viewed online on the Federal Bureau of Investigation's website (http://www.fbi.gov/ucr/ucr.htm)
2. *Uniform Crime Reports, op cit.*
3. Pen.L. §125.55
4. See Pen.L. §125.27
5. See Pen.L. §125.25(1)
6. See Pen.L. §125.20(1)
7. See Pen.L. §125.10
8. See Pen.L. §125.13
9. See Pen.L. §125.12
10. See Pen.L. §125.15(1)
11. See Pen.L. §125.25(3)
12. *People v. Walden*, 227 A.D.2d 887, 643 N.Y.S.2d 807 (4th Dep't 1996)
13. *People v. Boutin*, 75 N.Y. 2d 692, 556 N.Y.S.2d 1, 555 N.E.2d 253 (1990)
14. *Ibid*
15. Pen.L. §125.12(3)
16. Navigation Law §49A(2)(c)

17. Parks, Recreation and Historic Preservation Law §25.24(1)(a)
18. *People v. Gill*, 251 A.D. 2d 121, 674 N.Y.S.2d 651 (1st Dep't 1998)
19. See, e.g., *People v. Cobbs*, 174 A.D. 2d 751, 571 N.Y.S.2d 576 (2d Dep't 1991), in which the defendant threatened to cut the victim
20. See, e.g., *People v. Aveille*, 148 A.D. 2d 461, 538 N.Y.S.2d 615 (2d Dep't 1989), in which the defendant believed the victim had made sexual advances towards his wife
21. See, e.g., *People v. White*, 143 A.D. 2d 1066, 533 N.Y.S.2d 637 (2d Dep't 1998), in which the defendant fired four additional shots after the victim fell to the ground
22. Pen.L. §125.25(2)
23. Pen.L. §125.25(3)
24. *People v. Blake*, 44 A.D. 2d 606, 353 N.Y.S.2d 528 (2d Dep't 1974)
25. Pen.L. §125.25(4)
26. Pen.L. §125.27(1)(b)
27. *People v. Bell*, 172 Misc.2d 25, 656 N.Y.S. 2d 162 (Sup.Ct. Oneida County, 1997)
28. *Uniform Crime Reports, op cit.*
29. CPL §60.42
30. See Pen.L. §130.50 for a discussion of the crime of sodomy in the first degree
31. *Uniform Crime Reports, op cit.*
32. *People v. Mitchell*, 99 A.D. 2d 609, 472 N.Y.S.2d 166 (3d Dep't 1984)
33. *People v. Lumpkin*, 173 A.D.2d 738, 570 N.Y.S.2d 620 (1991)
34. *People v. Fields*, 179 A.D. 2d 458, 579 N.Y.S.2d 16 (1st Dep't 1992)
35. *People v. Williams*, 63 A.D.2d 1035, 406 N.Y.S.2d 341 (2d Dep't 1978)
36. *People v. Owusa*, 93 N.Y.2d 398, 690 N.Y.S.2d 863, 712 N.E.2d 1228 (1999)
37. Pen.L. §160.10(2)(b) and Pen.L. §160.15(4)
38. *Uniform Crime Reports, op cit.*
39. See e.g., *People v. Carney*, 179 A.D.2d 818, 579 N.Y.S.2d 157 (2d Dep't 1992); *People v. Langford*, 153 A.D.2d 908, 910-911, 545 N.Y.S.2d 610, 611-612 (2d Dep't 1989); and *People v. Karimi*, 204 A.D.2d 572, 614 N.Y.S.2d 210 (2d Dep't 1994)
40. *People v. Vercelletto*, 135 Misc.2d 40, 514 N.Y.S.2d 177 (Ulster Co.Ct.1987)
41. *People v. Spivey*, 81 N.Y.2d 356, 599 N.Y.S.2d 477, 615 N.E.2d 961 (1993)
42. *Ibid.* In this case, the defendant (Spivey) and three other men committed a robbery. Spivey was placed under arrest and was in the custody of a police officer. Meanwhile, another officer (Schumacher) followed the other three suspects and was feloniously assaulted by them. Although Spivey was in custody and not present when Officer Schumacher was assaulted, Spivey was found guilty of the felonious assault committed by the other offenders.
43. *People v. Hendrix*, 56 A.D.2d 580, 391 N.Y.S.2d (2d Dep't 1977)
44. The Vehicle and Traffic Code offenses discussed in this statute involve driving while intoxicated or when one's ability is impaired by drugs.
45. *Uniform Crime Reports, op cit.*
46. *People v. King*, 61 N.Y.2d 550, 555, 475 N.Y.S.2d 260, 262, 463 N.E.2d 601 (1984)
47. *People v. Gaines* 74 N.Y.2d 358, 362, 547 N.Y.S.2d 620, 622, 546 N.E.2d 913 (1989)
48. *People v. Brown*, 87 N.Y.2d 950, 641 N.Y.S.2d 225, 663 N.E.2d 1255 91996)
49. *Uniform Crime Reports, op cit.*
50. *People v. Jennings*, 69 N.Y.2d 103, 188, 512 N.Y.S.2d 652, 659, 504 N.E.2d 1079, 1086 (1986)
51. *People v. Olivo*, 59 N.Y.2d 309, 438 N.Y.S.2d 242, 420 N.E.2d 40 (1981)

52. See, e.g., *People v. O'Brien*, 102 Misc.2d 246, 423 N.Y.S.2d 135 (Dist.Ct., Nassau County, 1979)
53. Pen.L. §155.05(2)(b)
54. *People v. Dadon*, 167 Mis.2d 628, 640 N.Y.S.2d 425 (Crim. Ct. N.Y. County 1996)
55. See e.g., *People v. Campobello*, 154 A.D.2d 911, 546 N.Y.S.2d 62 (4th Dep't 1989)
56. Pen.L. §155.25
57. Pen.L. §155.30
58. Pen.L. §155.35
59. Pen.L. §155.40
60. Pen.L. §155.42
61. Pen.L. §155.20(1)
62. *Uniform Crime Reports, op cit.*
63. Pen.L. §155.30(8)
64. Pen.L. §165.06
65. Pen.L. §165.08
66. *Uniform Crime Reports, op cit.*
67. Pen.L. §140.00
68. Pen.L. §150.05(1)
69. Pen.L. §150.05(2)
70. Pen.L. §150.10(2)
71. Recent issues of the FBI's *Hate Crime Statistics* may be viewed online on the FBI's website (http://www.fbi.gov/ucr/ucr.htm)
72. Pen.L.§485.00
73. *Ibid*
74. Pen.L. §458.05(3)
75. New York State Division of Criminal Justice Services, *Hate Crime 2001* (http://criminaljustice.state.ny.us/crimnet/ojsa/hatecrimes/hatecrimes2001.pdf)
76. *Ibid*
77. *Ibid*

CHAPTER 4

THE POLICE IN NEW YORK

INTRODUCTION

There are many levels of police agencies in America, including federal law enforcement, state police, county sheriff's agencies, and city police. Article 9 of the New York State Constitution provides local governments within the state the right of "**home rule**." This means that any local government (county, city, town, or village), except a county which is contained entirely within a city, may have its own elected legislative body. One of the rights of home rule is the local control of emergency services; this means that any local government may set up its own local police department. Each department in New York has its own chief, its own organization, and its own policies and procedures. In addition to local and county departments, there are also a number of multi-jurisdictional law enforcement agencies. These include agencies such as the New York State Police, the New York City Reservoir Police, various park police departments, and railroad police.

In 2001, law enforcement agencies in the state of New York employed a total of 86,297 individuals, including both sworn and civilian personnel, and both full-time and part-time employees. The largest department in New York is the New York City Police Department, with over 56,000 employees, followed by the New York State Police, with slightly over 5,100 employees. Police in New York are predominately male; in 2001, only 13 percent of all sworn personnel in the state were female.[1]

Between 1992 and 2001, a total of 24 law enforcement officers were feloniously killed in the line of duty in the state of New York. These deaths all occurred prior to 1999; no officers were feloniously killed in New York between 1999 and 2001. A total of 20 officers were accidentally killed in New York between 1992 and 2001. None of these deaths occurred during 2001. A total of 1,097 officers were assaulted in New York during 2001 while performing law enforcement functions. The vast majority (almost 98 percent) involved personal weapons.[2]

Of course, this total pales beside the number of officers killed in New York on September 11, 2001 in the attacks on the World Trade Center. A total of 71 law enforcement officers died as a result of the terrorist attacks, including 23 officers of the New York Police Department. In addition, the attacks claimed the lives of 37 officers of the Port Authority of New York and New Jersey Police Department, five officers with the New York Office of Tax Enforcement, three officers of the State of New York Unified Court System, one New York City Fire Department fire marshal, one U.S. Secret Service agent, and one FBI agent.[3]

New York's status as the third most populous state in the country, and the fact that it houses the largest American city (New York City), creates a number of special law enforcement problems, including issues such as drugs, immigration, terrorism, and tourism. Because of this, a large number of federal law enforcement agencies have offices in New York and/or are involved in law enforcement activities within the state. This includes the Federal Bureau of Investigation, the Drug Enforcement Agency, and the Bureau of Alcohol, Tobacco, and Firearms. This results in a considerable amount of overlap among the various levels of law enforcement in the state.

LOCAL POLICING

The majority of the police departments in New York are local or city departments. Currently, most local cities, towns, and villages in New York maintain police departments. Every local department is independent of every other department. The goals, purposes, and priorities vary greatly among departments, with each local agency responding to the needs and desires of the population it serves. The New York City Police Department, a local city department, is the largest police agency in New York.

The New York City Police Department[4]

History of the New York City Police Department

New York City is currently the largest city in the United States and one of the leading centers of business in the world today. The stated mission of the **New York City Police Department (NYPD)** is:

> ...to enhance the quality of life in our City by working in partnership with the community and in accordance with constitutional rights to enforce the laws, preserve the peace, reduce fear, and provide for a safe environment.[5]

In 1845, New York City combined its separate day watch and night watch into a single city police force, the NYPD, in response to the city's growing crime problem. The department, which was based on the London Metropolitan Police, a paramilitary organization of uniformed officers, originally consisted of approximately 800 officers and is generally considered to be the first full-time 24-hour police force in the United States. In less than 30 years (by 1873) the NYPD would grow to almost 3,000 officers. The first chief of police, George W. Matsell, was a bookseller with no policing experience. The department was administered by the New York City Police Commission, which consisted of the mayor, the recorder, and a city judge. As officer appointments and tenure were frequently under the control of local politicians, the NYPD from the beginning faced problems of corruption, dissension, and division.

In 1856, twenty uniformed police officers were officially designated as detectives and assigned to a separate detective unit within the department. The NYPD Detective Bureau was formally created in 1882 by the state legislature. In 1887, members of the NYPD officially began carrying firearms while on duty, although many had been carrying such weapons unofficially for a number of years.

In 1895, Theodore Roosevelt became president of the Police Commission. His attempts to reform the department set the standard for the modern NYPD. During his two-year tenure, Roosevelt appointed more than 600 recruits to the NYPD, based on their physical and mental qualifications, rather than their political affiliation. Roosevelt also allowed ethnic minorities to enter the department and hired the first woman member of the NYPD. At that time, New York City consisted of only two boroughs, Manhattan and the Bronx. However, by 1889, 24 local governments and 18 separate police departments were consolidated into what would eventually become the five boroughs of the City of New York, and the NYPD grew to 6,400 officers.

During the 19th century, the NYPD was run by a Police Commission, a board consisting of four to six police commissioners. However, in 1901, the NYPD was placed under the jurisdiction of a single police commissioner. Since then, there have been a total of 41 commissioners. The most recent, Raymond W. Kelly, took office on January 1, 2002. Commissioner Kelly served a previous term as commissioner between September 1992 and January 1994 and is the first person ever to serve two separate non-consecutive terms.

The NYPD Today

Currently, the NYPD is the largest municipal police department in the United States. It is responsible for an area of approximately 320 square miles, covering the five boroughs of New York City: Manhattan, Brooklyn, Queens, Staten Island, and the Bronx. The NYPD employs almost 40,000 sworn officers and over 17,000 civilians.[6]

The NYPD is headed by a **Police Commissioner**, who reports directly to the mayor of the city. The other two top officials of the NYPD are the **First Deputy Commissioner** and the **Chief of Department**. The First Deputy Commissioner acts as the Police Commissioner's executive aid, assisting him in the administration of the NYPD. He supervises the department's disciplinary system and administers the major support functions of the department (e.g., budget, personnel, management). The First Deputy Commissioner also acts as the Police Commissioner during the commissioner's absence. The Chief of Department is the highest-ranking sworn member of the NYPD and is responsible for the crime control and prevention functions of the department.

The NYPD today is composed of nine major bureaus.

- Patrol Services Bureau
- Criminal Justice Bureau
- Detective Bureau
- Housing Bureau
- Internal Affairs Bureau
- Organized Crime Control Bureau
- Personnel Bureau
- Support Services Bureau
- Transportation Bureau

Under the **Patrol Services Bureau**, the five boroughs are divided into eight Patrol Borough Commands, which are further divided into separate precincts. The Bureau also has a number of other divisions, including Traffic Control, Highway Patrol, School Safety, Special Operations, and a Mounted Unit. The **Criminal Justice Bureau** acts as a liaison between the NYPD and other city and state criminal justice agencies, such as the District Attorney's Offices, the Division of Criminal Justice Services, and the New York State Office of Court Administration. The Bureau centralizes control of the department's criminal justice-related activities, supervises all police personnel assigned to court, provides warrant enforcement, and ensures that all arrested suspects are arraigned within the legal time parameters. The **Detective Bureau** investigates crimes, locates and apprehends suspects, locates missing persons, and recovers stolen property. There are approximately 3,000 detectives in the Bureau; they work with patrol officers in local precincts to investigate crimes and other incidents.

The NYPD's **Housing Bureau** is divided into nine Police Service Areas which are responsible for maintaining public safety in the New York City Housing Authority and for providing police services to public housing residents. The **Internal Affairs Bureau** is responsible for controlling corruption and misconduct within the department. The Bureau investigates complaints of police misconduct and allegations of corruption. The **Organized Crime Control Bureau** was established in 1971 as a result of the Knapp Commission hearings, which found widespread corruption throughout the NYPD. The department centralized all organized crime enforcement operations, unifying those enforcement operations which were most prone to corruption, such as vice, narcotics, auto theft, and traditional and non-traditional organized crime. The Bureau employs a module or team concept of investigation, which is designed to reduce the opportunity for corruption and provide supervisory accountability.

The **Personnel Bureau** is responsible for all departmental human resource functions, including recruitment, applicant processing, training, productivity, employee health, safety, and welfare programs, and other personnel issues. The Bureau has overall responsibility for hiring, managing, and maintaining NYPD employees. The duties of the **Support Services Bureau** include the maintenance and repair of the NYPD fleet of motor vehicles, the administration of the department's fuel dispensing system, the control of all property coming into the custody of the NYPD (contraband, found property, prisoners' property, confiscated property, decedents' property, etc.), the maintenance of department records (criminal records, stolen property records, etc.), and the printing of materials needed by the department on a daily basis (forms, daily orders, pamphlets, flyers, legal bulletins, etc.). The Support Services Bureau also holds regular public auctions of unclaimed and confiscated property. Finally, the **Transit Bureau** is responsible for patrolling the city's rapid transit system, which is the largest in the United States and one of the largest in the world.

In 1998, NYPD began a **Paid Detail Program** (also known as "Rent-a-Cop"), which allows off-duty uniformed employment of NYPD officers. The unit responsible for the program, the Paid Detail Unit, determines which organizations, events, and corporations may participate in the program, conducting background and credit checks of prospective vendors. All officers participating in the program are volunteers. Participating officers are off duty and acting as private contractors, although they do carry full law enforcement powers and are expected to perform only police-related duties. Currently, the cost of an off duty police officer or detective is $30 per hour. The vendor who hires the officer must also pay a 10 percent administrative charge to the City of New York.

Minimum requirements for the NYSP include the requirements that on the date of hire the applicant must:

- be at least 21 years of age and no more than 35 years of age
- be a U.S. citizen

- have a valid New York state driver's license with no restrictions
- have no felony convictions
- be a resident of one of the five boroughs of New York City or Nassau, Suffolk, Westchester, Rockland, Orange, or Putnam counties
- have 60 college credits and a 2.0 GPA or better, or have 2 years active military experience
- have an honorable discharge from the U.S. military (if applicable)

Applicants must first take a written test. Those passing the written exam must then pass a number of other examinations, including:

- a medical examination
- oral and written psychological examinations
- a physical agility test
- a background and character investigation
- a pre-hire interview

Applicants who are accepted by the NYPD attend the department's police academy and may earn up to 29 college credits. The beginning salary for a probationary NYPD officer is $34,514.

COUNTY POLICING

There are 55 separate sheriffs' departments in the state. In most counties in New York, sheriffs are elected by the voters in a general election. Therefore, partisan politics significantly influences county police agencies in the state. Most sheriff's departments in New York are full-service police agencies that provide police services to unincorporated areas of the county. However, although some of their duties, such as running the county jail, are mandated by the state, many of their actual responsibilities are determined by the government of the specific county. In addition, incorporated towns or cities that do not wish to set up their own local police department may contract out to their county sheriff's department for police services.

Article 13 of the New York State Constitution establishes the office of sheriff, stating that sheriffs shall be chosen by the electors of the county and will serve either three- or four-year terms, as directed by the legislature. They may hold no other office while serving as sheriff. Any elective sheriff may be removed from office by the state governor, after the sheriff has been given a copy of the charges and has had an opportunity of being heard in his or her defense. The sheriff is the oldest constitutional law enforcement officer of the county and is responsible for maintaining the peace in all townships, villages, and municipalities within his or her jurisdiction, and for the care and custody of all arrested persons pending court action. The sheriff also serves as the Chief Executive Officer of the Courts.

In most counties, there are no legal minimum training requirements which must be met by candidates running for sheriff. For example, candidates for sheriff are not required to have attended a police academy or to have any practical policing experience of any kind.

In many counties, the sheriff's department is not only responsible for providing law enforcement services to the county but also for running the county jail, maintaining security in all county courts, serving civil and criminal processes, and providing assistance when needed to local departments within the county. This assistance can range from operating a county-wide crime lab to assisting a local department with a criminal investigation. County sheriffs have police powers throughout the county, including within the boundaries of incorporated cities that maintain a city police force.

The Erie County Sheriff's Department[7]

The **Erie County Sheriff's Department** (ECSD) was established in February, 1821. The first sheriff of the district, which then included both Erie and Niagara counties, was John G. Camp. Shortly after this time, the district of Erie County was established. Camp continued in office as the Sheriff of Erie County until the end of 1822. There have been a total of 52 sheriffs in the county but probably the most famous was Grover Cleveland, who began his political career as Erie County Sheriff in 1871. He later became the mayor of the City of Buffalo, Governor of New York, and finally President of the United States.

The Erie County Sheriff is elected to a four-year term, must serve full time as sheriff, and may not hold any other public office during his or her tenure as sheriff. The ECSD is responsible for 1,046 square miles of land area, 90 miles of shoreline, and the waters along the shore. The department provides a wide variety of services to county residents.

One of the primary functions of the **Jail Management Division** of the ECSD is to maintain the **Erie County Holding Center**, a pre-trial maximum-security detention facility which can hold up to 680 inmates. It is the second-largest such facility in the state, outside of New York City. The Division also maintains the **Erie County Correctional Facility**, a medium-security facility with space for 1070 inmates. The Jail Management Division provides a variety of services to inmates in these facilities, including public and law library services, educational programs, religious services, recreation facilities, a commissary, alcohol and substance abuse programs, and various physical and mental health-related services. The ECSD is also responsible for transporting inmates between the two facilities and the various courts.

The **Patrol Services Division** is made up of uniformed officers who provide law enforcement services to the county. It includes several bureaus. The **Traffic Safety Bureau** attempts to create safe highways by enforcing the state seatbelt law, investigating departmental accidents and accidents involving public conveyances and county-owned vehicles, enforcing laws relating to commercial vehicles (weight laws, permits, etc.), and compiling data and performing research and statistical analysis for traffic and highway safety program planning. The **County Building Patrol** is responsible for providing security to some county buildings and shares with Holding Center officers the responsibility for transporting inmates between the Holding Center and the courts, county correctional facilities, the Erie County Medical Center, and county psychological centers. The **Narcotics and Intelligence Bureau** investigates illegal drug trafficking within the county and is responsible for the arrest and conviction of individuals possessing and/or dealing in illegal drugs. The Bureau works closely with other police agencies in the county and is available to provide local agencies with personnel and other assistance in local drug trafficking operations.

The **Investigative Services Bureau** is responsible for investigating all crimes reported to the Patrol Division. The Bureau also works closely with law enforcement agencies at various levels of government (local, state, and federal) and is available to provide assistance to all municipal departments within the county. The Bureau's Warrant Squad serves subpoenas, summonses, and warrants and is responsible for the extradition of felony suspects to other jurisdictions. The Bureau of Identification provides a variety of support services for departmental criminal investigations, including crime scene investigations, evidence processing (latent fingerprints, trace evidence, etc.), crime scene documentation, and the creation and maintenance of criminal history records and fingerprint files. The Identification Bureau is also available to cooperative with various agencies at all government levels. Other divisions within the Investigative Services Bureau include the **Environmental and Hazardous Materials Unit**, which trains ECSD personnel, as well as members of other agencies, on the identification and recognition of hazardous materials; the **Fire Investigation Unit**, which focuses on arson investigation and reduction; and the **Pistol Permit Unit**, which conducts the investigations required before pistol permits, gun dealer licenses, and gunsmith licenses can be issued or renewed.

By state mandate, all sheriffs' departments in New York maintain a **Civil Process Division**. This division serves and executes a wide variety of legal processes issued by and for various non-criminal courts in the state and for jurisdictions of other states and countries throughout the world. These include eviction warrants, court orders (contempt of court, seizure orders, etc.), income and property executions, and other notices, summonses, subpoenas, and petitions. The division acts as the enforcement arm of all civil courts, including small claims courts, city courts, county courts, and state and federal jurisdictions.

The ECSD **Court Division** maintains security and order in the county courts. Deputies assigned to this division are responsible for the security of the jury selection areas and the district attorney's offices, escorting defendants between the Holding Center and various courts, ensuring that jury members do not converse with non-court personnel after having been instructed by the judge in reference to the law, and sequestering jurors if they are unable to reach a verdict and must stay overnight.

The **Technology and Advancement Division** includes a number of specialized units, including the **Information Services Unit**, the **Communications Unit**, and the **Technical Services Unit**. In 1999, in response to a significant increase in computer-related crimes, the ECSD formed a **Computer Crime Unit**. The mission of this unit is to investigate the criminal use of computers and other related technologies, and to provide expert assistance and training to ECSD personnel and other law enforcement agencies. The unit focuses on crimes such as computer trespass, computer tampering ("criminal hacking"), child pornography over the Internet, telecommunications fraud, and the illegal sale of computer hardware or software. The unit recently set up a online "Cybertip" form to allow individuals to make online reports of computer crimes.

The **Violence Prevention Education and Domestic Violence Programs Division** has a broad focus, including not only domestic violence issues but also child and elder abuse, juvenile crime, and crime prevention education. One of the most well-known programs within the Division is the **"Operation Deadbeat Parent" Program**, which has received attention throughout the country. The program arrests individuals who have failed or refused to make court-ordered support payments to dependents (usually women and children). These dependents generally end up needing taxpayer-funded public assistance. Therefore, by forcing these individuals to meet their support payment schedule, the program has significantly reduced the burden on the taxpayers. The Division has also developed the **SE-NI-HEH Program**, which serves victims of domestic violence and elder abuse in the Native American community ("Se-ni-heh" means "Stop That" in the language of the Seneca Nation).

Nassau County Police Department[8]

The **Nassau County Police Department** (NCPD) was established in 1925. The first Chief of Police, Abram W. Skidmore, served from 1925 until 1945 (in 1938, his title was changed to the present title, Commissioner of Police). The original department had a total of 55 officers; by the time Commissioner Skidmore retired, there were over 650 officers employed in the NCPD. The department has had ten commissioners. The current commissioner, William J. Willett, joined the NCPD as a patrolman in 1953 and has served under every former commissioner except Skidmore.

The NCPD **Patrol Division** includes a number of specialized units, including a bicycle patrol, a Mounted Unit with 18 horses, an Air Bureau with four helicopters equipped for search and rescue, a Canine Unit with seven teams, and a Mobile Field Force that responds to civil disorders and other emergency situations. The first **Detective Division** was composed of ten of the original 55 NCPD officers. Today, it is responsible for investigating crimes reported to the Patrol Division. The **Support Division** provides administrative support, training, planning, and computer development.

NCPD is the largest county department in New York and one of the larger police departments in the entire country. In June 2003, the department included 2,507 sworn officers and 1,169 full- and part-time civilian employees. Requirements for employment with the NCPD include:

- the applicant must be at least 17 but no more than 35 years of age on the date of the required written examination (although exceptions are made for individuals who have served time in the military)

- the applicant must have been a resident of Nassau County, Suffolk County, Westchester County, or one of the five boroughs of New York City, for at least twelve months prior to the date of the required written exam and must maintain residency in these areas

- the applicant must be a citizen of the United States at the time of appointment to the department

- the applicant must have a valid New York State driver's license at the time of appointment to the department

- the applicant must submit to a background investigation, take a written examination, and pass other screening procedures as determined by the department

- the applicant must have a minimum of 32 college or university credits at the time of appointment to the department

Applicants who are accepted to the department attend the Nassau County Police Academy and receive 1200 hours of training. The starting salary for new recruits entering the academy is $21,000. This rises to $30,000 after six months of academy training and $35,000 after one year of employment. Officers who have been with the NCPD for 18 months receive $43,244, and those who have been with the department for seven years receive a base salary of $73,859.

STATE POLICING

There are two main types of **state police agencies** within the United States. Some states, such as North Carolina, separate or **decentralize** the functions and keep criminal investigations separate from the uniformed highway patrol. However, other states, including New York, operate one **centralized** or full-service state police agency which includes both highway patrol functions and criminal investigation.

The New York State Police[9]

History of the New York State Police

The **New York State Police** (NYSP) was established in 1917, in response to the 1913 murder of construction foreman Sam Howell during a payroll robbery. Howell was shot seven times after refusing to hand over the payroll to the offenders; he escaped with the payroll but later died of his wounds. At that time, Westchester County, the scene of the crime, was a rural area with no local police department. Because of this, although Howell identified his assailants prior to his death, they were never apprehended.

The crime resulted in the development of a movement to form a state police department to provide police protection to rural areas of New York state. In 1917, the Wells-Mills bill to appropriate $500,000 to establish a Department of State Police was introduced into the state senate, passing with one vote. It passed by a greater margin in the assembly and was signed into law by the governor on April 11, 1917, establishing the basic role of the new police force. This role remains relatively unchanged today.

> It shall be the duty of the superintendent of the state police and of members of the state police to prevent and detect crime and apprehend criminals. They shall also be subject to the call of the governor and are empowered to co-operate with any other department of the state or with local authorities.[10]

The first Superintendent, Major George F. Chandler, was appointed by the governor and confirmed by the senate. Chandler, a surgeon and military officer with no prior police training or experience, had more influence on the NYSP than any other single individual in the department's history. He developed selection methods, screened candidates, conducted physical examinations, designed the uniforms, wrote departmental procedures, bought the horses, and even came up with the designation of *trooper*. He even originated the procedure of having troopers wear pistols on a belt outside their uniforms. Prior to this time police officers around the country concealed their weapons; today it is standard practice to carry the weapon exposed. Chandler also emphasized professionalism and training for the state troopers, organizing the New York State School for Police, which eventually became the first police school in the United States to be certified by a state education board.

The NYSP began with a total of 237 mounted troopers to patrol the rural areas of the state. Their first assignment was the New York State Fair. They were then dispersed to substations around the state, working on horseback in pairs. Automobiles and motorcycles were added in 1918, although most officers still patrolled on horseback and mounted patrols would continue until 1948. However, the enforcement of vehicle and traffic laws increased in importance for troopers. By 1926, the NYSP had taken over all motor vehicle enforcement from the Motor Vehicle Bureau. In 1937, the first Traffic Bureau was established and the first formal course on traffic and vehicle enforcement was added to the training curriculum.

By 1919, the NYSP had become widely accepted by the rural population and had the strong support of the legislature and the state governor. However, organized labor continued to oppose the existence of the NYSP, due in great part to the department's responsibility for maintaining order during the frequent (and often violent) labor strikes that took place between 1919 and 1921. The NYSP was diligent in not showing any favoritism to either labor or management when confronting both strikers and guards employed by management, despite repeated attempts by both sides to involve troopers in violent actions. As a result, the NYSP gained a reputation of integrity, courage, and impartiality and by the mid-1920s was accepted state-wide as a valuable organization.

By 1928, each NYSP troop had its own identification section, which was available to assist local departments. The Bureau of Criminal Investigation was created in 1935 (then known as the Bureau of Investigation) and development of a crime laboratory was also authorized. Both were available to provide assistance to local departments as well as for conducting investigations of crimes under the jurisdiction of the NYSP.

During the early 1930s the NYSP became heavily involved in social service activities. The economic depression had severely affected many people living in rural areas of New York. Troop C surveyed their patrol areas and reported any families who needed food, clothing, or other basic necessities; they also raised money and obtained pledges of food and clothing to help these families. Their activities continued until 1933, when the establishment of various social service agencies took over much of the burden.

The opening of the New York State Thruway in 1954 significantly affected the department's duties as the NYSP assumed the responsibility for policing the Thruway. The 1950s and 1960s also found the NYSP focusing seriously on the problem of drug trafficking. The first dedicated narcotics enforcement unit was created in 1968 as a direct response to the increasing traffic in illegal drugs. Another key area was organized crime; the NYSP discovery of the organized crime leaders conference in Apalachin, New York, in 1957 led to the start of a national war on organized crime and directly contributed to the creation of the department's Criminal Intelligence Unit in 1958.

By the mid-1980s, the NYSP had grown to over 4,000 sworn troopers, making it the largest full-service state police department in the United States. The department focused on a variety of serious crime problems, including illegal drug trafficking, violent crime, child abuse and exploitation, computer crimes, consumer product tampering, and bias-motivated crimes. Highway safety was another priority. By the 1990s, violent crime (only some of which was drug related) had become one of the main priorities of the department. Several serial murderers during the early 1990s, as well as an increasing number of other violent crimes, led to the 1993 development of Violent Crime Investigative Teams to provide statewide assistance to police agencies that are investigating serious violent crimes, such as homicides, sexual assaults, abductions, and any serial violent crimes.

The NYSP Today

The responsibilities of the NYSP have increased dramatically as the department has expanded. Current mission priorities include crime prevention and law enforcement, a focus on highway safety (including both traffic enforcement and education), providing general assistance and protection to citizens in need, an emphasis on peacekeeping and order maintenance, and providing support to other departments and agencies in New York.

The NYSP has a wide variety of responsibilities. First, the department is a full-service law enforcement agency, providing direct police services statewide. The department's **Uniformed Force** provides primary police protection throughout many rural and suburban areas of the state. They have two primary responsibilities: the protection of life and property and the promotion of highway safety. To carry out these responsibilities, the Uniformed Force maintains regular preventive patrols, assists members of the public, provides emergency and disaster services, and responds to 911 calls for service which are made from cellular telephones. In many areas of the state, they are the primary law enforcement officers. The **Bureau of Criminal Investigation** (BCI) is the investigative branch of the NYSP, with over 900 investigative personnel. The BCI focuses on felony crimes, such as murder, assault, and rape, as well as cases relating to narcotics, child abuse, auto theft, consumer product tampering, organized crime, computer crimes, bias-related crimes, and violent and serial crimes. They also assist local and county departments which may need additional resources for investigations into major crimes.

The department also acts as a state highway patrol, with the responsibility of ensuring that highways are safe and maintaining safe and efficient traffic flow to prevent traffic accidents, fatalities, and injuries. To meet this responsibility, the department enforces the Vehicle and Traffic Law; conducts sobriety checkpoints and saturation patrols (to crack down on speeding, driving while intoxicated, etc.); conducts aerial patrols of the highways in the state; maintains dedicated interstate highway patrols; and employs hazardous materials experts and individuals specializing in vehicle weight and dimension regulations. The NYSP pays special attention to state, interstate, and controlled-access highways where the state police has primary presence and dedicated patrols. For example, Troop T of the NYSP is specifically assigned to the New York State Thruway.

The NYSP also provides a variety of services to the state. The department has a comprehensive driver safety education program; troopers make presentations to schools, senior citizen groups, civic organizations, and government agencies. The department also maintains data on causes of vehicle accidents both for internal departmental analysis and for use by other agencies.

As a state-wide agency, the NYSP is also responsible for providing technical and support services to local and county police departments throughout the state and to other state criminal justice agencies. The department may also assist other law enforcement agencies in New York in the investigation of serious crimes. The governor's mandate to crack down on trafficking in illegal drugs and guns has made that a primary concern of police departments throughout the state. The NYSP focuses on arresting drug traffickers; confiscating their drugs; seizing their illegally acquired assets; and identifying and apprehending violent, predatory, and serial offenders. To accomplish these tasks, the department maintains a number of specialized units. **Community Narcotics Enforcement Teams** are made up of trained undercover drug investigators who are available to help local police combat drug-trafficking and related violent crime within local communities. **Violent Crime Investigative Teams** include trained detectives who assist local departments in solving serious felonies, such as murders, assaults, rapes, and missing persons cases. The NYSP **Forensic Investigation Center** provides local departments with forensic science support, including crime laboratories, DNA analysis, and evidence collection. The **New York Statewide Police Information Network** gives local officers access to motor vehicle and driving records, and information on wants and warrants, escaped criminals, and stolen property. Other special units available to assist local departments include SCUBA divers, K-9 units, computer crime specialists, and hostage negotiators.

In 2001, the NYSP investigated over 116,000 reported criminal cases, conducted over 305,000 noncriminal investigations, and made almost 800,000 vehicle and traffic arrests.[11]

The minimum requirements for application to the NYSP include:

- a minimum age of 20 upon application and 21 upon appointment

- a maximum age of 30 when taking the examination (with an extension of up to six years for active military service)

- a high school diploma or equivalency diploma

- completion of at least 60 college credit hours at time of appointment (up to 30 credits may be waived for applicants who have two years of active military service and have received an honorable discharge or who have completed a Certified Police Officer Training Course)

- United States citizenship at time of application

- New York State residency at time of appointment

- a valid New York State driver's license at time of appointment

- 20/40 eyesight, correctable to 20/20, and no color deficiency

- conform to height and weight standards at time of appointment

- good moral character – a felony conviction results in automatic disqualification; convictions for other crimes and offenses may be evaluated during a background investigation

Applicants who meet these minimum requirements go through a rigorous selection procedure. This includes a written examination and a physical ability test, including sit-ups, push-ups, and a 1.5 mile run. Applicants who receive a conditional offer of appointment must then pass through three additional selection phases:

- a psychological evaluation, including written tests and an interview with a psychologist

- a background investigation, including a polygraph examination

- a medical examination, including vision, hearing, height/weight (must be proportional), and dental checks

Drug screening also occurs at various phases throughout the selection process.

Applicants who are selected for appointment attend a 25-week residential training program at the NYSP Academy and must complete successfully 1,079 hours of training. They then go through a 12-week Field Training and Evaluation Program. All new troopers are on probationary status for one year after their completion of Academy training.

The starting salary for a state trooper undergoing training at the Academy was $48,907 in 2003. Salary is automatically increased upon graduation from the Academy to $52,308. Additional increases follow after one year of service and after five years as a trooper. Troopers stationed in New York City and in certain counties receive additional location compensation.

The New York State Division of Criminal Justice Services[12]

The **New York State Division of Criminal Justice Services** (DCJS) is a state-wide criminal justice support agency which oversees a variety of law-enforcement related programs. The agency's responsibilities include maintaining the state's criminal history and fingerprint files; advising the Governor and the Director of Criminal Justice on programs that may improve the effectiveness of the criminal justice system; collecting and analyzing state-wide crime data; administering federal and state funds which are intended for the criminal justice system; conducting research on key criminal justice issues; and providing training to law enforcement officers and prosecutors throughout the state. The DCJS has five program bureaus:

- The Office of Justice Information Services
- The Office of Public Safety
- The Office of Strategic Planning
- The Office of Legal Services and Forensic Services
- The Office of Administration

Among the many functions of the DCJS is the oversight of several key state-wide programs. The **New York State Missing and Exploited Children Clearinghouse** maintains a database containing the state's register of missing children. Through this register, the Clearinghouse assists the public and the police in cases of child abduction and victimization. The Clearinghouse also plans and implements programs which combine federal, state, and local resources in the investigation of missing children cases. The DCJS also maintains the **New York State Sex Offender Registry**, which includes regularly updated information on sex offenders resident in the state. The **Internet Crimes Against Children Task Force** is a federally funded program that works in conjunction with the NYSP, the DCJS, and the state Attorney General's Office. It conducts investigations into situations where a computer or the Internet is being used to victimize children. These include crimes such as distributing indecent material to minors and child pornography. The task force also provides training for police officers and prosecutors, educates the public about internet safety, and helps to encourage statewide collaboration and cooperation.

POLICE TRAINING

New York was the first state in the United States to establish a set of basic training requirements for new police officers. In 1959, the legislature established the **Municipal Police Training Council** (MPTC), which is responsible for developing training standards for police officers in the state. According to statute, the MPTC is comprised of eight members, including:

- three appointed by the governor
- two appointed by the governor from a list of nominees submitted by the New York State Sheriffs' Association
- two appointed by the governor from a list of nominees submitted by the New York State Association of Chiefs of Police
- the commissioner of police of New York City (or a designated member of the department)

All members serve two year terms.[13]

The MPTC has a variety of functions and duties, including the responsibility for establishing minimum standards for appointment as a police officer in the state, developing minimum requirements for the basic police officer training course and for in-service training programs, and developing minimum qualifications for instructors.[14]

The current basic training course for police officers in New York includes a minimum of 510 hours, a significant improvement from the original 80-hour course that was mandated in 1960. Some large departments operate their own training academies but most officers attend a regional academy in the company of recruits from various other police and sheriff's departments in that part of the state. Many training programs offer more than the minimum number of training hours.

NOTES

1. *2001 Uniform Crime Reports* (http://www.fbi.gov/ucr/ucr.htm)
2. *Law Enforcement Officers Killed and Assaulted, 2001* (http://www.fbi.gov/ucr/killed/00leoka.pdf)
3. *Ibid*
4. Unless otherwise noted, information in this section was obtained from the web site of the New York City Police Department (http://www.nyc.gov/html/nypd/home.html)
5. New York City Police Museum home page (http://www.nycpolicemuseum.org/html/faq.html)
6. *2001 Uniform Crime Reports, op cit.*
7. Unless otherwise noted, information in this section was obtained from the web site of the Erie County Sheriff's Office (http://www.erie.gov/sheriff)
8. Unless otherwise noted, information in this section was obtained from the web site of the Nassau County Police Department (http://www.co.nassau.ny.us/police/index.html)
9. Unless otherwise noted, information in this section was obtained from the web site of the New York State Police (http://www.troopers.state.ny.us/index.html)
10. Executive Law, §223
11. *NYSP Annual Report 2001 (*http://www.troopers.state.ny.us/Intro/Annual/Annualindex.html*)*
12. Unless otherwise noted, information in this section was obtained from the web site of the Division of Criminal Justice Services (http://criminaljustice.state.ny.us/dcjs1.htm)
13. Executive Law, §839
14. Executive Law, §840

CHAPTER 5

THE COURT SYSTEM IN NEW YORK

The unified court system in New York, which includes the criminal courts, is similar to the federal system, although not identical. It includes a state court of appeals, a supreme court (or intermediate appellate court), and several levels of trial courts, including trial courts of limited jurisdiction, county courts, and family courts.

UNITED STATES FEDERAL COURTS

There are a number of federal courts which sit in New York. These should not be confused with the state trial and appellate courts.

There are several federal courts that sit in New York, although they are not specifically part of the New York State court system. There are four federal judicial districts in New York, each with a **federal district court**. These are:

- the Northern District Court, which serves 32 counties
- the Eastern District Court, which serves five counties
- the Southern District Court, which serves eight counties
- the Western District Court, which serves 17 counties.[1]

These are the trial courts of the federal system and are not related to state district courts.

The **U.S. Courts of Appeals** are the intermediate appellate court of the federal court system and have appellate jurisdiction only over federal laws. Judges in these courts serve life terms. They are nominated by the President of the United States and confirmed by the Senate. New York is part of the second judicial circuit, which includes all federal courts within New York, Connecticut, and Vermont.[2] The U.S. Court of Appeals should not be confused with the New York Court of Appeals, which is part of the New York Unified Court System and is discussed below.

THE HISTORY OF THE NEW YORK UNIFIED COURT SYSTEM

New York currently has what is known as a **unified court system**. However, this is a fairly new innovation in the state. During the colonial period, the supreme judicial authority for the state was held by the office of the state governor. Along with an advisory council, the governor established various inferior courts when necessary, and himself served as the court of last resort in the state. During this time, while New York was under English rule, the judicial system eventually developed into a structured series of courts to deal with all legal matters. These included county criminal courts (then known as courts of general sessions) and local courts (courts of special sessions). Judges rode circuit around the state and many areas were only able to hold court a few times each year.

In 1777, the first New York State Constitution was ratified. It kept the colonial court system intact, with only minor changes. However, other changes occurred over the years. For example, in 1784, the **Court for the Correction of Errors** was established, which replaced the governor as the highest court in the state.

A new constitution was ratified in 1821. This constitution established eight judicial circuits within the state, each with a circuit court presided over by a judge who was appointed by the governor with the consent of the state senate. Appeals of rulings and verdicts handed down by the circuit court were made to the supreme court of judicature, which consisted of one chief justice and two associate justices.

The third New York State Constitution, ratified in 1846, again reorganized the state court system. The Court for the Correction of Errors was abolished and a new two-tiered court system was created, establishing a new court of appeals as the highest appellate court in the state. A reorganized, elective supreme court became the highest court of original, unlimited jurisdiction for questions of both law and equity. Eight courts of intermediate appeal, one for each judicial district, were also established.

In 1869, a **Judiciary Article** was added to the state constitution, which once again revamped the state's court system. New York was divided into four departments, each of which had a supreme court general term to hear and decide appeals. The eight judicial districts were distributed among these four departments. This new court of appeals had seven elected judges, each of whom served a fourteen-year term. The number of judges in the supreme court was increased several times, in an effort to deal with the large number of cases in that court.

The organization of the supreme court was changed again when the fourth State Constitution was ratified in 1894. Various civil and criminal courts were replaced by trial terms of the supreme court. The second division of the court of appeals was also abolished by the new constitution and a new appellate division of the supreme court was created to hear those appeals which previously had been heard in the general terms of the supreme court.

In 1953, a **Temporary Commission on the Courts** was created and given the task of studying problems facing the New York judiciary. The commission's report suggested that the structure of the court system be simplified and court administration be centralized. As a result of the study, a new Judiciary Article was added to the state constitution in 1962. This article created the "Unified Court System" of the state of New York. Constitutional amendments ratified in 1978 and laws passed in both 1974 and 1978 have also impacted the central administration of the state's court system.

Currently, Article VI of the New York State Constitution states that:

> There shall be a unified court system for the state. The state-wide courts shall consist of the court of appeals, the supreme court including the appellate divisions thereof,

the court of claims, the county court, the surrogate's court and the family court, as hereinafter provided. The legislature shall establish in and for the city of New York, as part of the unified court system for the state, a single, city-wide court of civil jurisdiction and a single, city-wide court of criminal jurisdiction, as hereinafter provided, and may upon the request of the mayor and the local legislative body of the city of New York, merge the two courts into one city-wide court of both civil and criminal jurisdiction. The unified court system for the state shall also include the district, town, city and village courts outside the city of New York, as hereinafter provided.[3]

THE STRUCTURE OF THE NEW YORK UNIFIED COURT SYSTEM

The Unified Court System of the State of New York is a two-tiered system. It includes four primary appellate courts:

- **The Court of Appeals** – the highest court in the state
- **Appellate Divisions of the Supreme Court**
- **Appellate Terms of the Supreme Court**
- **County Court** – this is primarily a trial court but may hear appeals from local courts in some jurisdictions

There are also a wide variety of trial courts. Statewide trial courts in New York include:

- **The Supreme Court** – the trial court of unlimited original jurisdiction
- **The Court of Claims**
- **Family Court**
- **Surrogate's Court**

Some trial courts do not have statewide jurisdiction. There are two courts in New York City: the **Criminal Court** and the **Civil Court**. In addition, local courts outside New York City, which do not have statewide jurisdiction, include:

- **County Courts** – serving as both a trial and appellate court
- **City Courts**
- **District Courts**
- **Town and Village Courts**[4]

THE NEW YORK STATE COURT OF APPEALS

Unlike most states and the federal system, the appellate court of last resort in New York is not known as the "Supreme Court." Instead, the **New York State Court of Appeals** is the highest court in the state and is the court of last resort in New York. Its decisions are binding upon all other courts in the state. The court hears cases on appeal from the appellate division and from trial courts in capital cases. Its review is generally limited to questions of law, although in capital cases it may rule on both law and fact. The court of appeals also reviews determinations of the **Commission on Judicial Conduct**.[5]

History of the Court of Appeals

Originally, when New York was a colony under British Rule, the court of last resort was the **King's Privy Council**, which met in London, England. In most cases, however, appeals were made to the royal governor and his council, who sat as a court which was later termed the court for the correction of errors and appeals. The first New York State Constitution, ratified in 1777, replaced the governor and council with a new court which was known as the **Court for the Correction of Errors**. The court consisted of the lieutenant governor, all state senators, the chancellor, and the supreme court justices.

The court was abolished by the 1846 New York State Constitution, which created a new court of appeals composed of eight judges, four of whom were to be elected rather than appointed. They served eight-year terms and had no age limitation. The other four were appointed by the governor from among the supreme court justices and served one-year terms as ex-officio judges of the court of appeals. However, this procedure meant that each year half of the justices sitting on the court of appeals were replaced. In addition, every two years, the term of one of the elected judges would end and he would also have to be replaced. During the first 23 years the court of appeals was in operation, a total of 123 judges served as members of the court. In addition, as the ex-officio judges were selected from the supreme court, they frequently sat in review on appeals of their own decisions.

As a result, the **Judiciary Article of 1869** reorganized the court of appeals. The court had a chief judge and six associate judges, all of whom were elected. All judges served fourteen-year terms and faced mandatory retirement when they reached age 70. Five of the seven judges constituted a quorum. The agreement of at least four of the seven judges was necessary for a decision to be handed down. In addition, no judge was allowed to sit in review of his own decisions.

By the mid-1870s, a backlog of cases began to accumulate in the court of appeals. In 1874, appeals were limited to only those cases involving at least $500 (not including costs), unless the supreme court certified the case as involving an important question of law. In 1888, an amendment to the state constitution authorized the state governor to create a separate body of seven justices, known as the second division of the court of appeals. The second division, which was only designated if the court of appeals certified to the governor that the court calendar was overcrowded, assisted the court of appeals until it was no longer needed. The second division first sat in January 1889 and continued until fall 1890. Another second division was created in March 1891 and functioned until October 1892. During these years, the second division dealt with over 2,000 appeals.

However, the second division, which was effectively a temporary auxiliary to the court of appeals to deal with calendar backlog, did not solve the underlying problem of the rapidly increasing number of appeals. In 1894, a Constitutional Convention recommended the establishment of courts of intermediate appeal as a solution to the overcrowding problem faced by the court of appeals. It was felt that limiting the court of appeals jurisdiction, based on the amount of money involved, was inappropriate, as major issues of law may exist in cases involving small as well as large sums of money. As a result, the 1894 constitution divided New York into four judicial departments. Each contained an appellate court composed of five supreme court justices who served as the court of last resort within that department for all questions of fact. The court of appeals was limited to deciding on questions of law.

The court's jurisdiction was further limited by 1917 legislation which abolished appeals as of right unless a constitutional question was directly involved or unless there was a disagreement in the lower courts. The court at this time was solely a court of law, unless the penalty imposed was death or unless the appellate division made new factual findings. In 1921, another Judicial Convention again affected the court of appeals, allowing the court to bring in supreme court justices to sit temporarily on the court in the place of court members who were absent or temporarily unable to serve. The governor, at the request of the court of appeals, also had the power to appoint four supreme court justices to assist in dealing with case backlog. Since 1923, however, no additional justices have been designated by the governor.

In 1962 the state unified court system was established. An Administrative Board of the Judicial Conference was created to administer the new court system; the Board included the chief justice of the court of appeals as well as presiding justices of the four appellate divisions. In 1977, through a new constitutional amendment, the 1846 constitutional requirement that court of appeals judges be elected was repealed; currently judges of the court of appeals are selected by the state governor from a list of names that are recommended by the **Commission on Judicial Nomination** and approved by the New York State Senate. The amendment also provided that the chief judge of the court of appeals would be the Chief Judge of the State of New York as well as the Chief Judicial Officer of the Unified Court System. As a result, the chief judge, along with the Administrative Board, became responsible for establishing state-wide standards and policies for the administration of the court system. The chief administrator of the courts, who directs the Office of Court Administration and supervises the operation and administration of the trial courts, is appointed by the chief judge of the court of appeals.

In 1985, a new constitutional amendment was adopted that allowed the court to answer questions of New York law which were certified to the court by the United States Supreme Court, a U.S. Court of Appeals, or an appellate court of last resort in another state.

The Court of Appeals Today

The court of appeals is the highest court in the state. It focuses on broad issues of law rather than on individual factual disputes. Article VI, §3(a) of the New York State Constitution states that:

> The jurisdiction of the court of appeals shall be limited to the review of questions of law except where the judgment is of death, or where the appellate division, on reversing or modifying a final or interlocutory judgment in an action or a final or interlocutory order in a special proceeding, finds new facts and a final judgment or a final order pursuant thereto is entered; but the right to appeal shall not depend upon the amount involved.

In criminal cases, appeals may be taken directly from a court of original jurisdiction only when the offender has been sentenced to death. In non-capital criminal cases, appeals are taken from an appellate division or appellate term of the supreme court. This allows the court of appeals to focus on deciding important legal questions and maintaining uniformity in the state law. The court may select specific issues in a case to review or it may decide all the issues in a case. There are few grounds for appeals as of right; the court hears most appeals by its own permission, usually selecting cases which include difficult or unusual questions of law that have state-wide importance, or which involve issues over which lower courts are in conflict. The court also may choose to hear an appeal as a way of correcting an error made by a lower court. In addition, as stated above, the constitution gives the court the power to answer any questions of New York law which are certified to the court by a federal appellate court or a court of last resort in another state.[6]

According to Article VI, §2a of the New York State Constitution, the court of appeals is composed of seven judges (a chief judge and six associate judges), who are appointed by the governor to terms of fourteen years. Unlike United States Supreme Court justices, who serve life terms, judges on the New York Court of Appeals have a mandatory retirement age of 70.[7] The governor makes appointments to the court from a list of names submitted by the Commission on Judicial Nomination. All gubernatorial appointments must be confirmed by the New York State Senate. Any five of the seven judges constitute a quorum and the agreement of at least four of the judges is necessary for the court to reach a decision.[8] If a court of appeals judge is temporarily absent or unable to act, the court has the power to designate any supreme court justice to serve as an associate judge of the court of appeals during this period.

The court of appeals formally convenes in a courtroom in State Hall, in Albany, NY. There is one term of the court each year, which begins in January and continues in two-week sessions each month (generally excluding the month of July). Oral arguments are held during nine months of the year. The court generally sits in late August to hear and decide any cases that are related to primary elections. Between court sessions, the judges return to their home chambers for periods of three weeks. During these in-chambers sessions, the judges write opinions and prepare cases for the next session of the court. They also use this time to review requests for permission to appeal in criminal cases and to prepare recommendations for motions for leave to appeal in civil cases. In addition, this time is used for a variety of other judicial and professional responsibilities.[9]

During the court sessions in Albany, the judges hear oral arguments and meet confidentially in conference to deliberate and come to decisions which will become the law of the state. When the court is in Albany, oral arguments are heard Tuesday through Friday. Sessions are open to the public. The court of appeals is known as "a hot bench" because each of the judges has read through and thoroughly studied all the legal documents in the case prior to the attorneys' appearance in the courtroom. Because of this, judges frequently ask lawyers about specific legal points relating to the argument and the sessions often become lively question and answer sessions.

In 2002, the court of appeals dealt with over 4,250 matters. These included 176 appeals, of which 109 were civil and 67 were criminal. A total of 153 of these decisions were unanimous. The court also decided 1,352 motions, most of which were for leave to appeal in civil cases, and 2,724 criminal leave applications, of which 46 were granted. The 2002–2003 fiscal year budget appropriation was $13,138,335.[10]

THE NEW YORK STATE SUPREME COURT

In New York, the **Supreme Court** is the highest state trial court of original jurisdiction, with general jurisdiction in law and equity. It also serves as an appellate court.

History of the New York State Supreme Court

In 1691, the colonial assembly of New York established the **Supreme Court of Judicature**, commonly known as the Supreme Court, as the highest common-law court in the state to have both original and appellate jurisdiction. Original jurisdiction over criminal cases, some civil actions, and actions involving title to real property was shared with county-level courts. The supreme court also had appellate jurisdiction over all lower courts in the colony. Appeals from the supreme court were allowed only for civil cases involving sums greater than 100 English pounds (the sum was increased to 300 pounds after 1753). Appeals from the supreme court were made to the court for the correction of errors and appeals, and above that to the Privy Council in London. The supreme court included a chief justice and two associate justices who were appointed by the governor. In 1758, the number of associate justices was increased to three. The court sat twice yearly in New York City and also rode circuit, sitting in each county at least once a year to try civil and criminal cases.

Article 35 of the first New York State Constitution, ratified in 1777, maintained the supreme court of judicature as the highest court in the land with original jurisdiction, although it increased the number of justices to five. Between 1785 and 1841 a series of laws altered the number and location of regular terms to be held by the court. During these terms, the court ruled on points of law which had been raised during trial proceedings in the circuit courts or during pleading in the supreme court. The judges also reviewed cases appealed from various lower courts. The Constitution of 1822 again changed the organization of supreme court, reducing the number of justices to three.

In 1846, the third New York State Constitution abolished the court of chancery and transferred original jurisdiction for equity matters to the supreme court. The constitution established a new supreme court as the highest court of original jurisdiction for both equity and law. The new supreme court also heard cases appealed from county courts. The constitution established eight general terms of the supreme court (one for each judicial district) as courts of intermediate appeal. In 1869 a Judiciary Article was added to the constitution, becoming effective in 1870. The Article divided the state of New York into four departments, distributing the eight judicial districts among them. Each district included three justices and a presiding judge; New York City had five justices. While the jurisdiction of the supreme court was unchanged, judges were no longer allowed to sit in review of their own cases. The fourth state constitution, ratified in 1894, made further changes to the organization of the supreme court. One key change was the creation of an appellate division of the supreme court to hear all appeals that previously had been heard in the court's general terms.[11]

The Supreme Court Today

The supreme court is the principle trial court of the state of New York and also serves as the state's intermediate level appellate court. The structure and jurisdiction of the New York supreme court has changed little since the ratification of the 1894 state constitution, with the exception of changes in the number of justices and judicial districts. There is a branch of the supreme court in each county in New York. Article VI, §4a of the Constitution divides the state into four judicial departments and twelve judicial districts for appellate purposes. The boundaries of the departments may be changed by the legislature every ten years but the number of departments may not be altered except by a constitutional amendment. The court is divided into appellate divisions, appellate terms, and trial departments.

Article VI, §7a of the constitution outlines the jurisdiction of the supreme court, stating that:

> The supreme court shall have general original jurisdiction in law and equity and the appellate jurisdiction herein provided. In the city of New York, it shall have exclusive jurisdiction over crimes prosecuted by indictment, provided, however, that the legislature may grant to the city-wide court of criminal jurisdiction of the city of New York jurisdiction over misdemeanors prosecuted by indictment and to the family court in the city of New York jurisdiction over crimes and offenses by or against minors or between spouses or between parent and child or between members of the same family or household.

The Appellate Division of the Supreme Court

The **appellate division** of the supreme court is the intermediate court of appeals in New York. There are four appellate divisions, one in each of the four judicial departments in the state. Each appellate division is responsible for hearing most of the appeals from trial courts within its geographical area. Appellate division justices are appointed by the governor from among the justices elected to the supreme court. They serve terms of five years in the appellate division. The majority of the justices appointed to sit in any appellate division of the court must be residents of that judicial department. No more than five justices may sit on any case and four are required for a quorum.[12]

Each appellate division is responsible for admitting to practice and for disciplining all attorneys within its department. It hears both criminal and civil appeals from trial courts, and has the power to review both the facts and the law. In addition, the appellate division serves as a court of original jurisdiction for several very specific and limited areas, including the discipline, admission, and disbarment of attorneys, and Article 78 proceedings brought against a supreme court justice.[13]

The Appellate Term of the Supreme Court

The First and Second Judicial Departments, which include New York City and Nassau, Suffolk, Rockland, Westchester, Putnam, Dutchess, and Orange Counties, have an **appellate term** of the supreme court. The appellate term includes supreme court justices chosen by the Chief Administrator of the Courts with the approval of the Presiding Justice of the Appellate Division. The appellate terms hear appeals from both civil and criminal cases that originated in New York City criminal and civil courts or in certain district, city, town and village courts. No more than three appellate term justices may sit on a case and two are required for a quorum.[14]

The Supreme Court as a Trial Court

In addition to serving as an appellate court, the supreme court is the state-wide **trial court** with the broadest jurisdiction, including both civil and criminal cases. The court's jurisdiction is almost unlimited; it can hear almost any type of case brought before it with the exception of claims against the state, which must be brought before the court of claims. In the case of the ending of a marriage, the supreme court must be involved as it is the only court in New York which may grant a divorce, annulment, or separation. Because of the broad jurisdiction of the supreme court, attempts are generally made to divide the workload among the supreme court and the lower courts of limited jurisdiction.

The supreme court is divided into twelve judicial districts (not to be confused with judicial departments). Supreme court justices are elected by voters in their judicial districts for terms of fourteen years. Although they normally preside over trial terms in their own districts, elected supreme court justices have state-wide jurisdiction and may be assigned to serve anywhere in New York. The state legislature has the power to increase the number of justices in any judicial district of the supreme court. The legislature also has the power to decrease the number of supreme court justices in any judicial district, but they may not be fewer than the number designated in the constitution.[15]

TRIAL COURTS IN NEW YORK

Trial courts, or courts of original jurisdiction, hear original cases. The supreme court, discussed above, is only one of the many different trial courts found in the state. Some trial courts have statewide jurisdiction, while others have local jurisdiction.

Statewide Trial Courts

The Supreme Court

As discussed in the above section, the **supreme court** is also a trial court with almost unlimited original jurisdiction. It is a statewide court and has the broadest criminal and civil jurisdiction of any court in the state. With the exception of claims against the state, almost any type of case can be brought before the supreme court. It has statewide civil jurisdiction and in some parts of the state, including New York City, also exercises jurisdiction over felony charges. The supreme court is the only court which can grant a divorce, annulment, or separation, so it must be involved in all cases involving the ending of a marriage. In most situations, however, the supreme court generally hears only those cases which are outside the jurisdiction of other trial courts with more limited jurisdiction.

The Court of Claims

The New York State court system also has a **Court of Claims**, which has jurisdiction over civil claims for monetary damages against the State of New York or against some state government agencies, including the New York State Thruway Authority, the City University of New York, and the New York State Power Authority. Civil actions against other public authorities are generally heard in the supreme court. The Court of Claims has no jurisdiction over civil actions against local or county governmental agencies, corporations, or individuals.[16]

Cases heard in the Court of Claims are tried by a judge alone; there are no jury trials. This procedure dates back to the 1777 state constitution, which contained the principle of **sovereign immunity**. Based on English common law, this principle states that the government enjoys immunity from lawsuits and claims. In the Court of Claims Act, enacted in 1939, the state has waived immunity and has, under certain conditions, agreed to permit itself to be sued. Court of Claims judges are appointed by the state governor with the consent of the Senate and serve nine-year terms.[17]

Family Court

The **Family Court Act** established a **family court** in each county of the state.[18] Each of New York City's five boroughs also has a family court. Family courts were established in 1962 to replace the Children's Court and New York City's Domestic Relations Court. The court deals with most cases involving children between the ages of seven and sixteen who are charged with an offense which, if committed by an adult, would be a crime. The court also has jurisdiction over most legal matters which involve children and families. The types of cases handled by the family court include family offenses (e.g., domestic violence), family disputes, child protection (in cases of child abuse and/or neglect), paternity, custody, visitation, guardianship, child support issues (both in parental divorce situations and for children born out of wedlock), termination of parental rights, adoptions, cases involving persons in need of supervision (e.g., truants), and juvenile delinquency cases. Basically, the family court deals with all types of family problems with the exception of termination of a marriage; the state supreme court is the only court able to grant a divorce, separation, or annulment.

Family court judges serve ten-year terms. In most counties they are elected by the voters, although in New York City family court judges are appointed by the mayor. Each county must have at least one family court judge. Rather than trials, family court proceedings are known as hearings and are heard by judges. There are no juries in family court.[19]

Surrogate's Court

Each county in New York also has a **Surrogate's Court** which has jurisdiction over all cases and issues that relate to the affairs of deceased persons, regardless of whether or not a valid will exists. Matters dealt with in the surrogate's court include: will probate, estate administration, guardianship of minors and their property, adoptions, and the final settlement of estates. Surrogate court judges are elected by the voters of each county and serve terms of fourteen years in New York City and ten years elsewhere. They must be a resident of the county in which they are elected. Each county has at least one surrogate's court judge.[20]

New York City Courts

New York City has two city courts that have responsibilities which differ from courts in other parts of the state. The **Civil Court of the City of New York** has jurisdiction over civil matters that involve amounts up to $25,000 and cases involving real property within the city that is valued up to

$25,000. They may also have jurisdiction over other civil matters if they were referred to the civil court by the supreme court. New York City civil court judges are elected by city voters to a ten-year term and have jurisdiction throughout the city. The Civil Court also has a Housing Court to hear landlord-tenant cases and enforce housing codes as well as a Small Claims Court to hear cases brought by private individuals for amounts not exceeding $2,000.[21]

The **Criminal Court of the City of New York** has original jurisdiction over all criminal misdemeanors, violations, and petty offenses committed within the city. In addition, the court has preliminary jurisdiction over all felony arrests, conducts preliminary hearings in felony cases, and maintains jurisdiction until the grand jury votes an indictment, at which time the case is transferred to the county Supreme Court for trial or disposition. Criminal court judges also serve as magistrates for arraignments and may issue arrest warrants.[22] These judges are appointed by the New York City Mayor and serve ten-year terms. All judges must be residents of the city.[23]

Lower Courts Outside New York City

There are two types of lower courts. The various **trial courts of limited jurisdiction** handle misdemeanors, violations, and minor civil matters. They also preside over preliminary proceedings, such as arraignments, in felony cases, which are generally then prosecuted in a **county court**.

County Courts

Each county in the state outside of New York City has a **County Court**, which has almost unlimited jurisdiction over all crimes committed within that county. However, in most cases, misdemeanor trials, and preliminary proceedings for felony cases are handled by courts of limited jurisdiction. County courts have primary appellate jurisdiction on appeals from judgments from these courts of limited jurisdiction. They also have jurisdiction over those civil cases in which the amount in question is less than or equal to $25,000. The decisions of county courts are subject to review on appeal by the appellate division of the Supreme Court.

County court judges are elected by county voters to a ten-year term. The number of judges in the court varies according to the population of the county. In some counties with small populations, the county court judge may also serve as the judge for the family court and/or the surrogate court; in this case, the judge is referred to as a **multi-hat judge**. In other counties, two judges may share the responsibility for all three courts or may be elected to only one or two of the courts. In the more populous counties, judges are usually elected separately to each of the three courts.

District Courts

In Nassau County, and in the five western towns of Suffolk County, **District Courts** exercise limited jurisdiction over criminal and civil matters. In criminal cases, district courts may try all misdemeanors, violations, and offenses, and may hear preliminary matters in felony cases. In civil cases, the district court is limited to those involving amounts of no more than $15,000 and to small claims matters of no more than $3,000. They also have jurisdiction over landlord-tenant disputes and some matters involving property liens. District court judges are elected to six-year terms by district voters.[24]

City Courts

City Courts exist in 61 cities in New York (not including New York City). City courts have jurisdiction over criminal cases involving misdemeanors or minor violations and also hear preliminary matters in felony cases. City courts may hear civil cases which involve amounts up to $15,000; they also have jurisdiction over landlord-tenant disputes. City court judges must have been attorneys who have been licensed to practice law in New York for at least five years. They are elected by voters in the city; full-time city court judges serve terms of ten years while part-time judges are elected to six-year terms.[25]

Town and Village Courts

Town and Village Courts are also known as **Justice Courts**. They have very limited jurisdiction in both criminal and civil matters. They may handle misdemeanor traffic cases and minor criminal violations, and may conduct preliminary proceedings in felony cases. In civil matters, they hear cases which involve up to $3,000 worth of money or property. The court may also hear landlord-tenant cases, regardless of the amount of rent involved, but may not decides cases involving title to real property. Justice court judges are officially called "Justices of the Peace" but are often referred to as "Magistrates" or "Town Justices." They are not required to be lawyers, although they must go through special training. They serve four-year terms and are elected by voters in their locality.

OTHER COURT AGENCIES AND COMMISSIONS

The Commission on Judicial Nomination

The Commission on Judicial Nomination was established in Article VI, §2 of the New York State Constitution. The Commission evaluates candidates for appointment to the court of appeals and recommends to the governor those candidates considered to be qualified to serve as a court of appeals judge. The Commission is composed of twelve members who serve four-year terms. Of these, four are appointed by the governor; of these, two must be members of the New York State Bar while the other two may not be members of the bar. In addition, no more than two may be members of the same political party. Four members are appointed by the chief judge of the court of appeals, with the same conditions as apply to the members chosen by the governor. In addition, one each is appointed by the speaker of the assembly, the temporary president of the senate, the minority leader of the senate, and the minority leader of the assembly. Members of the Commission may not hold or have held any judicial office. The only exceptions to this rule are that the governor and the chief judge may each appoint one former judge or justice of the unified court system. In addition, during their period of service, no member may hold any elected public office for which he/she is compensated, nor may any member hold any office in any political party. No member of the commission may be eligible for appointment to any judicial office in any court in New York State during his or her period of service or for one year following.[26]

The Commission on Judicial Conduct

Article VI, §22a of the New York State Constitution provides for a **Commission on Judicial Conduct**. The commission receives, initiates, and investigates complaints regarding elected or appointed judges and justices of the state's unified court system. It has the authority to impose sanctions, including admonition, censure, and removal from office, on judges and justices, and may retire them for disability, subject to review by the Court of Appeals.

According to the New York State Constitution, the functions of the commission include:

> The commission on judicial conduct shall receive, initiate, investigate and hear complaints with respect to the conduct, qualifications, fitness to perform or performance of official duties of any judge or justice of the unified court system, in the manner provided by law; and, ... may determine that a judge or justice be admonished, censured or removed from office for cause, including, but not limited to, misconduct in office, persistent failure to perform his or her duties, habitual intemperance, and conduct, on or off the bench, prejudicial to the administration of justice, or that a judge or justice be retired for mental or physical disability preventing the proper performance of his or her judicial duties...[27]

The Commission consists of eleven members, four of whom are appointed by the governor and three by the chief judge of the court of appeals. Of the remainder of the Commission members, one is appointed by the temporary president of the state senate, one by the minority leader of the senate, one by the speaker of the assembly, and one by the minority leader of the assembly. At least four of the commission members must be judges, at least one must be an attorney in the state of New York, and at least two must be lay persons. Each member of the Commission is appointed for a four-year term.[28]

New York State Bar Association

The **New York State Bar Association** (NYSBA) has over 70,000 members and serves as the state-wide organization of the legal profession. It is both the oldest and the largest voluntary state bar organization in the United States.[29] According to the NYSBA,

> The Association's objectives, originally stated in its constitution adopted in 1877, are the same today. They are: to cultivate the science of jurisprudence, promote reform in the law, facilitate the administration of justice, and elevate the standards of integrity, honor, professional skill and courtesy in the legal profession.[30]

The NYSBA serves as an advocate for both the legal profession and for the public. Due to the increasing complexity of society and of the legal system, the Association's public role has increased significantly in recent years. During the 1990s, the Association developed programs dealing with a variety of public issues, including child abuse, the problems of the elderly, and governmental corruption. It is involved in public education, providing information to citizens about the courts, the law, the legal profession, and individual legal rights.

All lawyers who have been admitted to practice and who are in good standing before the bar of New York may become members of the State Bar. In addition, membership is also open to lawyers who are in good standing in any other state or country. Law students and graduated law students may also join the NYSBA, although graduated students must be admitted to practice within two years of graduation or they become ineligible for membership.

In addition to the NYSBA, there are a variety of other state-wide associations, including the New York State Association of Criminal Defense Lawyers, the New York State Defenders' Association, the New York State Trial Lawyers' Association, and the Women's Bar Association of New York. There are also a number of county-wide bar associations.

NEW YORK CRIMINAL COURT PROCEDURES

The basic procedures involved in a criminal trial, including the pretrial activities, are similar in most states. In New York, the criminal justice process begins when the police are notified (or in some other way discover) that a crime has been committed and they initiate an investigation into that crime. The procedures discussed in this section apply specifically to felony offenses; however, the procedures for misdemeanors are extremely similar.

Arrest and Booking

After the police have determined that a crime has in fact been committed and that a specific person committed the crime, they may place that individual under **arrest**. In some situations, the police may have obtained an **arrest warrant** from a judge. CPL §120 defines those situations in which a warrant of arrest may be issued and executed. However, in New York, as in most states, the vast majority of arrests are made by police officers acting without a warrant. There are a variety of situations in which it is lawful to make an arrest without a warrant; these are outlined in CPL §140.

Before being brought before a judge, the arrested individual taken to the county jail and undergoes processing, usually known as **booking**. This involves entering into the police record various facts about the suspect. The suspect will be photographed and fingerprinted and may be placed in a police lineup. At this time, the prosecutor will consult with the arresting officer. If the prosecutor decides there is sufficient evidence, he or she will prepare the charges against the defendant and will file a written **accusation** or **accusatory instrument** in the local criminal court.[31]

Arraignment

The first stage of the court process is known as the **arraignment**. This is generally held before a local court judge and typically occurs within 24 hours of arrest. The defendant has the right to legal representation at arraignment. If the defendant cannot afford to hire an attorney, the court at this time will appoint one from the Legal Aid Society, the Assigned Counsel Plan, or, if the defendant is charged with a serious homicide, the Capital Defender's Office.

At the arraignment, the **charges** outlined in the accusatory instrument are read, and the defendant is entitled to a written copy. The defendant will also be advised of his or her rights. At this time, the judge will also decide whether the defendant is entitled to any form of **pretrial release**, and if so, which type. In some cases, the judge may set bail; in other cases the defendants may request to be released on their own recognizance, without having to pay bail. The judge may also decide to **remand** the defendant to custody, which means the defendant will be held in jail without bail. According to CPL§520.10(2), there are two methods of fixing bail:

> (a) A court may designate the amount of the bail without designating the form or forms in which it may be posted...;
> (b) The court may direct that the bail be posted in any one of two or more of the forms specified in subdivision one, designated in the alternative, and may designate different amounts varying with the forms;

If the defendant is released, he or she is responsible for appearing in court when the judge sets a date and time. If the defendant does not appear, and does not notify the court, the judge may order a **bench warrant** for the defendant's arrest. A bench warrant tells the police to find and arrest the defendant and bring him or her to court. The bail posted by the defendant may be forfeited and the judge may choose to change bail conditions or even remand the defendant to custody. A bench warrant remains on the defendant's permanent record.

At this time, the defendant will also enter an initial **plea** to the charges. The primary plea options are guilty, not guilty, and *nolo contendere*. A plea of *nolo contendere* indicates that, while not admitting guilt, the defendant does not contest the charges. If a defendant enters a plea of guilty or *nolo contendere* at the arraignment, he or she waives the right to a trial and proceeds directly to the sentencing phase of the criminal court procedures.

Plea Bargaining

While **plea bargaining** is not a formal stage of the criminal justice process, it is an extremely important process in every state, including New York. Over 90 percent of all felony and misdemeanor convictions in New York are the result of guilty pleas. Generally, plea bargaining involves an attempt to resolve or dispose of a case without a trial. In most cases, the goal of the negotiation is to reach an agreement by which the defendant will enter a plea of guilty to a charge. This may be the original charge or a lesser or related charge. In exchange for this plea, the prosecutor may do one or more of the following:

- drop any other charges which have been filed against the defendant;

- make recommendations to the court concerning sentencing;

- agree not to oppose the defendant's request for a certain sentence; or

- agree to a specific sentence.

The defense attorney is responsible for advising the defendant of all plea offers and any other relevant matters that may affect the defendant's decision (e.g., the possible results of each plea). The defense attorney may not accept any plea bargain without the full consent of the defendant. The trial judge does not participate directly in plea bargaining. However, the judge is still an important element in the process because all plea bargains must be approved by the judge. Plea bargaining often begins at the arraignment stage but may continue up to and even during the trial.

After the Arraignment

Defendants who are charged with a felony and who have been arraigned in criminal court generally go before a **grand jury**. Occasionally, a **preliminary hearing** on a felony complaint may be held to determine whether or not the prosecutor has enough evidence to hold the defendant in jail while waiting for the grand jury to hear the case. If the defendant is in jail, either because s/he was remanded or because s/he was unable to post bail, the prosecutor must present evidence in the case to the grand jury no later than six days after the arrest. If the evidence is not presented to the grand jury within the six-day period, the defendant will be released from jail without bail unless the prosecutor can show a judge why the case could not be presented sooner.

A defendant charged with a felony may waive indictment, giving up his or her right to have the case presented to the grand jury. In these situations, the prosecutor will file a **Superior Court Information**.

Defendants who are charged with a misdemeanor, and who cannot post bail, will remain in jail for approximately five days. The prosecutor is required to provide the court with legal documents in support of the complaint filed by the arresting officer; if this is not done, the defendant will be released on his or her own recognizance. This does not mean that the case has been dismissed. Defendants who have been released on their own recognizance are still required to return to court on any date set by the judge.

The Grand Jury

In New York, grand jury proceedings are not open to the public. CPL §190.05 defines a grand jury as:

> a body consisting of not less than sixteen nor more than twenty-three persons, impaneled by a superior court and constituting a part of such court, the functions of which are to hear and examine evidence concerning offenses and concerning misconduct, nonfeasance and neglect in public office, whether criminal or otherwise, and to take action with respect to such evidence...

At the grand jury proceedings, the district attorney presents evidence to show that there is probable cause to believe both that a crime was committed and that the defendant committed it. The grand jury listens to the evidence and determines whether there is sufficient evidence to warrant a felony trial. If they decide that there is enough evidence, they vote an **indictment**.

Defendants appearing before the grand jury have the right to testify, although they are not required to do so. They have the right to have counsel present, but the defense attorney is required to remain silent during the defendant's testimony; defense counsel may not address the grand jury or object to questions put by the prosecution. A defendant may request that the grand jury hear witnesses willing to testify in his or her favor, but the defendant may not be present in the grand jury room during such testimony.

If the grand jury does not vote an indictment, the defendant is released from jail immediately. If an indictment is voted, the case is transferred to the supreme court for another arraignment. This arraignment is similar to that held by the criminal court. At this time, the defendant is formally charged with the crime or crimes which were voted by the grand jury and which are contained in the indictment. The defendant may plead either guilty or not guilty to each charge. Bail conditions may be reviewed and plea bargaining may occur. If the defendant does not plead guilty, the case is adjourned to a **calendar part**, a courtroom where the case will be scheduled for further proceedings.

Pre-Trial Motions

Plea bargaining may occur during the calendar part. At this time, the defense attorney also has the opportunity to engage in the **discovery process** by obtaining additional information about the prosecution's case and by inspecting any physical evidence possessed by the prosecutor. The discovery process is outlined in detail in CPL §240. Defense counsel may also ask the judge if the prosecutor presented sufficient evidence to the grand jury to allow for the filing of the indictment. To decide this, the judge must read the transcript of the grand jury proceeding. If the judge finds that there was insufficient evidence to show that the defendant committed the crime or crimes charged, the judge will dismiss the charges listed in the indictment. The judge may also reduce the indictment to less serious charges if the evidence shows that only lesser offenses were committed.

At this time, the defense attorney may file a motion asking that certain evidence be suppressed. Generally this will refer to property taken from the defendant by the police, statements made to the police by the defendant, or identification of the defendant by witnesses. The judge may order a suppression hearing to consider these pre-trial motions. There are several different types of hearings, depending on the type of motions made to the judge. At a **Mapp hearing** the judge hears evidence on the issue of whether property was legally seized by the police from the defendant. A **Huntley hearing** occurs when the defendant has made a statement to the police; the judge hears evidence to determine whether the police acted legally when the statement was made and whether the statement was voluntary. At a **Wade hearing**, the judge determines whether the police used fair and legal methods when they had witnesses identify the defendant as the offender who committed the crime in question. Finally, a **Dunaway hearing** allows the judge to hear evidence on the issue of whether the arrest was lawful.

The defendant has the right to be present at any of these hearings. The judge may hear testimony from police officers and from witnesses during the suppression hearing, the defense attorney is given the opportunity to cross-examine any prosecution witnesses, and the defendant may testify if he or she chooses. If the prosecutor is unable to prove that the police acted legally or if the defendant proves that the police acted illegally, the judge will suppress the evidence in question and it may not be introduced at trial. At this point, if the prosecutor has no other evidence against the defendant, and does not intend to appeal the decision of the judge, the prosecutor may file a motion asking the judge to dismiss the case.

In most cases, all pre-trial motions must be served or filed no later than 45 days after the arraignment and before the start of the trial.

If the defendant is charged with the crime of murder in the first degree, a sentence of death may not be imposed unless the prosecution has filed a **notice of intent to seek the death penalty**. According to CPL §250.40(2):

> In any prosecution in which the people seek a sentence of death, the people shall, within one hundred twenty days of the defendant's arraignment upon an indictment charging the defendant with murder in the first degree, serve upon the defendant and file with the court in which the indictment is pending a written notice of intention to seek the death penalty.

Once a notice of intent to seek the death penalty is filed, the defendant is entitled to an additional sixty days to file new motions or supplement pending motions.

The prosecution has the right to withdraw a notice of intent to seek the death penalty at any time; this is done by filing a written notice with the court and serving written notice upon the defendant. However, once the prosecution has withdrawn the notice of intent to seek the death penalty, it may not be re-filed at any time.

The Right to a Speedy Trial

CPL §30.20(1) states that "After a criminal action is commenced, the defendant is entitled to a speedy trial." In New York, the prosecutor is required to bring each case to trial within a certain specified period of time. If the defendant is charged with a felony (other than homicide), the prosecutor generally must be ready to try the case within six months of the date the felony complaint was filed in criminal court. If the defendant is charged with a misdemeanor, the prosecutor must be ready to try the case within 90 days of the date the misdemeanor complaint was filed in criminal court. However, if the defendant is responsible for delays in bringing the case to trial, these delay periods are not included in the six-month or 90-day maximum pre-trial period. If the prosecutor is not ready to try the case within the legally specified period, and the defendant is not responsible for the delay, the judge, upon a defense motion, must dismiss the case.[32]

The Trial

Less than ten percent of all felony and misdemeanor cases go to a formal criminal **trial**; the vast majority are disposed of by a plea of guilty on the part of the defendant. If the defendant enters a plea of not guilty and the case does go to trial, the procedure is similar regardless of the seriousness of the charge against the defendant.

If the defendant has chosen not to plead guilty to the charges, then once all pre-trial hearings are completed, the case will go to a **jury part** for trial. In New York defendants have the right to a jury trial in all cases except those involving Class B misdemeanors and violations. However, except in cases in which the charge is first degree murder (the only crime for which death is a possible sentence), the defendant has the right to waive a jury and be tried before the judge. This is known as a **bench trial.** Trials in New York are held in a public courtroom. According to CPL §260.20:

> A defendant must be personally present during the trial of an indictment; provided, however, that a defendant who conducts himself in so disorderly and disruptive a manner that his trial cannot be carried on with him in the courtroom may be removed from the courtroom if, after he has been warned by the court that he will be removed if he continues such conduct, he continues to engage in such conduct.

CPL §260.30 outlines the order of a jury trial. According to this statute, there are a total of eleven steps in a jury trial in New York:

1. The jury must be selected and sworn.
2. The court must deliver preliminary instructions to the jury.
3. The people must deliver an opening address to the jury.
4. The defendant may deliver an opening address to the jury.
5. The people must offer evidence in support of the indictment.
6. The defendant may offer evidence in his defense.
7. The people may offer evidence in rebuttal of the defense evidence, and the defendant may then offer evidence in rebuttal of the people's rebuttal evidence. The court may in its discretion permit the parties to offer further rebuttal or surrebuttal evidence in this pattern. In the interest of justice, the court may permit either party to offer evidence upon rebuttal which is not technically of a rebuttal nature but more properly a part of the offering party's original case.
8. At the conclusion of the evidence, the defendant may deliver a summation to the jury.
9. The people may then deliver a summation to the jury.
10. The court must then deliver a charge to the jury.
11. The jury must then retire to deliberate and, if possible, render a verdict.

Jury Selection

The first step in a trial is the **selection of the jury**. New York employs a trial jury of twelve individuals; if the trial is expected to be a long one, alternate jurors may also be selected. Alternate jurors are drawn from the same source, and in the same manner, as the original jurors. According to §506 of the New York Judiciary Law (J.L.), the names of prospective jurors are selected at random from the voter registration lists and from other available lists of county residents (e.g., lists of utility subscribers, licensed operators of motor vehicles, registered owners of motor vehicles, state and local taxpayers, persons applying for or receiving family assistance, medical assistance or safety net assistance, persons receiving state unemployment benefits, and persons who have volunteered to serve as jurors). J.L. §510 states that to serve as a juror in the state of New York, a person must meet the following qualifications:

1. Be a United States citizen and a resident of the county in which the defendant is being tried
2. Be at least 18 years of age

3. Have no felony convictions
4. Be able to understand and communicate in the English language

In addition, according to J.L. §524(a), any person who has served on a jury in any New York court or any federal court is not eligible to serve as a trial or grand juror in any court in New York's unified court system for four years. Federal, state, and city officials may be disqualified from serving as jurors. Some individuals, including lawyers, doctors, nurses, clergymen, police officers, and firemen, may be exempted from jury duty because of the nature of their occupations.

In New York, trials of defendants charged with a felony include twelve jurors and a minimum of two alternate jurors. If the defendant is charged with a Class A misdemeanor, the jury will include six jurors and two or more alternates. Class B misdemeanors and violations are tried before a judge and there is no jury.

The process of jury selection is known as *voir dire* and involves an examination of the prospective jurors by the court and by the attorneys for both the prosecution and the defense. The stated purpose of the *voir dire* is to determine whether each potential juror is impartial and will be able to render a fair verdict in a case. Potential jurors are placed under oath and then questioned by the judge, prosecutor, and defense counsel.

During the process, both the defense and the district attorneys are allowed to make challenges or to object to the inclusion of certain potential trial jurors. New York allows several types of challenges. The first type is a **challenge to the panel**. This occurs when an objection is made to the entire panel of prospective jurors. Such a challenge may only be made by the defendant and only when there is reason to believe that the drawing of the panel was in some way prejudicial to the defendant.[33]

If no challenge to the panel is made, the prosecution and the defense are given the opportunity to examine the prospective jurors. Each prospective juror is questioned by the judge, prosecutor, and defense counsel about whether s/he can be a fair and impartial juror in the case in question. After the examination is complete, two additional types of challenges are allowed. Both are directed against individual potential jurors. A **challenge for cause** is generally based on the attorney's belief that a potential juror is biased in some way that will prevent him or her from acting impartially and without prejudice during the trial. Challenges for cause of an individual juror may be made on any one of the following grounds:

   a. He does not have the qualifications required by the judiciary law; or
   b. He has a state of mind that is likely to preclude him from rendering an impartial verdict based upon the evidence adduced at the trial; or
   c. He is related within the sixth degree by consanguinity or affinity to the defendant, or to the person allegedly injured by the crime charged, or to a prospective witness at the trial, or to counsel for the people or for the defendant; or that he is or was a party adverse to any such person in a civil action; or that he has complained against or been accused by any such person in a criminal action; or that he bears some other relationship to any such person of such nature that it is likely to preclude him from rendering an impartial verdict; or
   d. He was a witness at the preliminary examination or before the grand jury or is to be a witness at the trial; or

e. He served on the grand jury which found the indictment in issue or served on a trial jury in a prior civil or criminal action involving the same incident charged in such indictment; or
f. The crime charged may be punishable by death and the prospective juror entertains such conscientious opinions either against or in favor of such punishment as to preclude such juror from rendering an impartial verdict or from properly exercising the discretion conferred upon such juror by law in the determination of a sentence...[34]

Peremptory challenges may be made by either attorney as a way of removing potential jurors from the jury panel without giving any reasons. When a peremptory challenge is made, the court is required to exclude the person challenged from service on the jury.[35] The number of peremptory challenges allowed depends on the charges against the defendant. When the highest crime charged is a Class A felony, the defense and the state are each allowed twenty peremptory challenges for the regular jurors and two for each alternate juror to be selected. If the highest crime charged is a Class B or C felony, each side is entitled to fifteen peremptory challenges for the regular jurors and two for each alternate juror to be selected. In all other cases, the defense and the state are each entitled to ten peremptory challenges for the regular jurors and two for each alternate juror to be selected.[36] Jurors may not be challenged based on their race, gender, religion, ethnicity, or sexual orientation.

After the selection of the jury is completed, the jurors are sworn in by the court and seated in the jury box.

The Preliminary Instructions to the Jury
The second stage of the trial is the preliminary instructions given by the court to the jury. This generally includes the trial procedure and the basic functions, duties, and conduct of the jury. According to CL §270.40, the instructions must include, among other things:

> admonitions that the jurors may not converse among themselves or with anyone else upon any subject connected with the trial; that they may not read or listen to any accounts or discussions of the case reported by newspapers or other news media; that they may not visit or view the premises or place where the offense or offenses charged were allegedly committed or any other premises or place involved in the case; that prior to discharge, they may not request, accept, agree to accept, or discuss with any person receiving or accepting, any payment or benefit in consideration for supplying any information concerning the trial; and that they must promptly report to the court any incident within their knowledge involving an attempt by any person improperly to influence any member of the jury.

Opening Statements
Both the prosecutor and the defense attorney are entitled to make an **opening statement** which provides all the participants in the trial, especially the jury, with an overview of the facts of the case. In the third step in the trial, the prosecution is required to deliver an opening address to the jury. In this address, the prosecutor generally tells the jury how he or she expects to prove the case against the defendant. Step four is optional; the defense has the option of delivering an opening statement but is not required to do so.

Presentation of the Prosecution's Evidence

After the opening statements are completed, the prosecution begins to present evidence in support of the charge that has been brought against the defendant. The prosecution presents first because the state is bringing the charge against the defendant and, because of the presumption of innocence, has assumed the burden of proof. In New York, evidence submitted into court may include the sworn testimony of witnesses as well as exhibits such as pictures, documents, or other objects. The judge determines the admissibility of each piece of evidence, based on the rules set forth in CPL §60. These rules are intended to ensure that unreliable evidence, or evidence that was illegally obtained, is not received in court.

The district attorney generally begins with the **direct examination** of the prosecution's first witness, who is obviously expected to give evidence to support the state's case against the defendant. After the district attorney finishes questioning the witness, the defense is allowed to **cross-examine** the same witness. If the prosecutor wishes, s/he may then return to ask the witness more questions in a process that is known as **re-direct examination**. Following this, the defense attorney has the option to question the witness once more during the **re-cross examination**. This procedure is repeated for each witness called by the prosecution.

Presentation of the Defense's Evidence

After the prosecution has presented all its evidence and called all its witnesses, the defense may then offer evidence. Although the prosecution is required to present evidence in support of the indictment, the presentation of evidence in defense of the defendant is optional. Generally, the defense begins by putting forth a motion to dismiss all charges or to acquit, on the grounds that the evidence offered by the prosecution was insufficient. If the motion is denied, the defense presents its evidence. The procedure for the presentation of the evidence by the defense is similar to that of the prosecution: direct examination, cross examination, re-direct, and re-cross. The defendant is not required to testify at any point in the trial; both the U.S. Constitution and the New York State Constitution protect the defendant against self-incrimination.

Rebuttal

Rebuttal is the seventh stage of the trial proceeding. After the defense has presented its evidence, each side is given the opportunity to offer rebutting testimony or evidence. First, the prosecutor may present additional evidence that may nullify or challenge the evidence presented by the defense. After the prosecution rebuttal is complete, the defense is given the opportunity to present its rebuttal. At the discretion of the court, each side may be given the opportunity to present additional rebuttal evidence, known as **surrebuttal**, in the same pattern.

Closing Arguments

Once all the evidence is presented, each side is given the opportunity to make a **closing argument** or **summation.** In the closing arguments, the attorneys review and summarize the evidence that best supports their side of the case and discuss any inferences that may be drawn from that evidence. In New York (as in most, but not all, states), the defense presents closing arguments first, with the goal of trying to persuade the jury to acquit the defendant. When the defense has completed its closing arguments, the prosecution is given the option of delivering a summation to the jury, to try to persuade the jury to convict the defendant. Closing arguments are optional for both the prosecution and defense.

Charging the Jury

After the final arguments are completed, the judge has the opportunity to provide instructions to the jury regarding any legal issues or points of law which the jury must follow when deciding on a verdict. This step is also known as **jury instruction** or **charging the jury**. According to CPL §300.10(2), the court's charge to the jury must include the following elements:

1. the fundamental legal principles which apply to all criminal cases (including the presumption of innocence, the requirement that guilt be proven beyond a reasonable doubt, and that the jury may not consider matters relating to sentence or punishment when determining the defendant's guilt or innocence)

2. the fact that no inferences unfavorable to the defendant may be drawn from the defendant's choice not to testify in his or her own behalf (this will only be stated upon the request of a defendant who did not testify in his or her own behalf)

3. the material legal principles that apply to the particular case being tried

4. an explanation of the application of the law to the facts

However, the court is not required to summarize or refer to the evidence in any way other than is necessary for the required explanations.

According to CPL §300.10(3), if the defendant has raised the affirmative defense of lack of criminal responsibility by reason of mental disease or defect, the court must include the following statement, without any elaboration, in the charge to the jury:

> A jury during its deliberations must never consider or speculate concerning matters relating to the consequences of its verdict. However, because of the lack of common knowledge regarding the consequences of a verdict of not responsible by reason of mental disease or defect, I charge you that if this verdict is rendered by you there will be hearings as to the defendant's present mental condition and, where appropriate, involuntary commitment proceedings.

In addition, the instructions to the jury must include a definition of each offense included in the indictment and the court must instruct the jury to render a separate verdict for each count and, if applicable, for each defendant. The possible verdicts that the jury may render are:

1. Guilty of the offense submitted (or of a specified one of two or more submitted offenses where applicable)
2. Not guilty
3. Not responsible by reason of mental disease or defect (where applicable)[37]

Jury Deliberation

After the judge has given instructions to, or charged, the jury, the jury is required by statute to retire to a place outside of the courtroom for **deliberation** upon the verdict.[38] During the deliberations, the jurors discuss the case and attempt to come to agreement on a verdict concerning the guilt or innocence of the defendant. When the jury retires for deliberation, they may take with them any exhibits which were placed into evidence at the trial as well as a written list, prepared by the court, containing the offenses and the possible verdicts. At any time during the jury deliberations, the jury may ask the court for additional information or instructions regarding the law or any other matter they consider relevant to their consideration of the case. If requests for information or instructions are made, the court must require the jury to return to the courtroom, provide notice to the prosecutor and defense counsel, and then, in the presence of the defendant, provide whatever requested information or instruction that the court feels is appropriate.

If the jurors come to an agreement on a verdict, they then return to the courtroom. In New York, the jury verdict must be unanimous. Therefore, all of the jurors must agree on a verdict of guilty before the defendant can be convicted of the charge. The verdict must be read in the courtroom in the presence of the court, the prosecutor, the defense counsel, and the defendant. Before the verdict is rendered and announced by the jury foreman, s/he must be asked whether the jury has agreed upon a verdict and s/he must answer in the affirmative.

After the verdict is rendered, the jurors must be collectively asked whether this is their verdict. In addition, either the defense or the prosecution is entitled to request a poll of the individual members of the jury to ensure that each member of the jury agrees with the verdict and that no member was coerced or intimidated into agreeing, or agreed simply out of exhaustion. If in either the collective or individual poll, any juror responds negatively, the court must refuse to accept the verdict and direct the jury to resume deliberations.

If the verdict of the jury is not guilty, the trial is over and the defendant must be immediately discharged from custody or, if s/he is released on bail, the court must exonerate the bail. Because of the state and federal constitutional protections against double jeopardy, the defendant may never be tried in state court for those same charges.

If the verdict handed down is one of not responsible by reason of mental disease or defect, further proceedings against the defendant may follow. These are outlined in detail in CPL §330.20.

A Non-Jury Trial

CPL §320 discusses the procedures used in non-jury, or **bench trials**. The statute states that any defendant, with the exception of those charged with murder in the first degree, may waive his or her right to a jury trial at any time prior to the start of the trial and may consent to a trial without a jury in the superior court in which the indictment is pending. Defendants charged with first-degree murder do not have the option of waiving their right to a jury trial.

A **waiver of a jury trial** must be done in writing and must be signed by the defendant in the presence of the court and with the court's approval. If the court fails to approve the waiver, it must state on the record the reasons.

Bench trials are conducted by one judge in the superior court in which the indictment is pending. According to CPL §320.20(3), the order of a bench trial is:

1. Both sides must be given the opportunity to deliver opening statements to the court.

2. Both sides must be given the opportunity to present evidence.

3. Both sides must be given the opportunity to deliver summations or closing arguments.

4. The court must consider the case and render a verdict.

Proceedings Between the Verdict and the Sentence

If the defendant is found guilty, s/he will be sentenced. However, after a verdict of guilty is rendered and before the sentencing phase of the trial, the defendant may make a **post-trial motion** to set aside or modify the verdict. If the judge sets aside the verdict, the defendant may be entitled to a dismissal, a reduction of the charges, or a new trial. These motions are rarely granted.

Sentencing

In all cases where a defendant is convicted of a felony offense, the judge must order a **pre-sentence investigation**, to be completed by the New York Department of Probation. The judge may not pronounce **sentence** until s/he has received the pre-sentence report. If the court has received the pre-sentence report at the time of conviction, the defendant may be sentenced at the time of conviction. If the sentencing report has not been received, the judge will set a date for a sentencing hearing. If the case is a misdemeanor, a pre-sentence report is not required in most cases. The trial court judge may pass sentence immediately.

If the defendant has been convicted of murder in the first degree, a crime for which the death penalty is a possible sentence, a sentencing hearing will be held before a jury. In a capital crime, it is up to the jury to determine whether the defendant will be sentenced to death or to life imprisonment without the possibility of parole.

If the defendant was between the ages of 13 and 15 at the time of the offense, s/he will be sentenced as a juvenile offender. If the defendant was between the ages of 14 and 18 at the time of the crime, s/he may be entitled to be treated as a youthful offender. If the defendant is treated as a youthful offender, the offense will not appear on his or her record, and s/he may receive a lower sentence. However, juveniles between the ages of 16 and 19 may be processed either as youthful offenders or as adults.

The sentencing process is discussed in more detail in the next chapter of this supplement.

Appeals

In New York, after sentence has been handed down, defendants have the right to **appeal** either the conviction or the sentence. The defendant has the right to appeal regardless of:

- the crime of which s/he was convicted;
- the sentence received; and
- whether s/he was convicted after a trial or by a plea of guilty.

In some cases, the defendant may be asked to give up his or her right to appeal as a part of the plea bargain. However, even if this is the case, the defendant may be permitted to have the appellate court review certain issues regarding the case.

An appeal does not involve retrying a case or even re-examining the factual issues surrounding the crime; it only involves an examination or review of the legal issues involved in the case. The purpose of an appeal is to make certain that the defendant received a fair trial and that s/he was not deprived of any constitutional rights at any time. The appellate court reviews the proceedings of the trial court.

In non-capital cases, notice of intent to appeal must be filed within 30 days of the sentencing. Special appellate rules apply to cases for which a sentence of death was imposed.

One possible result of an appeal is an **affirmance**. In this situation, the appellate court has found that the defendant received a fair trial, that there was enough evidence to prove guilt, or that the guilty plea was properly taken. The defendant may have a limited right to seek further appeal to the court of appeals. If the court of appeals decides not to review the case, or if it also affirms the conviction, the defendant has reached the end of the New York State appellate process.

If the conviction is **reversed**, the case may be dismissed, the defendant may receive a new trial or hearing, or the guilty plea may be vacated. The court may also modify the conviction, resulting in a reduction in the conviction offense and/or a lower sentence.

During the appeal process, the offender may make an **application for a stay**. This is a request to be released from prison pending a decision on the appeal. An application for a stay may not be made if the offender was convicted of a Class A felony. Only one such application is permitted during the appeal. However, if the appeal continues to the court of appeals, the offender may make another application for a stay.

In certain circumstances, even if the charges were dismissed, the prosecutor may be permitted to appeal the case, through a procedure known as a **People's Appeal**. If this is successful, the charges against the defendant may be revived and the case may continue. Because of the constitutional protection against double jeopardy, the prosecutor is prohibited from appealing an acquittal.

NOTES

1. 28 U.S.C. 112
2. U.S. Court of Appeals for the Second Circuit (http://www.tourolaw.edu/2ndCircuit/)
3. New York State Constitution, Article VI, §1a
4. Court structure (http://www.courts.state.ny.us/courts/structure.shtml)

5. *2002 Annual Report of the Clerk of Court to the Judges of the Court of Appeals of the State of New York* (http://www.nycourts.gov/ctapps/2002AnnRep.pdf)
6. *Ibid*
7. New York State Constitution, Article VI §25b
8. New York State Constitution, Article VI, §2a
9. *2002 Annual Report of the Clerk of Court to the Judges of the Court of Appeals of the State of New York, op cit.*
10. *Ibid*
11. *"Duely & Constantly Kept" A History of the New York Supreme Court, 1691-1847.* (http://www.nycourts.gov/history/elecbook/duely/pg1.htm)
12. New York State Constitution, Article VI, §4b
13. This refers to Article 78 of the Civil Practice Law and Rules
14. New York State Constitution, Article VI, §8c
15. New York State Constitution, Article VI, §6
16. New York State Consolidated Laws, Court of Claims Act, Article II, §9
17. New York State Consolidated Laws, Court of Claims Act, Article I, §2
18. New York State Consolidated Laws, Family Court Act, Part 1, §113
19. New York State Constitution, Article VI, §13
20. New York State Constitution, Article VI, §12
21. New York City Courts (http://www.nycourts.gov/courts/nyc/)
22. New York State Consolidated Laws, New York City Criminal Court, Article II, §20
23. New York State Consolidated Laws, New York City Criminal Court, Article II, §22
24. Suffolk County District court (http://www.nycourts.gov/courts/10jd/suffolk/dist/index.shtml)
25. Elmira City Court (http://www.nycourts.gov/6jd/CountyMaps/chemung/city/default.html)
26. New York State Constitution, Article VI, §2d
27. New York State Constitution, Article VI, §22a
28. New York State Constitution, Article VI, §22b
29. New York State Bar Association home page (http://www.nysba.org/)
30. *Ibid*
31. Muldoon, G. And S.J. Feuerstein (2002). *Handling a criminal case in New York.* New York: Thomson West, §1:57
32. CPL §30.30
33. CPL §270.10
34. CPL §270.20(1)
35. CPL §270.25(1)
36. CPL §270.25(2)
37. CPL §300.10(4)
38. CPL §310.10(1)

CHAPTER 6

SENTENCING IN NEW YORK

INTRODUCTION

According to §380.20 of the New York Criminal Procedure Law, in every case in which a conviction has been entered, either because a criminal defendant pled guilty or was found guilty in court by a judge or jury, the court is required to pronounce **sentence**. If the defendant has been found guilty on multiple counts, the court is required to pronounce sentence on each count. In most cases, the sentence is determined by the judge. However, if the defendant has been convicted of murder in the first degree, sentence is pronounced by a jury.

THE SENTENCING REFORM ACT OF 1995

In 1995, the New York State Legislature passed the **Sentencing Reform Act**, which significantly altered the sentencing laws in New York. The Act identifies four classes of felony offenders:

- first-time felony offenders
- second-time felony/first-time violent felony offenders
- second-time felony/second-time violent felony offenders
- persistent violent felony offenders (those with at least three violent felony convictions)

The Act increased sentences for all categories of violent felony offenders. First-time felony offenders receive indeterminate sentences on the first conviction. The Act requires that the minimum sentence must be one-half the maximum sentence imposed; the old law gave all first-time felons a sentence of one-third the maximum sentence. The Act doubled the minimum prison sentence for persistent violent offenders; the maximum sentence was already fixed at life in prison.

Determinate sentencing is required for all second-time felony/first-time violent felony offenders as well as all second-time felony/second-time violent felony offenders. Under the old laws, these offenders were given indeterminate sentences. The Act also eliminated parole eligibility for repeat violent felons, requiring them to serve at least 85 percent of their sentences. This is intended to create more "**truth in sentencing**," so that the sentence imposed by the court is the one actually served by the defendant. For example, under the old sentencing law, a repeat offender convicted of armed robbery could be released from prison after serving only 4.5 years; under the new law, the court must impose a sentence of at least eight years and the offender must serve at least seven years in prison.

Many of the provisions of the Sentencing Reform Act of 1995 are scheduled to be repealed in 2005 unless they are specifically renewed by the legislature.[1]

During the same legislative session, the legislature also restored the death penalty in New York and introduced a sentence of life imprisonment without parole.[2]

JENNA'S LAW

In 1998, the state passed the **Sentencing Reform Act of 1998**, also known as "**Jenna's Law**," which eliminated parole for all first-time violent felony offenders. Parole release for second-time violent felony offenders had been abolished by the 1995 Sentencing Reform Act. The law was named after Jenna Grieshaber-Honnis, who was allegedly murdered by a violent felon out on parole.

Jenna's Law states that any violent felony offender who committed crimes on or after September 1, 1998, must receive a determinate sentence, is ineligible for parole and conditional release, must serve a minimum of six-sevenths of the court-imposed sentence before being released, and must serve a period of post-release supervision of between 18 months and five years. While on post-release supervision, the offender is overseen by the New York State Division of Parole. Violations of the conditions of supervision may result in the offender being re-incarcerated for a fixed prison term of between six months and the remainder of the post-release supervision term, for a maximum of five years. Pen.L. §70.45 discusses the terms of post-release supervision and outlines the methods for calculating the length of the supervision period. The state is also required to notify a crime victim when his or her attacker is scheduled to be released from custody.

Although it most cases Jenna's Law requires a determinate sentence be imposed on offenders convicted of violent felony offenses, it makes an exception in cases where the defendant is a victim of domestic violence. The abuse must be a factor in causing the defendant to commit the violent felony and the victim of the violent felony must be a member of the same family or household as the defendant (e.g., the defendant is a battered wife who commits a violent felony against her spouse).[3]

Under Jenna's Law, the four categories of felony offenders are:

- violent felony offenders (first offense)
- second violent felony offender
- second felony offender
- persistent violent felony offender

The sentencing provisions outlined under the Sentencing Reform Act of 1995 apply to all offenders whose felony or violent felony crimes were committed prior to September 1, 1998.

TYPES OF SENTENCES

There are a variety of sentences that may be imposed upon offenders convicted in New York. The specific sentence imposed by the court depends on many factors, including the offender's background, the circumstances of the crime, and the victim's attitude. Types of sentences include:

- fines
- restitution and/or reparation
- conditional discharge
- *unconditional discharge*
- probation
- incarceration in a jail or prison
- death

Combinations of these sentences are also allowed. For example, a judge may order both imprisonment and a fine, or order an offender on probation to pay a fine as well as victim restitution.[4]

Defendants who are sentenced to **probation** are released from custody and supervised by the probation department for a period of time specified by the court. They are required to obey a set of conditions. Offenders who are sentenced to a **conditional discharge** are also released from jail and required to obey specific conditions but will not be supervised by the county probation department. In some situations, an offender may be given a split sentence, which includes a jail term followed by a period of probation. Both probation and conditional discharge are conditional sentences. If the sentenced offender violates any of the conditions imposed by the court, s/he may be re-sentenced to a term of incarceration in a jail or prison.

Offenders who are sentenced to an **unconditional discharge** are released without any conditions. Offenders may also be ordered to pay a **fine**, or to pay **restitution** to the victim; these may be imposed either alone or with another type of sentence. Offenders who have prior convictions may receive longer sentences than first-time offenders.

WHEN SENTENCING OCCURS

If the defendant enters a plea of guilty to a crime, or if the defendant pleads not guilty and is then found guilty at a criminal trial, s/he will be sentenced by the judge unless the charge is murder in the first degree and death is a possible sentence. If the defendant is convicted of murder in the first degree and death is a possible sentence, a sentencing hearing will be held before a jury, who will decide whether the offender will receive a sentence of death or life imprisonment without the possibility of parole.

In all cases where death is not a possible sentence, the county probation department conducts a pre-sentence investigation, often including an interview with the offender, and prepares a **pre-sentence report** for the judge. This report contains information about the offender's background and about the circumstances of the crime. In addition, both the defense attorney and the prosecutor may prepare pre-sentence memoranda for the judge.

If the offender was between thirteen and fifteen years of age at the time of the offense, s/he will be sentenced as a **juvenile offender**. If the offender was between the ages of fourteen and eighteen, s/he may also be entitled to be treated as a **youthful offender**. Therefore, an offender who is at least sixteen years of age is considered to be a **youth** rather than a **juvenile**. When an offender is treated as a youthful offender, his or her offense does not appear on his or her record and s/he may receive a lower sentence. Offenders who are at least nineteen years old are considered to be adults, rather than youths.

According to CPL §380.30(1), "sentence must be pronounced without unreasonable delay." At the time of the conviction, the court is required to do one of the following:

- fix a date on which the sentence will be pronounced
- fix a date for a pre-sentence proceeding
- pronounce sentence on the date of conviction[5]

Under certain circumstances, the offender may be sentenced at the time the conviction is pronounced. These include situations in which a fingerprint report or a pre-sentence report is not required or when the required reports have already been received by the court.[6]

For those cases where sentence is not pronounced immediately at the time of the conviction, the Criminal Procedure Law does not specify the timing of the delay between conviction and sentencing. In other words, the law does not define "unreasonable delay."

According to CPL §380.40, the defendant must be present in person when the sentence is pronounced. However, the law goes on to state one exception to this requirement. When the offense for which the offender is being sentenced is a misdemeanor or a petty offense, the defendant may waive his or her right to be personally present. At the time sentence is pronounced, both the prosecutor and the defense attorney are entitled to an opportunity to make a statement to the court regarding the sentence. The court must also give the defendant the opportunity to make a statement os his or her own behalf.[7] The right of the victim to make a statement at the sentencing hearing is discussed below, in the section on the rights of the victim.

RESTITUTION, REPARATION, AND FINES

Several types of sentences require the offender to make some type of financial payment, either to the court or to the victim of the crime. A **fine** is a monetary payment made to the state. **Restitution** is a monetary payment made to the victim as a way of financially repaying the victim for a loss sustained as a result of the crime. It is limited to the fruits of the defendant's crime.[8] **Reparation** involves compensating the victim for some harm that resulted from the crime and is limited to any out of pocket losses sustained by the victim as a result of the crime.[9] The death of the victim does not end the offender's requirement to pay restitution or reparation. If the victim dies before payments are completed, the offender must continue to make payments to the estate of the deceased victim.

For some crimes, such as certain violations of the New York Vehicle and Traffic Laws, a fine may be the only penalty imposed on the offender by the court. However, it is also possible for the court to impose a financial penalty upon an offender in addition to another penalty. According to Pen.L. §60.01(2)(c),

> In any case where the court imposes a sentence of probation, conditional discharge, or a sentence of intermittent imprisonment, it may also impose a fine...

Section 80 of the Penal Law discusses the topic of fines and outlines the amount that may be imposed for various offenses. Excessive fines are prohibited both by the U.S. Constitution and by the New York State Constitution.[10] The amount of the fine which the court may impose is based on the seriousness of the conviction offense. Pen.L. §80.00(1) discusses fines that may be imposed on felony offenders:

> A sentence to pay a fine for a felony shall be a sentence to pay an amount, fixed by the court, not exceeding the higher of
> a. five thousand dollars; or
> b. double the amount of the defendant's gain from the commission of the crime; or
> c. if the conviction is for any felony defined in article two hundred twenty or two hundred twenty-one of this chapter, according to the following schedule:
>   • for A-I felonies, one hundred thousand dollars;
>   • for A-II felonies, fifty thousand dollars;
>   • for B felonies, thirty thousand dollars;
>   • for C felonies, fifteen thousand dollars.
>
> When imposing a fine pursuant to the provisions of this paragraph, the court shall consider the profit gained by defendant's conduct, whether the amount of the fine is disproportionate to the conduct in which defendant engaged, its impact on any victims, and defendant's economic circumstances, including the defendant's ability to pay, the effect of the fine upon his or her immediate family or any other persons to whom the defendant owes an obligation of support.

Articles 220 and 221 of the Penal Law focus on offenses involving marijuana and controlled substances. Thus, the maximum fine for a felony offender is usually $5,000, unless the offender has been convicted of one of the controlled substance or marijuana offenses defined in these articles. In those cases, the maximum fine is increased to as much as $100,000. In addition, if the offender gained money or property as a result of the crime, the court is not bound by the statutory maximums and may impose a sentence of up to twice the amount gained by the offender.

Pen.L. §80.05 specifies fines for misdemeanors and violations. In general, offenders convicted of a Class A misdemeanor may be sentenced to pay a fine of up to $1,000, offenders convicted of a Class B misdemeanor may be sentenced to pay a fine of up to $500, and offenders convicted of a violation may be sentenced to pay a fine of up to $250.

If the defendant being fined is a corporation, these statutes do not apply. The fine structure for corporations is discussed in Pen.L. §80.10.

New York currently is attempting to increase the use of restitution and reparation. Pen.L. §60.27(1) states that:

> In addition to any of the dispositions authorized by this article, the court shall consider restitution or reparation to the victim of the crime and may require restitution or reparation as part of the sentence imposed upon a person convicted of an offense, and .... require the defendant to make restitution of the fruits of his or her offense or reparation for the actual out-of-pocket loss caused thereby...

While this statute does not mandate the use of restitution or reparation, it does require the court to consider imposing them. The amount of the restitution or reparation is to be determined is outlined in Pen.L. §60.27(2). In addition, when the court orders a defendant to pay restitution or reparation, it must also order the defendant to pay a surcharge of five percent of the amount ordered to the official designated to collect the restitution or reparation. The purpose of the surcharge is to cover the cost of collection and administration.[11]

When the court orders the defendant to pay a fine, or to make victim restitution or reparation, the sentence may also include the requirement that if the defendant fails to pay the required amount, s/he may be imprisoned until such time as the fine, restitution, or reparation is paid.[12]

It is possible for the court to impose both a fine (payment to the state) and either restitution or reparation (payment to the victim) on the same defendant. If the offender is allowed to pay the financial penalties on a schedule of payments, rather than being required to pay the entire amount at the time sentence is pronounced, the payment of any assigned restitution or reparation takes priority over the payment of the fine.[13]

CONCURRENT VERSUS CONSECUTIVE SENTENCES

If an offender is convicted of multiple offenses, the court may impose a separate sentence for each offense. If these sentences imposed involve terms of imprisonment, the court has the option of requiring the sentences to be served either concurrently or consecutively. **Concurrent sentences** are served at the same time. **Consecutive sentences** are served in succession, one after the other. For example, consider an offender who is sentenced to two determinate terms, one of three years and one of four years. If the sentences are to be served concurrently, then the earliest conditional release is 3.4 years (85 percent of four years) and the controlling maximum term is four years. If however, the sentences are to be served consecutively, then the earliest conditional release is six years (85 percent of seven years) and the controlling maximum term is seven years.

In most situations, the court has considerable discretion in deciding whether multiple sentences will be served concurrently or consecutively. However, in some circumstances, the law sets forth specific requirements and removes the discretion from the court.[14]

For example, Pen.L. §70.25(2) presents a situation in which concurrent sentences are mandated, stating that:

> When more than one sentence of imprisonment is imposed on a person for two or more offenses committed through a single act or omission, or through an act or omission which in itself constituted one of the offenses and also was a material element of the other, the sentences, except if one or more of such sentences is for a violation of section 270.20 of this chapter, must run concurrently.

Thus, in the case of *People v. Laureano*,[15] a defendant who pled guilty to first degree manslaughter and first degree robbery of the same victim received concurrent sentences for the two offenses under this statute. However, in the case of *People v. Arroyo*,[16] the court imposed consecutive sentences for conspiracy to murder and attempted murder (of the same victim). The court held that the crime of conspiracy to murder was completed before the offenders committed the attempted murder.

There also are situations in which the courts are required to impose consecutive sentences. For example, Pen.L. §70.25(2-b) requires that the court impose consecutive sentences:

> When a person is convicted of a violent felony offense committed after arraignment and while released on recognizance or bail, but committed prior to the imposition of sentence on a pending felony charge....

Thus, if an offender is convicted of a violent felony offense that was committed while s/he was out on bail or released on recognizance on a felony charge for which s/he has not yet been sentenced, the sentences must run consecutively. However, the statute does give the court the option of imposing concurrent sentences if there are mitigating circumstances or if the defendant's participation in the violent felony offense was relatively minor.

SENTENCES OF INCARCERATION

Both the Sentencing Reform Act of 1995 and Jenna's Law significantly affected the penalties for offenders who receive indeterminate sentences of incarceration. The sentence range is dependent upon the type or class of felony that was committed and whether the crime is the offender's first felony or a repeat crime.

Much of the recent sentencing reform in New York has focused on violent felony offenders (offenders who have been convicted of a violent felony offense). This includes not only repeat offenders but also those who have no prior felony convictions at all, or who have prior convictions in the distant past (generally more than ten years ago, not including time spent incarcerated). Under the Sentencing Reform Act of 1995, these offenders received indeterminate sentences. However, Jenna's Law changed this to require all violent felony offenders receive determinate sentences of imprisonment. An **indeterminate sentence** is one in which the court imposes both minimum and maximum periods or terms of imprisonment. The maximum term of an indeterminate sentence must be at least three years.[17] A **determinate sentence** consists of a fixed period or term of imprisonment to be served at a state correctional facility. The statutes also allow for the imposition of a **definite sentence**, which is a fixed term of imprisonment that is served at a local correctional facility. In most cases, the maximum term of a definite sentence is one year.[18]

Section 70 of the Penal Law outlines the terms of sentences for felony offenders (including second and persistent felony offenders) as well as violent felony offenders (including second and persistent violent felony offenders). Pen.L. §70.01(2) and (3) list the minimum and maximum terms of sentences for **felony offenders:**

- **Class A-I felony** – an authorized minimum term of 15 to 25 years, and an authorized maximum term of life imprisonment

- **Class A-II felony** – an authorized minimum term of 3 years to 8 years and 4 months, and an authorized maximum term of life imprisonment

- **Class B felony** – an authorized minimum term of 1 year to 8 years and 4 months, and an authorized maximum term of twenty-five years

- **Class C felony** – an authorized minimum term of 1 to 5 years, and an authorized maximum term of fifteen years

- **Class D felony** – an authorized minimum term of 1 year to 2 years and 4 months, and an authorized maximum term of seven years

- **Class E felony** – an authorized minimum term of 1 year to 1 year and 4 months, and an authorized maximum term of four years

Pen.L. §70.02(3) mandates terms of imprisonment for **violent felony offenders**. Note that there are no Class A violent felony offenses in the New York Penal Law.

- **Class B violent felonies** – a determinate sentence of not less than five years nor more than twenty-five years

- **Class C violent felonies** – a determinate sentence of not less than three and one-half years nor more than fifteen years

- **Class D violent felonies** – a determinate sentence of not less than two years or more than seven years

- **Class E violent felonies** – a determinate sentence of not less than one and one-half years or more than four years

Any offender serving a determinate sentence must serve at least six-sevenths of the imposed sentence and is ineligible for release on parole or conditional release. Once released from imprisonment, the offender must serve a period of post-release supervision. Generally, this period is five years for a Class B or C felony and three years for a Class D or E felony. The court may impose shorter periods, but not less than two and one-half years for a Class B or C felony and one and one-half years for Class D or E felonies.[19]

The New York Penal Law has separate sentencing structures for various categories of repeat offenders, including sentence enhancement in many categories. Pen.L. §70.06 discusses **second felony offenders**. A second felony offender is defined by Pen.L. §70.06(1)(a) as:

> a person, other than a second violent felony offender as defined in section 70.04, who stands convicted of a felony defined in this chapter, other than a class A-I felony, after having previously been subjected to one or more predicate felony convictions...

Essentially, this statute states that any defendant who is convicted of a felony and who was previously convicted of and sentenced for another felony, must be sentenced as a second felony offender. To qualify under this definition, the offender must have a prior felony conviction in New York or in any other jurisdiction of an offense for which a sentence to a term of imprisonment for at least one year, or a sentence of death is authorized in New York (regardless of whether the sentence was actually imposed). The sentence upon the prior conviction must have been imposed before the offender committed the present felony offense but must have been imposed not more than ten years before the present felony offense. This ten-year period does not include any period of time when the offender was incarcerated. The statute lists specific minimum and maximum sentence lengths for each felony class.

A **second violent felony offender** is defined by Pen.L. §70.04(1)(a) as:

> a person who stands convicted of a violent felony offense ... after having previously been subjected to a predicate violent felony conviction as defined in paragraph (b) of this subdivision.

The prior violent felony conviction includes any violent felony offense for which a sentence of imprisonment for at least one year or a sentence of death is authorized, regardless of whether such a sentence actually was imposed. In addition, even though there are no Class A violent felonies in New York, a prior conviction of a Class A felony will serve as a predicate offense for this statute. Sentence upon the prior conviction must have been imposed before the offender committed the present violent felony offense but must have been imposed not more than ten years before the present violent felony offense, not including any period of time when the offender was incarcerated.

Under the Sentencing Reform Act of 1995, all second violent felony offenders and second felony offenders receive determinate sentences and may not be released before serving at least six-sevenths of the sentence term. Under Jenna's Law, if the violent felony offense was committed on or after September 1, 1998, the offender will be released to a period of post-release supervision.

Pen.L. §70.10(1) defines a **persistent felony offender** as:

> ...a person, other than a persistent violent felony offender ..., who stands convicted of a felony after having previously been convicted of two or more felonies...

Essentially, this category applies to an offender who is convicted of a felony and who has at least two prior felony convictions. The statute authorizes the court to sentence the offender to the sentence of imprisonment authorized for a Class A-I felony, when

> ...the court has found, ... that a person is a persistent felony offender, and when it is of the opinion that the history and character of the defendant and the nature and circumstances of his criminal conduct indicate that extended incarceration and life-time supervision will best serve the public interest...[20]

Finally, a **persistent violent felony offender** is defined by Pen.L. §70.08(1) as:

> (a) a person who stands convicted of a violent felony offense as defined in subdivision one of section 70.02 after having previously been subjected to two or more predicate violent felony convictions as defined in paragraph (b) of subdivision one of section 70.04.
>
> (b) For the purpose of determining whether a person has two or more predicate violent felony convictions, the criteria set forth in paragraph (b) of subdivision one of section 70.04 shall apply.

Thus, a persistent violent felony offender is one who has at least three convictions for violent felony crimes. The Court of Appeals, in the case of *People v. Morse*[21], limited persistent violent felony offender treatment to an offender who has committed felony offenses in the following sequence:

1. The offender was first sentenced on a conviction for a violent felony offense.

2. The offender next committed another violent felony offense and was sentenced on that second violent felony offense.

3. The offender committed a third violent felony offense.

An offender convicted of a third violent felony offense in the above sequence must be sentenced as a persistent violent felony offender, even if s/he did not receive sentences of incarceration for the previous crimes and even if s/he was not treated as a second violent felony offender at the time of sentencing for the second violent felony offense. Persistent violent felony offenders receive indeterminate sentences with a maximum term of life in prison. Minimum terms for Class B, C, and D felonies are outlined in Pen.L. §70.08(3). The statute does not define a *minimum sentence range* for Class E violent felony offenses; however, the courts have held that a defendant who has been convicted of a Class E violent felony offense may be sentenced as a persistent violent felony offender and must be sentenced to a term of two years to life in prison.

THE RIGHTS OF THE VICTIM DURING SENTENCING

The Right to Be Heard

During the sentencing phase of a criminal trial, the court is required to provide the prosecutor, the defense counsel, and the defendant the opportunity to make statements. In addition, if the defendant is being sentenced for a felony, the victim, under certain circumstances, may also have the right to make a statement. CPL §380.50(2)(b) states that:

> If the defendant is being sentenced for a felony the court, if requested at least ten days prior to the sentencing date, shall accord the victim the right to make a statement with regard to any matter relevant to the question of sentence ...

The statement made by the victim must be made before any statement is made by the defendant or defense counsel.[22]

If the offender has been charged with a homicide, a member of the victim's family or the victim's legal guardian has the right to make a statement on the victim's behalf. This right also holds if the victim is a child or suffers from a mental or physical disability that makes it impractical for him or her to appear in court.

Victim Impact Statements

A **victim impact statement** is a written report or verbal statement given to the sentencing judge for consideration when sentencing the defendant. The statement includes admissible evidence concerning the impact or effects of the crime upon the victim. In New York, a judge is not allowed to pronounce sentence upon a felony offender, or sentence any defendant to probation, until s/he has received a pre-sentence report prepared by the probation department.[23] In most cases, this report must include a victim impact statement.[24] The report includes information about any physical injury or economic loss that the victim suffered, as well as information concerning the victim's views as to what form of punishment he or she feels is appropriate. If the victim is unable to assist the probation department in the preparation of the victim impact statement (if, for example, the crime was a homicide and the victim is dead), the victim's family may provide the information. The prosecutor must provide the victim (or the victim's family) with a copy of the victim impact statement prior to the sentencing of the offender.

If the offender is a youth who has been determined by the Family Court to be a juvenile delinquent, the judge may not pass sentence until a victim impact statement is prepared. The judge is required to consider the statement when determining whether the youth needs supervision, treatment, or confinement.

In New York, victims are also allowed to make a statement at a parole hearing. Victims have the right either to meet with a member of the Board of Parole or to submit a written, video, or audio taped statement regarding the impact of the crime. If requested, the Board of Parole will inform victims of parole interview dates, Board decisions, and release dates of the offenders who victimized them.[25]

The Right to Restitution

During the sentencing phase of a trial, the judge is required to consider imposing the requirement of **restitution** or **reparation** to the victim as an element of the sentence.[26] This generally involves requiring the offender to pay a sum of money to the victim as a consequence of the crime (e.g., reimbursement for medical expenses or lost wages). When the court imposes a sentence including restitution, the victim and the offender do not deal directly with each other; the defendant makes all payments to a public agency which then transfers the money to the victim. In most jurisdictions, this agency is the probation department.

The defendant may be ordered to pay restitution in a lump sum or to make payments over a period of time. Restitution may be ordered even if the judge sentences the offender to a fine or a term of imprisonment in jail or prison. If the offender is given a sentence of incarceration, restitution is collected from his or her earnings while in prison and after release.

Pen.L. §60.27(5) limits the amount of restitution or reparation that may be ordered by the court. In most cases, the maximum amount an offender may be sentenced to pay is $15,000 in the case of a felony conviction and $10,000 for any other offense. However, the statute does specify situations in which the court may order the offender to pay a larger amount of restitution. In addition, even if the judge has ordered the offender to make restitution, the victim still has the right to file a civil suit against the offender for damages that are in excess of this amount.

The Right to Compensation

In addition to restitution, victims may be eligible for **victim compensation** from the **New York State Crime Victims Board (CVB)**. Compensation is a state-authorized payment intended to cover unreimbursed expenses that are related to the crime. Eligible expenses may include loss of earnings or support, counseling services, medical expenses not covered by insurance, the cost of securing and/or cleaning up a crime scene, court transportation expenses, domestic violence shelter use costs, burial expenses, and the repair or replacement of essential personal property.[27]

The CVB has three categories or types of claims. **Personal injury claims** involve crimes in which an innocent person was injured, **death claims** involve crimes that resulted in the death of an innocent person, and **essential personal property loss claims** are specifically focused crimes in which the essential personal property of an elderly (aged sixty or above) or disabled crime victim was damaged or loss. Essential personal property includes eyeglasses, hearing aids, wheelchairs, medication, and other items necessary for the victim's health and well-being.[28]

The CVB specifically identifies individuals who may be eligible for victim compensation. These include:

- a victim of a crime who has sustained personal injury
- a victim of unlawful imprisonment in the first degree
- a victim of a first or second degree kidnaping
- a victim of a stalking offense
- an elderly or disabled crime victim who suffered loss of or damage to essential personal property
- a surviving relative or other person dependant upon a victim who died as a direct result of the crime
- the person who incurred burial expenses of an innocent victim who died as a direct result of a crime
- a child (under the age of 18) victim or witness of a crime, or the child's parent, guardian, or sibling.[29]

For an individual to be awarded compensation, s/he must be an innocent victim of the crime. Therefore, an individual who was injured while participating in a crime is not eligible for compensation. The CVB also requires that, to be eligible for compensation, the victim must report the crime to a criminal justice agency within one week, unless there is adequate justification for delay. A compensation claim may be filed by the crime victim or the immediate family of a victim who has died as the result of a crime. Only costs which have not been reimbursed from some other source may be claimed for compensation.

Basically, for an award of compensation to be considered by the CVB, it must be shown that:

- a crime was committed

- the crime resulted in personal physical injury or death to a victim, or loss of essential personal property to an eligible victim

- the crime was reported to a criminal justice agency within one week

- the victim did not sustain the injury, death, or loss while participating in the crime.[30]

Victims may receive compensation for a wide variety of expenses, although there are upper limits placed on the amount that may be provided. These include:

- medical, occupational rehabilitation, and counseling service expenses not covered by other insurance programs

- lost earnings or loss of support (up to $600 per week, with a total maximum compensation of $30,000)

- burial expenses up to $6,000 for crimes committed on or after November 1, 1996 (for crimes prior to that date, the burial compensation allowance is $2,000)

- repair or replacement of essential personal property (up to $500)

- transportation expenses related to necessary court appearances

- expenses related to the use of services of a domestic violence shelter

- expenses relating to the cleanup of a crime scene (up to $2,500)

- fees for an attorney to represent the victim before the CVB (up to $1,000)[31]

In some cases, a victim would suffer significant financial hardship if forced to wait for compensation benefits. If the victim is potentially eligible for compensation, the CVB may provide emergency benefits for such victims.

NOTES

1. Greenberg, R.A. (2002). *New York Criminal Law*. New York: WestGroup.
2. *Ibid*
3. Pen.L. §60.12(1)
4. Pen.L. §60.01 and Pen.L. §60.27
5. CPL §380.30(2)
6. CPL §308.30(3)
7. CPL §380.50
8. Pen.L. §60.27(1)
9. *Ibid*
10. U.S. Constitution, Amendment VII; New York State Constitution, Article I, §5
11. Pen.L. §60.27(8)
12. CPL §420.10(3)
13. CPL § 420.10(1)(b)
14. These situations are discussed in Pen.L. §70.25(2-a) through Pen.L. §70.25(2-e)
15. *People v. Laureano*, 87 N.Y.2d 640, 642 N.Y.S.2d 150, 664 N.E.2d 1212 (1996)
16. *People v. Arroyo*, 93 N.Y.2d 990, 695 N.Y.S.2d 537, 717 N.E.2d 696 (1999)
17. Pen.L. §70.02(2)
18. Pen.L. §70.15(1)
19. Pen.L. §70.45
20. Pen.L. §70.10(2)
21. *People v. Morse*, 62 N.Y.2d 205, 476 N.Y.S.2d 505, 465 N.E.2d 12 (1984)
22. CPL §380.50(2)(c)
23. CPL §390.20(1)
24. CPL §390.30(3)(b)
25. New York State Division of Parole, Victim Impact Unit webpage (http://parole.state.ny.us/victimimpact.html)
26. Pen.L. §60.27(1)
27. New York State Crime Victim's Board home page (http://www.cvb.state.ny.us)
28. *Ibid*
29. *Ibid*
30. *Ibid*
31. *Ibid*

CHAPTER 7

CAPITAL PUNISHMENT IN NEW YORK

THE HISTORY OF CAPITAL PUNISHMENT IN NEW YORK

During the colonial period, many of the original 13 colonies, including New York, used the death penalty to punish criminal offenders. In 1664, New York Colony passed the **Duke's Laws** which allowed the death penalty for a wide variety of offenses, including denying the "true God," striking one's father or mother, perjury in a capital trial, raising arms to resist the authority of the King, and various types of killings.[1] The primary method of death during this period was hanging. However, executions were rare events and pardons or reprieves were fairly common. In 18th century New York, over 50 percent of condemned offenders received some sort of mercy. Some were pardoned on the condition they leave the province, others were forced to enlist in the army or navy.

One of the reforms that followed the Revolutionary War was a move to abolish capital punishment throughout the nation. While the movement was not totally successful, the use of the death penalty was significantly reduced. In 1788, the list of capital offenses in New York was restricted to murder, treason, rape, buggery, burglary, larceny from a church, arson, mayhem, and certain types of counterfeiting and forgery. In 1796, New York limited the death penalty to only the crimes of murder and treason; in 1813, first degree arson (the burning of an inhabited dwelling) was added to this list.

In 1841, an attempt was made to abolish the death penalty in New York. Petitions were sent to the legislature and heavy lobbying and debate surrounded the topic. Although the death penalty survived, it still applied to only the above three crimes (treason, murder, and arson in the first degree). By 1863, murder was divided into two degrees and only the first category was considered to be a capital crime. Arson was removed from the list of capital offenses during that year. However, New York's capital punishment law was still considered to be extremely harsh because the imposition of a capital sentence was mandatory. Neither the court nor the jury were given any discretion to commute the sentence to one of life imprisonment regardless of mitigating circumstances.

During the latter part of the 19th century, the formal use of the death penalty declined in New York. However, executions were still carried out and, in New York, some were, for all practical purposes, carried out in public. Even those that were ostensibly private were not always carefully screened from the public view. For example, although executions carried out at the Tombs in New York City were supposedly private, members of the public would crowd into neighboring buildings to look down over the walls of the prison and watch the hanging being carried out.

In 1881, a dentist and former steamboat engineer, Dr. Albert Southwick, observed an elderly drunkard touch the terminals of an electric generator in Buffalo, NY. The man was killed quickly and apparently painlessly. Dr. Southwick described the incident to a state senator, who passed the information on to the governor of New York. In 1885, the governor asked the state legislature to consider how electricity might replace hanging as a more humane way of executing condemned criminals. One year later, the New York State Legislature enacted Chapter 352 of the Laws of 1886. This act appointed a commission whose purpose was to investigate humane methods of effecting the death sentence in capital cases and to report its findings to the legislature. The commission's report, which was completed in 1888, provided a detailed analysis of the various methods of execution. As a result of the report, on June 4, 1888, the New York State Legislature passed Chapter 489 of the Laws of New York of 1888. The law established **electrocution** as the only method of execution to be used in New York, replacing hanging. As a result, New York became the first state to introduce the electric chair as an alternative means of carrying out a capital sentence. This also increased the privacy of the death, as the electric chair was located in a small room within the prison; the gallows were generally placed in the prison yard.[2]

In spring 1889, Joseph Chappleau became the first person sentenced to die under the new electrical execution law. However, his sentence was later commuted to life imprisonment. In 1890, William Kemmler became the first offender to be put to death in the new electric chair in New York. The first application of the electric current was flawed and Kemmler did not die until a second application of current was made.[3] In 1899 Martha Place became the first woman to be executed by electricity.[4] Another famous offender who died in New York's electric chair was Leon Czolgosz, who was executed on October 29, 1901, six weeks after he assassinated President William McKinley.

Kemmler was put to death in Auburn Prison, the location of the first electric chair used in New York. Other electric chairs were soon added at Sing Sing Prison (where Martha Price was executed) and at Dannemora (Clinton) Prison. In the 1920s, the Auburn electric chair was destroyed in a prison fire. The original Dannemora electric chair was later moved to the state prison guard training facility in Albany, New York.

In 1937, the New York State Legislature passed a law allowing the jury, upon conviction of certain types of first degree murder (felony murder or depraved recklessness) or of kidnapping (which had recently been made a capital offense), to recommend life imprisonment instead of death. However, this recommendation was not binding upon the court; the judge had the option of rejecting the recommendation and imposing the death penalty. In addition, the death penalty remained a mandatory punishment for premeditated first degree murder and for treason.

Between 1890 and 1963, a total of 695 individuals were put to death in the electric chair in New York.[5] Of these, 329 died during the 33-year period between 1930 and 1963.

On June 29, 1972, the U.S. Supreme Court case of *Furman v. Georgia* challenged the constitutionality of capital punishment in the United States.[6] The Court ruled that the death penalty, as it was administered, constituted "cruel and unusual punishment" and therefore was a violation of the Eighth Amendment of the U.S. Constitution. As a result of this decision, New York state death penalty statutes were voided and capital punishment in New York was stopped. Four years later, on January 15, 1976, the Court ruled in the case of *Gregg v. Georgia* that capital punishment did not invariably violate the Constitution and reinstated the death penalty.[7]

In 1974, Pen.L. §60.06 was revised to mandate a sentence of death for any individual convicted of first degree murder. The statute did not permit the sentencing court to consider mitigating circumstances. As a result, this statute was declared unconstitutional in 1997.[8] Between 1977 and 1995, New York did not have a constitutionally acceptable death penalty statute. During this period, New York state governors, including Governor Mario Cuomo, consistently vetoed all capital punishment legislation. However, the restoration of the death penalty was a key campaign promise of George Pataki, contributing to his election as governor of New York in 1994. In 1995, after the Sentencing Reform Act of 1995 was passed by the New York State Legislature, it was signed into law by Governor George Pataki on March 7, 1995.[9] This Act put into effect a new capital punishment law for the state, making New York the 38th state to legalize the death penalty. The law allows the court to sentence an offender convicted of a Class A-1 felony to death or to life imprisonment without the possibility of parole and also permits other appropriate sentences of imprisonment. The law became effective with all crimes committed on or after September 1, 1995 and stipulated the use of **lethal injection** as the primary method of execution. Correction Law (COR) §658 states that:

> The punishment of death shall be inflicted by lethal injection; that is, by the intravenous injection of a substance or substances in a lethal quantity into the body of a person convicted until such person is dead.

The new law mandates a bifurcated, or two-stage, criminal proceeding, separating the determination of guilt or innocence from the determination of the sentence. The law requires that both hearings be held before the same court but in certain extraordinary cases the judge does have the right to discharge the jury and impanel a new jury. The law also requires that the sentence of death be imposed by a unanimous verdict of the sentencing jury.[10]

CAPITAL PUNISHMENT IN NEW YORK TODAY

New York only permits a sentence of death for the crime of murder if at least one of thirteen aggravating circumstances are present. These are outlined in Pen.L. §125.27. Five of these aggravating factors relate, at least in part, to the killing of a member of a specified group. Essentially, the status of the victim is the aggravating factor. These include the following:

- the intended victim was a police officer engaged in the performance of his or her duties and the defendant knew or reasonably should have known this;

- the intended victim was a peace officer engaged in the performance of his or her duties and the defendant knew or reasonably should have known this;

- the intended victim was an employee of a state or local correctional institution engaged in the performance of his or her duties and the defendant knew or reasonably should have known this;

- the intended victim was a witness to a crime and was killed either to prevent him or her from testifying in a criminal proceeding or in retribution for previous criminal testimony, or the intended victim was an immediate family member of a witness who was killed either to influence the testimony of the witness or in retribution for prior testimony;

- the victim was a judge who was killed because of his or her office.

Two aggravating factors relate to past or present characteristics of the offender. These include:

- at the time of the killing the defendant was in custody under a sentence of life imprisonment, or a sentence of at least 15 years to life, or was under such a sentence but had escaped from custody and had not yet been caught and returned to confinement;

- before committing this murder, the defendant had a prior conviction for first or second degree murder in New York or any other state.

Four of the aggravating factors relate to the circumstances surrounding the killing, or the criminal transaction that relates to the killing, including:

- the victim was killed while the defendant was committing or attempting to commit one of a list of serious felonies, and the killing was in furtherance of the felony;

- the defendant, during the commission or attempted commission of a listed serious felony, intentionally caused the death of an additional victim who was not a participant in the crime;

- the defendant intentionally tortured the victim prior to the death;

- the victim was killed in the furtherance of an act of terrorism.

The final two factors deal with the issues of contract killers and serial killers:

- the defendant either committed murder for hire or hired another person to commit the murder;

- the *defendant* was a "serial killer" who *intentionally killed two or more* persons within the state of New York in separate but similar events within a period of 24 months.

In addition, the death penalty may not be imposed upon a convicted offender unless the prosecution, within 120 days of the defendant's arraignment on a charge of first degree murder, files a written notice of intent to seek the death penalty. This notice may be withdrawn at any time but *once withdrawn, may not be filed again.*[11]

Felony murder is not in and of itself a capital crime, probably because the felony murder statute does not require intent to kill, only to commit the underlying felony.[12] While murder committed in the course of a felony may be considered an aggravating circumstance to first degree murder, thus elevating it to a capital offense, the murder must be intentional.[13]

In all capital cases, both the verdict of guilt or innocence and the sentence of death is determined by the jury. Therefore, if a defendant is charged with the crime of murder in the first degree, s/he may not waive his or her right to a jury trial.

New York limits administration of the death penalty to certain categories of offenders. First, the state only allows the death penalty to be administered to offenders who are more than 18 years of age. According to Pen.L. §125.27(b), one of the statutory elements for the charge of first degree murder is that "The defendant was more than eighteen years old at the time of the commission of the crime." The wording of the statute does not make it clear whether this refers to an individual who is 18 years and one day old or to an individual who is at least 19 years of age. However, the courts have consistently held that the former condition applies.[14] Secondly, individuals who have been determined to be mentally incompetent individuals are excluded from capital sentencing unless they have committed murder while in a correctional facility. COR §656(1) defines "incompetent" as

> when, as a result of mental disease or defect, he lacks the mental capacity to understand the nature and effect of the death penalty and why it is to be carried out.

Finally, COR §657(1) specifically states that "A sentence of death may not be carried out upon a woman while she is pregnant."

In December 1998, the Court of Appeals heard appeals in the case of *Hynes v. Tomei*,[15] the first death penalty case brought to the court since the 1995 statute became effective. In this case, the court unanimously voted to strike down the plea bargaining provisions of New York's capital punishment law. The provisions in question allowed defendants charged with first degree murder to enter a plea of guilty only when the sentence agreed upon was life imprisonment without parole (or some other specified term of imprisonment). Because a sentence of death may only be handed down as the result of a jury trial, once the prosecutor filed a notice of intent to seek the death penalty, the result of these provisions was that only those defendants who pleaded not guilty and went to trial by jury risked a death sentence. The judges felt that the provisions encouraged offenders to plead guilty, thereby violating their constitutional rights under the Fifth and Sixth Amendments to the United States Constitution. Effectively, those offenders who exercised their Fifth Amendment protection against self-incrimination and their Sixth Amendment right to trial by jury were penalized by the possibility of receiving a death sentence. The Court's ruling did not affect the use of the death penalty itself; prosecutions in capital offenses were allowed to continue.

The Court's decision in this case limits but does not eliminate the use of plea bargaining. Defendants may not plead guilty to the crime of first-degree murder as long as a notice of intent to seek the death penalty is pending. However, defendants may plead guilty to a lesser offense at any time and may plead guilty to first-degree murder either before a notice of intent is filed or after it has been withdrawn. A death notice may not be reinstated once withdrawn, even if the defendant eventually backs out of or reneges on the plea deal. As district attorneys throughout New York may be reluctant to risk withdrawing the death notice and relying on the defendant's good faith, the prosecutor's discretion to negotiate plea agreements with defendants accused of a capital crime is clearly limited, and plea bargaining in cases where the death notice has already been filed may be severely curtailed.

Offenders who choose to make an appeal may appeal from the trial court of original jurisdiction directly to the New York Court of Appeals, without first going through an appellate division or appellate term of the New York Supreme Court.

In the vast majority of cases, district attorneys do not seek the death penalty. Between September 1996 (when capital punishment was reinstated in New York) and August 2003, district attorneys in New York formally investigated a total of 799 cases with the possibility of seeking the death penalty. Of these, a notice of intent to seek the death penalty was filed in 50 cases; another 41 cases are still under evaluation. There were a total of 18 capital trials during this period, 15 of which proceeded to both guilt and penalty phases, and seven defendants have been sentenced to death by lethal execution. Of these, three are black, three are white, and one is Hispanic. They are all male. The sentence of the first defendant sentenced to death, Darrell Harris, has since been vacated by the Court of Appeals. The other six cases are pending before the Court. Since 1995, the death penalty has been sought against only two women. Both defendants pled guilty and were not sentenced to death.[16]

NEW YORK'S DEATH ROW

New York's "death row" is known as the **Unit for Condemned Persons** (UCP). As of July 1, 2003, the UCP houses a total of six inmates under a sentence of death. Of the six inmates, three are white, two are black, and one is Hispanic.[17] The last execution in New York was in 1963.

There is no specific statute that requires the **New York Department of Corrections** (DOCS) to confine all condemned offenders to the UPC. According to COR §652(2), the convicted person:

> may, in the commissioner's discretion, either be kept isolated from the general prison population in a designated institution or confined as otherwise provided by law. The commissioner, in his discretion, may determine that the safety and security of the facility, or of the inmate population, or of the staff, or of the inmate, would not be jeopardized by the inmate's confinement within the general prison population.

However, although this statute does allow condemned offenders to be incarcerated within the general prison population, the procedure used by DOCS places all condemned inmates in the UCP and later allows for release to the general population.[18]

The UPC is housed within the Clinton Correctional Facility, located in Dannemora, New York. This is a male facility. Currently, there are no women under a sentence of death in the state. However, a UPC for condemned women has been established at the Bedford Hills Correctional Facility in Westchester County in case of future need.

The Clinton UPC cells include a living area of approximately 78 square feet, containing a toilet, sink, and bed. Attached to each cell is a small visiting and showering area, which is separated from the living area by a sliding door that is electronically controlled by the corrections officers. Inmates may only access the visiting and showering cubicle when the door has been opened by an officer. Inmates have no contact with non-UPC inmates and are separated from visitors by a clear Plexiglas window. UPC cells are neither air conditioned nor fan-cooled.[19]

Inmates are under constant video and audio surveillance and are unable to turn off the lights in their cells. These remain on constantly throughout the day and night. The showers are open cubicles with no curtains, so that inmates can be monitored while showering. UPC inmates are in lockdown for 23 hours every day. They are allowed one hour of solitary outdoor daily exercise in a 2,000 square foot area.

UPC inmates are limited to visits from five categories of individuals:

- legal counsel
- immediate family
- the media
- individuals with a court order
- spiritual advisors

Immediate family consists of spouse, parents (including step-parents, foster parents, and legal guardians), grandparents, siblings, children, and grandchildren.

UPC inmates are allowed one visit per week, not including visits from legal counsel. However, the immediate family restriction means that friends may not visit. Thus, "for those inmates who are estranged from their immediate families, or whose families live in distant parts of the State, the 'immediate family only policy' effectively means no visitors at all."[20] Visitation restrictions placed on UPC inmates are not shared by those in the general prison population. Non-condemned inmates may have visits from friends, may have some direct physical contact with their visitors, and may have multiple visitation periods.

UPC inmates also have more limited commissary privileges, compared to those in the general prison population. All inmates may spend $55 on commissary items each month. However, while general population prisoners may purchase any items available for sale, UPC inmates are limited in their discretionary food purchase to only $15 per month. On UPC, all meals are served within the course of one eight-hour work shift. Because up to sixteen hours may pass between dinner and breakfast on UPC, this restriction does present difficulties for UPC inmates.[21]

LEGAL PROCEDURES RELATING TO EXECUTIONS IN NEW YORK

Once a defendant has been sentenced to death, the sentencing judge makes out a warrant of death directed to the commissioner of corrections. This warrant, which must be prepared within seven days of the sentencing hearing, states the crime of which the defendant has been convicted, the sentence imposed (death), appoints a week during which the sentence must be carried out, and commands the commissioner to execute the sentence during that week.[22] According to COR §651,

> The week of execution appointed in the warrant shall be not less than thirty days and not more than sixty days after the issuance of the warrant. The date of execution within said week shall be left to the discretion of the commissioner, but the date and hour of the execution shall be announced publicly no later than seven days prior to said execution.

The only person authorized to reprieve a sentence of death is the governor of the state.[23] The governor has the legal right to consult with the district attorney, the defense attorney, and the attorney general of the state regarding suspension or reprieve of execution.[24]

Individuals permitted to witness an execution are strictly controlled by statute.[25] No individual under the age of 18 is permitted to witness an execution. Individuals authorized to attend an execution include:

- the commissioner
- individuals, including corrections officers, designated by the commissioner assist in the execution in some way (e.g., to act as execution technicians)
- one or more licensed physicians
- a justice of the supreme court who is selected and invited by the commissioner
- the convicted offender's counsel
- the district attorney of the county in which the offender was convicted
- the sheriff of the county in which the offender was convicted
- six adult citizens selected and invited by the commissioner
- two clergymen, at the request of the convicted offender
- any four relatives or friends named by the convicted offender, unless the commissioner determines that the presence of one or more of these individuals would create a threat to the safety and security of the institution.

Unlike some states, New York does not permit friends and family of the victim to attend the execution.

NOTES

1. Reggio, Michael H. (1999). *History of the death penalty*. PBS Online. Available online at (http://www.pbs.org/wgbh/pages/frontline/shows/execution/readings/history.html)
2. MacLeod, Marlee. *The electric chair*. Court TV's Crime Library. Available online at (http://www.crimelibrary.com/notorious_murders/not_guilty/chair/)
3. *Ibid*
4. Gado, Mark. *Stone upon stone: Sing Sing Prison*. Court TV's Crime Library. Available online at (http://www.crimelibrary.com/notorious_murders/famous/sing_sing/)
5. MacLeod, *op cit*.
6. *Furman v. Georgia*, 408 U.S. 238 (1972)

7. *Gregg v. Georgia*, 428 U.S. 153 (1976)
8. *People v. Davis*, 43 N.Y.2d 17 (1977)
9. "Press Release: Governor Pataki Signs Death Penalty Into Law," March 7, 1995 (http://www.state.ny.us/governor/press/deathpn.htm)
10. CPL §400.27
11. CPL §250.40
12. Pen.L. §125.25(3)
13. Pen.L. §125.27(a)(8)
14. See e.g., *People v. Mower*, 280 A.D. 2d 25, 719 N.Y.S.2d 780 (3d Dept 2001) and *People v. Gatti*, 277 A.D.2d 1041, 716 N.Y.S.2d 182 (4th Dept 2000)
15. *Hynes v. Tomei*, 92 N.Y.2d 613, 684 N.Y.S.2d 177, 706 N.E.2d 1201 (1998)
16. The Capital Defender Office (2003). *Capital punishment in New York State: Statistics from eight years of representation.* Available online at (http://www.nycdo.org/8yr.html)
17. The Criminal Justice Project (2002). *Death Row U.S.A.: Summer 2003.* NAACP Legal Defense and Educational Fund, Inc. Available online at (http://www.deathpenaltyinfo.org/DEATHROWUSArecent.pdf)
18. *Dying twice: Conditions on New York's death row* (http://www.abcny.org/currentarticle/dying%20_twice2.html)
19. *Ibid*
20. *Ibid*
21. *Ibid*
22. COR §650(1)
23. COR §655
24. COR §654
25. COR §660

CHAPTER 8

CORRECTIONS IN NEW YORK

INTRODUCTION

There are several state agencies that are relevant to a study of corrections in New York. The state's correctional programs are administered by the **New York State Department of Correctional Services** (DOCS). This agency is responsible for the confinement and supervision of inmates held in 70 state correctional facilities throughout the state. There are a number of divisions within DOCS, including Corcraft, which is the Division of Correctional Industries that provides employment for inmates within the state correctional system.

The **New York State Commission of Correction** oversees the operation of all correctional facilities in the state, including both state and local facilities. The **New York State Division of Parole** administers the parole system within the state.

Jails and probation are run at the county level, with a separate agency for each county in the state.

PRISONS IN NEW YORK

The New York State Commission of Correction

The **New York State Commission of Correction** is the state agency responsible for all correctional agencies and programs within the state. The mission of the Commission is to:

- Oversee the operation of all State and local correctional facilities.

- Advise the Governor on policies and programs for improving the administration of correctional facilities.

- Promulgate rules and regulations establishing minimum standards for the care, custody, treatment, supervision, and discipline of all persons confined in State and local correctional facilities.

- Inspect these facilities to ensure adherence to standards.

- Examine facility operations to ensure adherence to laws governing inmates' rights.

- Recommend ways to assist in the development of facility programs for the effective employment of inmates.[1]

In 1894, the New York State Constitution, along with additional legislation, provided for the formation of a **State Commission of Prisons**. The Commission was composed of eight members who were appointed by the governor. Members were responsible for inspecting all penal institutions within the state and ensuring that these institutes were administered in an efficient and humane manner. In 1901 the membership of the Commission was reduced to three members, who also served as a **Board of Commissioners for Paroled Prisoners**. This was abolished in 1908 and replaced by an independent **Board of Parole for State Prisons**. At the same time, the Commission's membership was increased to seven individuals, again all appointed by the governor.

The **Department of Correction** was created in 1926. At the same time, the Commission of Prisons was renamed the **Commission of Correction**. The Commissioner of the new Department of Correction served as the chair of the Commission, which was placed administratively within the Department of Correction but which had independent powers of visitation and inspection of penal facilities. In 1973, Article 3 of the New York State Correction Law (COR) removed the Commission from the administrative jurisdiction of the Department of Correction and established it as an independent agency within the state's executive department.[2]

The functions, powers, and duties of the Commission are outlined in COR §45. In addition to the goals outlined in its mission, the Commission also oversees the development of new jail facilities, assists in implementing new correctional technologies, and trains correctional officers. Currently, the Commission has three full-time members as well as necessary staff. Each of the three members is appointed by the governor with the advice and consent of the state Senate. One commissioner is designated by the governor to serve as the chair of the Commission. The other commissioners chair the **Medical Review Board** (MRB) and the **Citizen's Policy and Complaint Review Council** (CPCRC), which are organizations within the Commission.[3] The three members of the Commission serve five-year terms and may be reappointed once. No member of the Commission may serve for more than ten years.[4]

The CPCRC is responsible for the investigation and review of complaints and grievances filed against local correctional facilities and was created as a way of providing for public participation in facility oversight. The Council is composed of nine members who are appointed by the governor with the advice and consent of the senate. The members, who hold office for five years, must include:

- one individual who served in the U.S. Armed Forces in Indochina at any time between January 1, 1963 through May 7, 1975 and who did not receive a dishonorable discharge, or a licensed mental health professional with professional training or experience in post-traumatic stress syndrome

- one attorney admitted to practice in the state of New York

- one former inmate of a correctional facility

- one former corrections officer

- one former resident of a secure youth facility

- one former employee of the division for youth who supervised youth in a secure residential facility.[5]

The MRB is responsible for the investigation of the death of any inmate in a correctional facility. The Board also investigates and make recommendations regarding the delivery of medical care to inmates.[6] The Board is composed of six members who are appointed by the governor with the advice and consent of the senate. The members, who hold office for five years, must include:

- one physician who is licensed to practice in the state of New York

- one physician who is licensed to practice in the state of New York and who is a board certified forensic pathologist

- one physician who is licensed to practice in the state of New York and who is a board certified forensic psychologist

- one attorney admitted to practice in the state of New York

- two members appointed at large.[7]

The New York State Department of Correctional Services

The **New York State Department of Correctional Services** (DOCS) is responsible for overseeing all inmates held in state correctional facilities. The mission of the Department is:

To provide for public protection by administering a network of correctional facilities that:

- Retain inmates in safe custody until released by law;

- Offer inmates an opportunity to improve their employment potential and their ability to function in a non-criminal fashion;

- Offer staff a variety of opportunities for career enrichment and advancement; and,

- Offer stable and humane "community" environments in which all participants, staff and inmates, can perform their required tasks with a sense of satisfaction.[8]

DOCS runs a total of 70 state correctional facilities which are located throughout the state. These facilities house inmates who are sentenced to terms of incarceration of more than one year. As of September 30, 2003, there were 65,655 inmates for which DOCS was responsible.[9]

DOCS facilities are classified by security level, including minimum, medium, and maximum security. The majority of the institutions hold only male offenders. Of the 70 facilities, only five are specifically designated as women's institutions: one minimum-security institution, three medium-security facilities, and one maximum-security institution. In addition, there are two facilities that house both men and women; one is the Lakeview Shock Incarceration Correctional Facility and the other is the Willard Drug Treatment Center.[10]

Corcraft

Corcraft Products is the trade name of the **Division of Correctional Industries**, which is the manufacturing division of the DOCS. The primary purpose of Corcraft is to provide employment opportunities for inmates within the state-wide correctional system to work in real-world situations. Inmates produce a wide variety of goods and services for sale to state agencies.[11]

Many of the products made by Corcraft employees are sold to the DOCS, such as clothing and uniforms for inmates and correctional officers, cleaning supplies, furniture, and prescription eyeglasses. Some products are also sold to other state agencies and to local governments (for example, license plates). Corcraft products and services may not be sold on the open market to private organizations or to private individuals, and the program does not compete unreasonably with private labor and manufacturers.

By fulfilling its mission, Corcraft helps to reduce the cost of incarceration to the taxpayer. At the same time, inmates receive the opportunity for productive employment as well as learning job skills and work habits that may benefit them upon their release from prison.

The conditions under which inmates work are made to be as similar as possible to those in the outside world. Corcraft inmate employees are required to punch time clocks and to work standard seven-hour shifts, five days per week. Overtime is rare, but may be authorized in extraordinary circumstances to meet specified deadlines. The inmates are paid an hourly wage, which ranges from $0.16 to $0.45, depending on the inmate's job title and time in grade. Productivity bonuses are also possible.[12]

Products made by Corcraft employees include:

- seating (office chairs, lounge furniture, classroom and educational seating, etc.);

- tables (computer tables, folding tables, typewriter tables, etc.);

- storage (filing cabinets, storage lockers, shelving, etc.);

- desks (secretarial desks, executive desks, credenzas, bookcases, etc.);

- miscellaneous office products (bulletin boards, etc.); and

- janitorial and maintenance products (soaps, floor wax remover, laundry detergent, glass cleaner, liquid hand soap, etc.).

In addition, several service industries are administered by Corcraft, including optical services, printing and engraving, screening and ADA signage, asbestos removal, and construction.[13]

Newgate Prison

In 1796, a major revision of the New York State Penal Code significantly reduced the number of capital crimes in the state from sixteen to two (murder and treason) and substituted punishments of life imprisonment (either with hard labor or solitary confinement) for crimes that had formerly been punished by a sentence of death. Other felonies were also punished by various terms of imprisonment. As a result, the state began to establish prisons based on the model developed in Philadelphia with the **Walnut Street Jail**. The first state prison in New York, the **Greenwich State Prison**, was constructed in 1797 overlooking the Hudson River in a rural area which is now Greenwich Village. It was commonly known as **Newgate**, after the London prison. Newgate Prison rejected the colonial approach to crime and punishment, which emphasized deterrence and did not consider reformation or rehabilitation to be an aim of punishment. The program emphasized education, religion and moral instruction, and a prison labor program.

Within five years, Newgate was suffering from problems of overcrowding. In addition, private industry was becoming vehemently opposed to prison labor. Other problems included the prison's inability to manage special classes of offenders. Female prisoners were housed separately but were a continual problem for prison management. Insane and deranged offenders were also difficult to handle.

In 1824 a legislative commission recommended that Newgate Prison be abandoned. When the new **Sing Sing Prison** was completed in 1828, all male inmates of Newgate were moved to Sing Sing. Female inmates were temporarily contracted out to New York City. Newgate Prison was sold to New York City for use as a jail and was later demolished.[14]

Auburn Prison

In 1817, overcrowding problems with Newgate prison led to the construction of the new **Auburn Prison**, located in Auburn, NY. The **Auburn system**, with new concepts of prison architecture and prison routines, was devised in response to the then-dominant **Pennsylvania system**. The Auburn system emphasized solitary confinement but also allowed for congregate work, permitting inmates to leave their solitary cells during the day to work in prison shops. The prison philosophy emphasized a total domination of the inmate, mind, body, and spirit, through absolute silence, strict routine and regimentation, and swift punishment for any rule violation. One feature of the system was the use of the "lockstep," which was created at Auburn Prison.

Auburn housed both male and female offenders. However, the female prisoners were housed in an attic. The attic windows were kept sealed at all times, so the attic was dark and stifling. Once a day, a prison keeper, assisted by several male prisoners, would go to the attic with food and supplies for the prisoners. Women inmates were given work, primarily picking wool, knitting, and spooling. However, because of the absence of prison officers, the women were not constrained to silence. It is known that at least one woman inmate became pregnant while housed in the attic.

In 1832, Auburn Prison hired a female matron, without waiting for the Legislature to approve an appropriation for her salary. The south wing of the prison was remodeled to hold women inmates, but their conditions were still highly unpleasant. In 1838, a female unit was opened at Sing Sing Prison and the women were moved from Auburn to the new unit. However, in 1892, women prisoners were returned to Auburn and the Auburn Prison for Women continued to function for the next 40 years, closing in 1933.[15]

The first electric chair was installed at Auburn Prison; the first execution occurred on August 6, 1890. A total of 55 offenders, both men and women, were executed at Auburn, including Leon Czolgosz, who assassinated President William McKinley in 1901.[16]

By the early part of the 20th century, the prison was totally transformed, with all elements of the original Auburn system disappearing, including the mandatory silence, the lockstep, and even the striped inmate uniforms. In 1929, there were two serious riots at Auburn. In the first, two inmates were killed, and one inmate, five correctional officers, and three firemen were wounded. In the second riot, the inmates were armed with guns that had been hidden during the first riot. They took eight hostages, including the warden. A total of eight prisoners were killed and nine people, including two inmates, were wounded. Three inmates were later executed for their roles in this riot.

After these riots, extensive reconstruction took place at Auburn prison, including the construction of new cell blocks in 1941. Currently, Auburn Prison serves as a male maximum-security facility, housing 1,800 adult male offenders. Among the other industries in which Auburn inmates are involved is the production of plates for the State Department of Motor Vehicles. Approximately 100 inmates are employed in the Plate Shop, generating approximately nine million dollars per year in revenues.[17]

Sing Sing Prison

The third state prison to be constructed in New York, **Sing Sing** was built on an abandoned mining site on the banks of the Hudson River. One hundred convicts from Auburn Prison, living in temporary barracks, constructed the new institution, completing the first cell block in 1828. The entire prison was built using only prison labor under the supervision of Elan Lynds, who had been warden of Auburn. Lynds, who was engaged by the state legislature to build Sing Sing, had been criticized for his cruel treatment of inmates at Auburn. As early as 1828, these problems resurfaced at Sing Sing, and Lynds was charged with cruelty, mismanagement, and keeping prisoners on short rations. However, although Lynds resigned in 1830, he returned to the prison in the 1840s, and again ran it harshly and with extreme severity, closing the prison's Sunday School and library and even eliminating the inmates' correspondence privileges. The silent system originally developed at Auburn was also used at Sing Sing.

Sing Sing originally had no quarters for female inmates and custody of women prisoners was contracted out to New York City. In 1837, a women's wing was built at Sing Sing but it quickly became overcrowded. At least five children are known to have been born in the prison and the prison inspectors frequently left them in the prison with their mothers where they almost inevitably died. Only one of the children born in prison prior to the mid-1840s is known to have survived. Although there were some attempts at more humane treatment for female offenders during the mid-1840s, these quickly disappeared under the attack of more severe prison administrators. In 1877, the women's wing at Sing Sing was closed and women felony offenders were again housed in local jails.[18]

Prior to 1914, executions took place at Sing Sing, as well as at Auburn and Clinton Correctional Facilities. All three facilities had electric chairs. The first inmate executed in the Sing Sing electric chair was Harris A. Smiler, who was one of four inmates electrocuted on July 7, 1891. Martha Place, the first woman to die in the electric chair, was executed at Sing Sing in 1899.[19] After 1914, all death sentences were carried out in the electric chair at Sing Sing. The chair was last used in 1963. The electric chair was moved from Sing Sing to Green Haven in 1971, although it was never used in that location.[20]

In the 20th century, modernization reached Sing Sing Prison. The lockstep was abolished in 1900, the striped uniform in 1904, and the rule of silence in 1914. Eventually, prisoners were allowed to remain out of their cells during weekends, given the freedom of the yard. In 1983, a riot at Sing Sing significantly affected the prison. A total of 17 correctional officers were held hostage. The riot ended after 53 hours of negotiations. Safety and security programs were modified and enhanced following the riot.

Sing Sing is currently a maximum security institution. It has a medium-security annex known as Tappan, which opened in the 1970s. Including the Tappan annex, Sing Sing has a staff of nearly 1,000 and houses approximately 2,300 male felony offenders. Sing Sing currently houses a Special Needs Unit, which was the first prison medical ward for inmates infected with HIV. In addition, another unique program is the Masters in Theology curriculum, which is sponsored by the New York State Theological Seminary and entails no costs to state taxpayers. In September 1995, an offshoot program, the Certificate in Ministry, was started.[21]

The Elmira Reformatory

In 1876, New York opened the **Elmira Reformatory**, located in Elmira, NY. The institution, which was based on the theory of reform, emphasized the use of rewards rather than punishments to encourage offenders. Elmira also emphasized the use of inmate classification, individualized treatment, indeterminate rather than fixed sentences, and parole.

The concept of the reformatory was developed by **Zebulon Brockway**, who served as its first warden. Originally, 30 inmates were transferred to Elmira from Auburn Prison; others later followed to finish the construction of the new reformatory. The facility was limited to first offenders between 16 and 30 years of age. The Elmira program used a three-grade system. All new inmates were placed in the middle or second grade. They could earn promotion to first grade, which brought extra privileges, by six months of perfect marks in school, work, and deportment. Another six months of perfect marks were needed to earn eligibility for parole. Unsatisfactory marks could result in demotion to the third grade; third grade inmates were required to wear a red suit, march in lockstep, and lost visiting and correspondence privileges. The Elmira education program eventually included instruction in 34 different trades. In addition, elementary classes were offered as well as advanced courses in subjects such as geography, natural sciences, geometry, bookkeeping, physiology, ethics, psychology, history, and literature. In 1883, the world's first prisoner newspaper, *The Summary*, began publication at Elmira. The reformatory was also the first correctional institution to use games such as baseball, basketball, football, and track and field as "treatment" rather than merely recreation.

In the 1880s, Elmira faced severe problems of overcrowding. By the late 1890s the prison was approximately 300 inmates over capacity, even after several additions and expansions were made to the original cell blocks. At the same time, the increasing popularity of probation as a judicial option meant that many of the young first offenders for whom the Elmira program was designed were diverted instead. In 1894, accusations of cruelty and brutality towards inmates by Brockway led to formal hearings. Although Brockway was officially cleared of all charges, the appointment of new members to the reformatory's board of managers in 1899 led to sweeping changes, and Brockway lost much of his earlier autonomy. He retired in 1900.

In an attempt to deal with overcrowding at Elmira, the New York State Legislature approved a second reformatory. The **Eastern New York Reformatory** was opened at Napanoch in 1900, receiving inmates by transfer from Elmira. Because the transferred inmates were to assist in the construction of the new reformatory, Elmira sent only older and stronger inmates. Thus, by chance precedent was established. Napanoch was used for recidivists, parole violators, and other troublemakers, while Elmira concentrated on the younger offenders for whom there was believed to be more hope.

In 1945, a reception center, used for the inmate classification program originally initiated by Brockway and refined over the years, was established on the grounds of Elmira. In 1970, the reception center and the reformatory were joined together administratively and the entire complex was renamed the **Elmira Correctional and Reception Center**. Elmira continued to concentrate on younger offenders until the early 1990s, when the DOCS established several under-21 facilities. Currently, the population of Elmira averages approximately 35 years of age.

Elmira is now a general prison facility for adult male offenders. It includes academic, industrial, and vocational programs, as well as an extensive substance abuse treatment program. The facility offers basic education classes and pre-GED programs, as well as programs for Spanish-speaking inmates to improve their English language skills. Elmira operates a printing plant, a foundry, and a paint brush and roller cover shop. Inmates are able to receive occupational training in carpentry and building construction, computer programming, custodial maintenance, electrical trades, painting, plumbing and heating, printing, small engine repair, and welding.[22]

JAILS IN NEW YORK

Each county in New York has a **jail** system, most of which are operated by sheriffs. County jails in New York have four primary functions:

- to book arrested suspects
- to house some defendants awaiting trial (those who were not granted pretrial release)
- to punish convicted offenders who are sentenced to incarceration in a local facility
- to hold inmates awaiting transfer to other facilities

Most county jail systems in New York are locally funded, operated, and controlled. However, unlike many other states, county jails in New York are regulated by the state. They are required to comply with state-wide standards for the construction and operation of jail facilities and for staff training.

The county jails share the responsibility for administering sanctions to convicted offenders with the state prison system. In most cases, the county correctional agencies have larger caseloads than the state agencies. As of September 30, 2003, there were a total of 30,415 inmates incarcerated in county correctional facilities, including those operated by the New York City Department of Correction in the five boroughs of New York City.[23]

Many of the jails in New York are old and somewhat rundown. Most suffer from problems of overcrowding. Segregation of inmates is a frequent issue as well. Obviously juveniles and adults are rarely housed together, and males and females are also housed separately from each other. However, many jails do not segregate pre-trial detainees from convicted offenders, or separate offenders who are serving short sentences of incarceration for a minor offense from serious felony offenders who are awaiting transfer to a state prison.

The New York City Department of Correction

The **New York City Department of Correction** (NYC DOC) is larger than the prison systems of 35 of the 50 states in the United States. On September 30, 2003, NYC DOC facilities housed a total of 13,947 inmates.[24] NYC DOC has over 10,000 uniformed staff and 1,500 civilian employees.[25]

The NYC DOC houses both males and females who are at least 16 years of age. There are three main categories of inmates in NYC DOC facilities. In FY 2002, approximately 70 percent of the population was composed of pre-trial detainees, individuals who have been arraigned on criminal charges and who either were unable to post bail or were remanded without bail pending trial. NYC DOC also houses all offenders who were sentenced in New York City to terms of up to one year. In FY 2002, this category comprised approximately 17 percent of the population of the NYC DOC. Finally, approximately 13 percent of the inmates were offenders sentenced to prison terms of more than one year and who were housed in NYC DOC facilities until they were transferred to a state institution.[26]

Prior to 1895, the **New York City Department of Charities and Correction** supervised penal institutions as well as a variety of charity facilities. However, in that year, the Department was divided into two separate agencies. The **Department of Public Charities** was given jurisdiction over all hospitals and almshouses in the city, while the **Department of Correction** had jurisdiction over all New York City penal institutions, including the Penitentiary and Workhouse on Blackwell's Island (now called Roosevelt Island); the City Prison in Manhattan (the Tombs); and five District Prisons and the City Cemetery (Potter's Field) on Hart Island, off City Island in the Bronx. At that time, Queens, Brooklyn, and Richmond Counties were not yet incorporated into the City of New York. Therefore, all penal facilities in those areas fell under the jurisdiction of their respective county sheriffs.[27]

In the mid-1930s, the penitentiary and workhouse on Blackwell's Island were abandoned. The inmates were transferred to the newly constructed **City Penitentiary** on Rikers Island, in Queens. Since that time, the majority of inmates have been housed on **Riker's Island**. There are ten major facilities on the island, with a combined capacity of approximately 17,000 inmates. They include a jail for sentenced males, a jail for sentenced and detainee females, and a detention center for adolescent males between the ages of 16 and 18. The other seven jails house adult male detainees. In addition, two floating detention centers, which are converted Staten Island ferries, are docked off the northern tip of the island. Each has a capacity of 162 inmates and serves as an annex to one of the seven adult male detainee jails.

In addition to the facilities on Rikers Island, the NYC DOC also operates six borough jails, two in the Bronx (including one floating 800-bed barge), two in Brooklyn, one in Queens, and one in Manhattan. These six jails have a combined capacity of approximately 4,000 offenders. The Department also operates fifteen **court detention facilities**, or **court pens**, which are located in the Criminal Court, Supreme Court, and Family Court buildings in each borough. An additional facility is located in the special Narcotics Court in Manhattan. These courthouse facilities are designed to hold inmates who are scheduled for participation in the day's court proceedings.

The Department also operates four hospital prison wards. Individuals who are seriously ill, or who require intensive psychiatric observation, are housed in prison wards operated in three hospitals in the city: Elmhurst General Hospital, Kings County Hospital, and Bellevue Hospital. A semi-secure chronic care unit is located at Goldwater Hospital on Roosevelt Island. In addition, high-security inmates, detainees, and offenders who have less serious medical problems, as well as persons with AIDS who do not require hospitalization, are housed in the North Infirmary Command on Rikers Island.[28]

In 1927, the NYC DOC became the first in the United States to establish a **Correction Officer Training School**. Originally, instruction was provided by the New York Police Department. In the 1930s, the Department began to develop an independent curriculum. By 1943, classes included general deportment, care of uniforms and equipment, duties and responsibilities of various assigned posts, and seminars by guest speakers on sociology, penology, parole, probation, and fingerprinting.

Between 1947 and 1955, the training expanded. Recruits trained for a period of five weeks, and new civilian clerks went through a two week orientation program. In 1961, firearms training was provided on a voluntary basis to all uniformed correctional officers, and in 1963, a new course emphasizing the legal responsibilities involved in the use of a weapon was added.

The Academy has moved many times over the years. It is currently located in Queens and provides both pre-service and in-service training to uniformed and civilian corrections staff. The current training program for uniformed correctional officers is 15 weeks long and includes topics such as interpersonal communications, sciences, human relations, cultural awareness, legal principles, inmate programs, firearms and tactics, CPR/First Aid, physical conditioning, and various security skills, as well as on-the-job training.[29]

During Fiscal Year 2002, a total of 108,464 inmates were admitted to NYC DOC facilities, placing the Department at 96.9 percent of capacity. The average daily population was 13,934 during FY 2002. The average length of stay of detainees was 45.2 days, and the average length of stay of city sentenced offenders was 39.0 days. The average age of an inmate in an NUYC DOC facility during FY 2002 was 31.3 years of age. Approximately 58 percent of the inmates were African American, 30 percent were Latino, nine percent were white, and 1.5 percent fell into some other racial category. The average annual cost of maintaining an inmate during FY 2002 was $62,595.[30]

PAROLE IN NEW YORK

In New York, **parole** is operated at the state level. Parole is not a sentence but rather a form of early release from a sentence of incarceration. Parole is not only a mechanism for facilitating release from prison but also a way to exercise community control over offenders who have received early release from prison.

New York has allowed early release of inmates since 1817, when the state legislature passed the first "good time" law in America. This law reduced the length of the sentence of imprisonment for inmates with good behavior. In 1876 the state first began to use indeterminate sentences of imprisonment, which allowed inmates who had served at least the minimum term imposed by the court to be released on parole. While paid parole officers did not yet exist, parolees did report regularly (usually once per month) to volunteer "guardians." The **New York Division of Parole** was established in 1930, although it was not until 1945 that all statewide parole functions were consolidated and not until 1967 that the New York City Parole Commission was incorporated into the Division. In 1971 the Division was merged with DOCS, but the **Parole Reform Act of 1977** reestablished the Division as a separate and independent agency. The following year the Division was also given the responsibility for the release decision and post-release supervision of juveniles convicted of some serious felonies.[31]

Within the DOP is an administrative unit known as the **Board of Parole** which consists of 19 full time members, all of whom must have a college degree and at least five years of experience in criminology, law enforcement, sociology, law, social work, psychology, medicine, or one of several other fields specified by statute. Members are appointed by the governor with the advice and consent of the Senate and serve six year terms.[32]

Essentially, the Board determines who receives parole, sets release conditions, and has the power to revoke parole. Division staff have the responsibility for supervising those inmates released on parole or conditional release. According to the Division website, "The parolee population is largely minority, poorly educated, underemployed, and concentrated in urban New York." Currently, the Division is responsible for supervising approximately 45,000 parolees throughout the state. In addition, Division staff have responsibility for approximately 14,700 additional inmates who are participating in DOCS work release programs, are parolees from other states, or are inmates who are soon to be released on parole.[33]

Offenders placed on parole will be required to comply with a variety of conditions set forth by the Board of Parole. Some of these are known as **general conditions**, and apply to all individuals who are released on parole. These include:

- I will proceed directly to the area to which I have been released and, within twenty-four hours of my release, make my arrival report to that office of the Division of Parole unless other instructions are designated on my release agreement.

- I will make office and/or written reports as directed.

- I will not leave the State of New York or any other state to which I am released or transferred, or any area defined in writing by my Parole Officer without permission.

- I will permit my Parole Officer to visit me at my residence and/or place of employment and I will permit the search and inspection of my person, residence, and property. I will discuss any proposed changes in my residence, employment, or program status with my Parole Officer. I understand that I have an immediate and continuing duty to notify my Parole Officer of any changes in my residence, employment, or program status when circumstances beyond my control make prior discussion impossible.

- I will reply promptly, fully, and truthfully to any inquiry of, or communication by, my Parole Officer or other representative of the Division of Parole.

- I will notify my Parole Officer immediately any time I am in contact with, or arrested by, any law enforcement agency. I understand that I have a continuing duty to notify my Parole Officer of such contact or arrest.

- I will not be in the company of, or fraternize with, any person I know to have a criminal record or whom I know to have been adjudicated a Youthful Offender, except for accidental encounters in public places, work, school, or in any other instance without the permission of my Parole Officer.

- I will not behave in such manner as to violate the provisions of any law to which I am subject which provides for a penalty of imprisonment, nor will my behavior threaten the safety or well-being of myself or others.

- I will not own, possess, or purchase any shotgun, rifle, or firearm of any type without the written permission of my Parole Officer. In addition, I will not own, possess, or purchase any dangerous instrument or deadly weapon as defined in the Penal Law or any dangerous knife, dirk, razor, stiletto, or imitation pistol. In addition, I will not own, possess or purchase any instrument readily capable of causing injury without a satisfactory explanation for ownership, possession or purchase.

- In the event that I leave the jurisdiction of the State of New York, I hereby waive my right to resist extradition to the State of New York from any state in the Union and from any territory or country outside the United States. This waiver shall be in full force and effect until I am discharged from Parole or Conditional Release. I fully understand that I have the right under the Constitution of the United States and under law to contest an effort to extradite me from another state and return me to New York, and I freely and knowingly waive this right as a condition of my Parole or Conditional Release.

- I will not use or possess any drug paraphernalia or use or possess any controlled substance without proper medical authorization.

- I will follow my special conditions as specified by the Board of Parole, my Parole Officer or other representative.

- I will fully comply with the instructions of my Parole Officer and obey such special additional written conditions as he/she, a member of the Board of Parole, or an authorized representative of the Division of Parole, may impose.[34]

In addition to the general conditions of parole, both the Board and the parolee's Field Parole Officer have the right to assign additional **special conditions** of parole that may be specifically relevant to the individual parolee. Special conditions might include a curfew, attendance at Alcoholics Anonymous or similar counseling program meetings, a prohibition against being in a specific geographic area, a prohibition against associating with a specific individual, or a prohibition against using alcohol.[35]

Jenna's Law has had a significant impact on the Division. The Law eliminated discretionary release for violent felony offenders and requires that these offenders must serve a term of post-release supervision of between 1.5 and five years. The Division is responsible for the supervision of these offenders during their post-release supervision period.

Each offender is assigned a **facility parole officer** prior to release. The duty of this officer is to help prepare the inmate for his or her release into the community. When the inmate is discharged, a **field parole officer** is assigned. The parole officer holds regular office visits with the parolee, and also meets with the parolee, and his or her family, at their home. The parole officer may also visit the parolee's place of employment and may help the parolee obtain any necessary services (vocational training, rehabilitation services, drug or alcohol counseling, etc.).

PROBATION IN NEW YORK

Unlike parole, **probation** is a sentence imposed by the court. It is a form of community corrections because the sentence is served in the community rather than in a correctional institution. Thus, probation, which is a cost-effective alternative to incarceration, is a sentence which the court imposes in place of incarceration and which allows the offender to serve his or her sentence in the community under the supervision of the court. Offenders on probation are required to abide by various statutory and court-ordered conditions.

Probation services in New York are provided at the county level, although they are regulated and supervised by a state agency, the **New York State Division of Probation and Correctional Alternatives**. New York has 58 probation departments, including 57 county probation departments and the New York City Department of Probation. These agencies provide a variety of services to the Criminal and Family Courts. According to Executive Law (Exec.L.) §256(1),

> Each county shall maintain or provide for a probation agency or agencies to perform probation services therein, including intake, investigation, pre-sentence reports, supervision, conciliation, social treatment and such other functions as are assigned to probation agencies pursuant to law.

Exec.L. §256(3) does allow for several counties to establish and operate a joint county probation department to perform all probation services for all the participating counties.

Probation departments assist the courts by helping to identify offenders who are poor risks for probation, identifying offenders who are suitable candidates for probation, and recommending appropriate sanctions (including custodial sentences, fines, restitution, and community service). When an offender is sentenced to probation, the assigned probation officer develops a supervision plan which is tailored to the offender's individual needs and which is intended to guide the offender toward becoming a law-abiding citizen. Services provided to the courts by probation departments include:

- Supervising juveniles and adults who receive a court ordered sentence of probation.

- Conducting family court intake services to determine if cases can be resolved without filing a family court petition for Juvenile Delinquent and Persons in Need of Supervision (PINS) cases.

- Conducting pre-disposition investigations for juveniles and certain adults before family courts.

- Conducting pre-plea or presentence investigations for defendants before criminal courts.

- Collecting restitution and other fees from probationers and non-probationers as ordered by the court.

- Where appropriate, being responsible for operating pre-trial release services and community service programs.[36]

In some cases, the county government or the courts may order probation departments to perform other functions as well, such as operating pre-trial release services or community service sentencing programs.

CPL §410.10(1) states that:

> When the court pronounces a sentence of probation or of conditional discharge it must specify as part of the sentence the conditions to be complied with...

The court has the right to modify the conditions of probation at any time during the probationary period, although the offender must be personally present in court at the time of the modification, unless the modification is only to eliminate or relax one or more conditions.[37]

Section 65.10 of the New York State Penal Law outlines the conditions of probation and conditional discharge. The law states that:

> The conditions of probation and of conditional discharge shall be such as the court, in its discretion, deems reasonably necessary to insure that the defendant will lead a law-abiding life or to assist him to do so.[38]

The statute also requires the court to consider imposing restitution or reparation as a condition of probation. In addition, the statute states that the court may require that the defendant conform to any or all of the following conditions:

(a) Avoid injurious or vicious habits;

(b) Refrain from frequenting unlawful or disreputable places or consorting with disreputable persons;

(c) Work faithfully at a suitable employment or faithfully pursue a course of study or of vocational training that will equip him for suitable employment;

(d) Undergo available medical or psychiatric treatment and remain in a specified institution, when required for that purpose;

(e) Participate in an alcohol or substance abuse program or an intervention program approved by the court...;

(f) Support his dependents and meet other family responsibilities;

(g) Make restitution of the fruits of his or her offense or make reparation, in an amount he can afford to pay, for the actual out-of-pocket loss caused thereby...

(h) Perform services for a public or not-for-profit corporation, association, institution or agency...;

(i) If a person under the age of twenty-one years, (i) resides with his parents or in a suitable foster home or hostel as referred to in section two hundred forty-four of the executive law, (ii) attends school, (iii) spends such part of the period of the sentence as the court may direct, but not exceeding two years, in a facility made available by the division for youth pursuant to article nineteen-G of the executive law, provided that admission to such facility may be made only with the prior consent of the division for youth, (iv) attend a non-residential program for such hours and pursuant to a schedule prescribed by the court as suitable for a program of rehabilitation of youth, (v) contribute to his own support in any home, foster home or hostel;

(j) Post a bond or other security for the performance of any or all conditions imposed;

(k) Observe certain specified conditions of conduct as set forth in an order of protection....

(k-1) Install and maintain a functioning ignition interlock device ... in any vehicle owned or operated on a regular basis by the defendant...

(l) Satisfy any other conditions reasonably related to his rehabilitation.[39]

In addition, the court may impose conditions specifically relating to the supervision of the offender on probation. These may include requiring the offender to:

(a) Report to a probation officer as directed by the court or the probation officer and permit the probation officer to visit him at his place of abode or elsewhere;

(b) Remain within the jurisdiction of the court unless granted permission to leave by the court or the probation officer; and

(c) Answer all reasonable inquiries by the probation officer and notify the probation officer prior to any change in address or employment.[40]

The court may also require the probationer to use an electronic monitoring device, but only if the court determines that this requirement will increase public safety or probationer control or surveillance. In addition, the court may impose any other reasonable conditions which it deems to be necessary.[41]

The New York State Division of Probation and Correctional Alternatives

The **New York State Division of Probation and Correctional Alternatives** (DPCA) is responsible for supervising the operation of all local probation agencies, as well as overseeing a variety of correctional alternative programs throughout the state. The DPCA also runs a state aid funding program which provides state funds to approved local probation services and to municipalities and private non-profit agencies which have approved alternative-to-incarceration services. Programs funded by the DPCA include local probation departments, alternative to incarceration services, juvenile and adult intensive supervision programs, and programs providing supervision and treatment to specially targeted offender populations. All funded programs are designed to reduce the state's reliance on detention and incarceration in a way that is consistent with public safety.[42]

The mission of the Division is to promote and facilitate the delivery of community corrections programs throughout the state. The State Director of the DPCA also serves as the chairman of the New York State Probation Commission.[43] Members of the Probation Commission are appointed by the governor and provide advice and consultation to the State Director on all matters relating to probation in New York State.[44]

The New York City Department of Probation

The **New York City Department of Probation** is responsible for supervising all adults and juveniles placed on probation by the family court, supreme court, and criminal courts in New York City. It is the second largest probation department in the country. Only Los Angeles has a larger probation department than New York City. The Department provides probationers with counseling and job training as well as referrals to various community-based services, such as employment counseling and substance abuse treatment programs. The Department is also responsible for informing the court when an offender fails to live up to the court-imposed conditions of his or her probation. Department officers prepare pre-sentencing background reports that judges use in determining the appropriate sanctions for both adult and juvenile offenders. When an offender is required, as a special condition of probation, to pay restitution, the Department is responsible for collecting and distributing payments of restitution.[45]

The Department was created by Exec.L. §255(1), which states that:

> There is hereby created a department of probation in and for the city of New York to have charge of all probation work in the supreme, family and criminal courts in the counties of Bronx, Kings, New York, Queens and Richmond.

The head of the Department is appointed by the mayor of New York City.[46]

The Department's **Intensive Supervision Program** (ISP) is used primarily for higher-risk felony offenders who require a higher level of supervision in the community than is given to most probationers. Low-risk felony offenders who violate the conditions of regular probation may also be placed on ISP, although a second violation of probation conditions generally leads to incarceration.

An offender on ISP is required to meet with probation officers on a frequent basis both at Department offices and in the offender's home.

The Department supervises juveniles as well as adults on probation. Juvenile programs run by the New York City Department of Probation will be discussed in the next chapter.

NOTES

1. New York State Commission of Corrections home page (http://www.scoc.state.ny.us/)
2. *Ibid*
3. *Ibid*
4. COR §41
5. COR §42
6. COR §47(1)
7. COR §43
8. New York State Department of Correctional Services home page (http://www.docs.state.ny.us/)
9. New York State Commission of Corrections home page, *op cit.*
10. New York State Department of Correctional Services home page, *op cit.*
11. Corcraft Products home page (http://www.corcraft.org/index.html)
12. *Ibid*
13. *Ibid*
14. History of Newgate – New York's First Prison (http://www.geocities.com/MotorCity/Downs/3548/facility/newgate.html)
15. History of Auburn Correctional Facility (http://www.geocities.com/MotorCity/Downs/3548/facility/auburn.html)
16. Miskell, John N. (1996). *Executions in Auburn Prison, Auburn, New York: 1890–1916* (http://www.correctionhistory.org/auburn&osborne/miskell/jnmchair_index.html)
17. History of Auburn Correctional Facility, *op cit.*
18. History of Sing Sing Correctional Facility (http://www.geocities.com/MotorCity/Downs/3548/facility/singsing.html)
19. Gado, Mark. *Stone upon stone: Sing Sing Prison.* Court TV's Crime Library. Available online at (http://www.crimelibrary.com/notorious_murders/famous/sing_sing/)
20. History of Sing Sing Correctional Facility, *op cit.*
21. *Ibid*
22. History of Elmira Correctional Facility (http://www.geocities.com/MotorCity/Downs/3548/facility/elmira.html)
23. New York State Department of Correctional Services home page, *op cit.*
24. *Ibid*
25. New York City Department of Correction home page (http://www.ci.nyc.ny.us/html/doc/home.html)
26. *Ibid*
27. *Ibid*
28. *Ibid*

29. City of New York Correction Academy (http://www.correctionhistory.org/html/chronicl/nycdoc/html/academy2.html)
30. New York City Department of Correction home page, *op cit.*
31. New York State Division of Parole home page (http://parole.state.ny.us/index.html)
32. Exec.L. §259-b
33. New York State Division of Parole home page, *op cit.*
34. *New York State Parole Handbook* (http://parole.state.ny.us/parolehandbook.htm)
35. *Ibid*
36. New York State Division of Probation and Correctional Alternatives home page (http://dpca.state.ny.us/index.htm)
37. CPL §410.20(1)
38. Pen.L. §65.10(1)
39. Pen.L. §65.10(2)
40. Pen.L. §65.10(3)
41. Pen.L. §65.10(4) and (5)
42. New York State Division of Probation and Correctional Alternatives home page, *op cit.*
43. Exec.L. §240(1)
44. Exec.L. §242
45. New York City Department of Probation home page (http://www.nyc.gov/html/prob/home.html)
46. Exec.L. §255(2)

CHAPTER 9

THE JUVENILE JUSTICE SYSTEM IN NEW YORK

INTRODUCTION

In New York, a person who is under the age of sixteen cannot, in most cases, be held criminally responsible for his or her conduct.[1] If a person between the ages of seven and fifteen commits a criminal act and is found to need supervision, treatment, or confinement, he or she is considered to be a **juvenile delinquent** (JD). Family Court (Fam.Ct.) §301.2(1) defines a juvenile delinquent as:

> a person over seven and less than sixteen years of age, who, having committed an act that would constitute a crime if committed by an adult,
> (a) is not criminally responsible for such conduct by reason of infancy, or
> (b) is the defendant in an action ordered removed from a criminal court to the family court...

Acts committed by a juvenile delinquent are known as **delinquent acts**. Juvenile delinquency cases are heard in Family Court rather than in an adult trial court.

In 1978, the New York State Legislature passed the Juvenile Offender Act, which created a new category of **juvenile offender** (JO). The Act stated that, in some situations, a juvenile who is at least thirteen years of age may be held criminally responsible for his or her actions. According to Pen.L. §30.00(2):

> A person thirteen, fourteen or fifteen years of age is criminally responsible for acts constituting murder in the second degree ... provided that the underlying crime for the murder charge is one for which such person is criminally responsible; and a person fourteen or fifteen years of age is criminally responsible for ... kidnapping in the first degree ... arson in the first degree ... assault in the first degree ... manslaughter in the first degree ... rape in the first degree ... sodomy in the first degree ... aggravated sexual abuse ... burglary in the first degree ... burglary in the second degree ... arson in the second degree ... robbery in the first degree ... robbery in the second degree ... or ...an attempt to commit murder in the second degree or kidnapping in the first degree.

The statute also includes several crimes involving criminal possession of a firearm or other dangerous weapon.

The majority of juvenile offenders in New York are aged fourteen or fifteen; a thirteen-year-old individual can only be held criminally responsible for certain types of second degree murder. Because of the seriousness of these crimes, juvenile offenders are treated as adults by the courts. JO cases are heard in a criminal court or in the supreme court by a special youth part judge, although the criminal court does have the option of sending the case back to family court. Juvenile offenders are subject to more serious penalties than juvenile delinquents. However, while they are charged as adults, juvenile offenders must be housed with other juveniles. Essentially, the treatment of a juvenile offender in court is similar to the adult trial procedure discussed in Chapter 5, although a juvenile offender sentenced to a term of imprisonment will be held in a secure facility maintained by the Office of Children and Family Services, rather than in an adult correctional facility under the Department of Correction.

New York also recognizes a category known as **youthful offender** (YO). An individual may be found to be a youthful offender by the court; it is not a statutory status. A **youth** is defined in CPL §720.10(1) as:

> a person charged with a crime alleged to have been committed when he was at least sixteen years old and less than nineteen years old or a person charged with being a juvenile offender...

Thus, the term "youth" includes juvenile offenders as well as individuals between the ages of sixteen and eighteen.

An **eligible youth** is essentially a youth who is eligible to be found by the court to be a youthful offender. All youth are considered to be eligible unless they fall into one of the following categories:

1. The present conviction, which is to be replaced by a YO finding, is for a Class A-I felony, a Class A-II felony, certain armed felonies, first degree rape, first degree sodomy, or aggravated sexual abuse (although there are several exceptions to this).

2. The youth has a prior felony conviction and sentence.

3. The youth has previously been found a YO by the court after being convicted of a felony, or has been found by the family court to be a juvenile delinquent.[2]

The court has the option of making a **youthful offender finding** if:

(a) If in the opinion of the court the interest of justice would be served by relieving the eligible youth from the onus of a criminal record and by not imposing an indeterminate term of imprisonment of more than four years, the court may, in its discretion, find the eligible youth is a youthful offender; and
(b) Where the conviction is had in a local criminal court and the eligible youth had not prior to commencement of trial or entry of a plea of guilty been convicted of a crime or found a youthful offender, the court must find he is a youthful offender.[3]

There is a clear difference between a juvenile offender and a youthful offender. A juvenile offender is a youth between the ages of thirteen and fifteen who committed one of the offenses specified in Pen.L. §30.00(2). A youthful offender may be a juvenile offender but may also be an individual who was between sixteen and eighteen years of age when the crime was committed.

New York also has another category for juveniles: **persons in need of supervision** (PINS). A person in need of supervision is defined by Fam.Ct. §712(a) as:

> A person less than eighteen years of age who does not attend school ... or who is incorrigible, ungovernable or habitually disobedient and beyond the lawful control of a parent or other person legally responsible for such child's care, or other lawful authority, or who violates the provisions of section 221.05 of the penal law.

Pen.L. §221.05 refers to the unlawful possession of marijuana. Except for juveniles who violate this statute, most PINS are juveniles who have committed **status offenses**, behaviors which are crimes only if they are committed by juveniles.

NEW YORK FAMILY COURT

The Family Court was established by the Family Court Act. Each county in New York has a **Family Court**, as do each of the five boroughs of New York City. Family Courts handle most legal matters that affect families and children, including adoptions, guardianship, foster care approval and review, domestic violence, termination of parental rights, and various child protective proceedings. The only family-related matter not handled by Family Court is the termination of a marriage. The state supreme court is the only court that can grant a divorce or separation or annul a marriage. Family Courts also handle most cases that involve juvenile delinquents and PINS.

Family Court judges serve terms of ten years. In New York City, they are appointed by the mayor while in other counties, they are elected.[4] Proceedings in Family Court are heard by judges only; there are no juries in family court. An accused child is called a **respondent** and the victim is known as the **complainant**. The case is generally presented by the county attorney (or in New York City the "corporation counsel"), although in some counties the assistant district attorney may present the case against the juvenile if the charges are extremely serious.

During 2001, there were a total of 683,390 cases filed in Family Court in New York. The majority of the cases (80 percent) involved paternity, support, custody, and family offenses (e.g., domestic violence). Juvenile delinquency and designated felony cases comprised approximately 3 percent of these cases while PINS cases comprised approximately 2 percent.[5]

Juvenile Delinquency Proceedings in Family Court

The juvenile justice system differs in several key ways from the adult criminal justice system. A juvenile delinquent is **taken into custody**, rather than arrested, goes through an **intake process**, and then faces one of three immediate dispositions:

1. The juvenile may be brought directly to Family Court.

2. The juvenile may be held overnight in juvenile detention until the next court day.

3. The juvenile may be released to the custody of a parent or guardian with instructions to come to court on a given day.

The complainant, the police officer, and the respondent are all interviewed by **probation intake workers**. The content of these interviews is not disclosed unless there is a finding of delinquency by the Family Court. The probation officers use this information to determine if the case can be **adjusted** or settled without going through the court, although this generally only happens if the case does not involve serious violent actions on the part of the juvenile. They may also refer the various parties in the case to other agencies or social services.

If the case is not adjusted, the county attorney or probation department will prepare and file a **juvenile delinquency petition** with the court. The petition includes a description of the acts the juvenile is accused of committing. If Family Court agrees to hear the case, a date and time will be set for the **intake hearing** or **first hearing**. At this hearing, the juvenile must be represented, either by an attorney hired by the child's parent or guardian, or by a court-appointed attorney if the parent or guardian cannot afford to hire a lawyer. During the intake hearing, the court decides if the child can be remanded to the custody of the parents until the **fact finding hearing** or if the child must be detained in a secure or non-secure facility. Recommendations from the probation officer are considered by the court in making this decision; generally the child will be detained if the court decides that the child might commit a crime prior to the hearing or is unlikely to return to court for the hearing if released.

If the court decides that the child must be detained or **remanded** prior to the fact finding hearing, the court may hold a **probable cause hearing** to determine whether there is probable cause to hold the child in detention. Bail is not set on juvenile delinquency cases in Family Court.

The case then proceeds to a **fact finding hearing**, which is equivalent to an adult criminal trial. The case is heard by a judge; juveniles in New York do not have the right to a jury trial. At the fact finding hearing, the judge attempts to determine whether the child did commit the acts outlined in the petition. If the prosecutor proves the case against the juvenile beyond a reasonable doubt, the judge will make a finding that the juvenile did commit the acts (or some of the acts) that were described in the petition and will set a date for a **dispositional hearing**. The judge may also order the Probation Department to prepare a report on the child's behavior at home and at school. If the prosecutor does not prove the case against the respondent, the judge will dismiss the petition against the child. Prior to the dispositional hearing the judge has the option of remanding the respondent to a juvenile detention facility or paroling the respondent to the custody of a parent or guardian.

At the dispositional hearing, the judge hears the report of the probation officer and may hear testimony from the child's parent or guardian, or other individuals who have important information. The judge must determine whether the respondent is a juvenile delinquent in need of supervision, treatment, or placement in a secure or non-secure facility. There are several possible outcomes at a dispositional hearing:

1. The judge may determine that even though the respondent committed the acts described in the petition, he or she is not in need of treatment, supervision, or confinement, and dismiss the case.

2. The judge may determine that the respondent is a juvenile delinquent who does need supervision, treatment, or confinement, and will make an appropriate disposition.

3. The court may order an **adjournment in contemplation of dismissal** and place the case on hold for up to six months before deciding whether or not the petition should be dismissed.

If the judge finds the respondent to be a juvenile delinquent in need of supervision, treatment, or confinement, there are several options for disposition. One option is to give the respondent a **conditional discharge**, which allows the juvenile to live at home without court supervision, although he or she must abide by certain conditions set by the court. Another option is to give an **order of probation**, allowing the respondent to live at home while under supervision by the Probation Department. The court may also place the respondent in custody outside the home. In addition, the judge may order the juvenile to pay restitution for any damages resulting from his or her delinquent actions. The judge determines the appropriate disposition for the respondent and signs a **dispositional order**.

If the juvenile violations the conditions of the dispositional order, a **violation petition** may be filed against the child by the probation officer or social service agency and the juvenile will be brought before the court for a new dispositional hearing. If it is proved that the juvenile violated the original dispositional order, the court has the right to order a different, and possibly more severe, disposition.

A finding of juvenile delinquency is not the same as a criminal conviction. In most cases, the juvenile will have no criminal record, although the most serious charges, which are known as **designated felonies**, will become part of the juvenile's criminal record.

Juveniles do have the right to appeal the court's final decision and disposition orders. Appeals from Family Court are reviewed by the Appellate Division of the Supreme Court. Although parties in an appeal do not testify, they have the right to be present at appellate arguments.

Persons in Need of Supervision

PINS proceedings also are heard in Family Court. The procedure is similar to that for a juvenile delinquent. A parent or guardian may file a **PINS petition** with the Family Court. In addition, a petition may be filed by the child's school district, a peace officer or police officer, any person who has been injured by the child, or any social service agency with which the child may have been placed. A PINS petition includes a written description of the circumstances of the case, including a description of the juvenile's behavior, and asks the court to find the child to be in need of supervision.

However, prior to filing such a petition, the child and his or her family (or other complaining parties) generally are required to go through the process of **PINS diversion**. This involves meeting with a member of the Probation Department in an attempt to resolve the existing problems and divert the case from formal court processing. The probation officer may recommend the juvenile be referred to community or government programs. Diversion proceedings may last up to 90 days and a petition may not be filed until the probation officer has determined that the process has failed. If the diversion process is successful, no petition is filed and there is no case in Family Court.

After a PINS petition is filed, the juvenile has the right to be represented by an attorney. Attorneys appointed by the court to represent PINS are known as **law guardians**. The court may also decide to remove the child from the custody of the parent or guardian while awaiting the hearing and to place him/her with a relative or in a non-secure juvenile facility. The court may not place the child in a secure facility.

As with a juvenile delinquency case, a PINS trial is known as a **fact-finding hearing**. Its purpose is to determine whether the statements made in the PINS petition are true. Both the juvenile and the complainant may testify at this hearing and have the right to present evidence and call witnesses. If the Family Court judge decides that the statements made in the petition are true, and that the juvenile did commit the acts outlined in the petition, the judge will set a date for a **dispositional hearing**. The judge may also order the Probation Department to prepare a report on the child, outlining the child's home life, school attendance, and general behavior both at home and at school.

Just because the judge determines that the juvenile committed the acts of which he or she is accused, it does not automatically mean that the juvenile is considered to be a PINS. This determination is made at the dispositional hearing. At this hearing, the judge examines the report prepared by the Probation Department and hears testimony and evidence presented by witnesses who have information about the child. The judge may at this point determine that the child does not need supervision or treatment and may dismiss the case. However, if the judge determines that the juvenile is in need of treatment or supervision, he or she has the authority to place the juvenile in a residential facility, such as a foster group home, for up to 18 months, or to place the child on probation and allow them to live at home. Juveniles who are at least ten years of age may be ordered to pay for any property damage they may have caused or to perform community service. Finally, the judge has the authority to place the case on hold for up to six months before making a disposition, or to discharge the juvenile with simply a warning. After making a determination of disposition, the judge signs a **dispositional order** outlining the results of the hearing.

The dispositional order outlines the terms mandated by the court for the juvenile (e.g., community service, payment of restitution, serving a term of probation). If the juvenile fails to obey the terms outlined in the dispositional order, a **violation petition** may be filed against the child by the probation officer or social service agency and the juvenile will be brought before the court for a new dispositional hearing. If it is proved that the juvenile violated the original dispositional order, the court has the right to change the order and require additional supervision or treatment.

SENTENCING OF JUVENILE OFFENDERS

In New York, juveniles who have committed felony offenses receive indeterminate sentences.[6] The actual length of the sentence depends on the type of crime committed. Pen.L. §70.05(2) discusses the maximum term of the indeterminate sentence, stating that:

> The maximum term of an indeterminate sentence for a juvenile offender shall be at least three years and the term shall be fixed as follows:
> (a) For the class A felony of murder in the second degree, the term shall be life imprisonment;
> (b) For the class A felony of arson in the first degree, or for the class A felony of kidnapping in the first degree the term shall be fixed by the court, and shall be at least twelve years but shall not exceed fifteen years;
> (c) For a class B felony, the term shall be fixed by the court, and shall not exceed ten years;
> (d) For a class C felony, the term shall be fixed by the court, and shall not exceed seven years, and
> (e) For a class D felony, the term shall be fixed by the court and shall not exceed four years.

Pen.L. §70.05(3) specifies the minimum period of imprisonment of the indeterminate sentence as follows:

> The minimum period of imprisonment under an indeterminate sentence for a juvenile offender shall be specified in the sentence as follows:
> (a) For the class A felony of murder in the second degree, the minimum period of imprisonment shall be fixed by the court and shall be not less than five years but shall not exceed nine years;
> (b) For the class A felony of arson in the first degree, or for the class A felony of kidnapping in the first degree, the minimum period of imprisonment shall be fixed by the court and shall be not less than four years but shall not exceed six years; and
> (c) For a class B, C or D felony, the minimum period of imprisonment shall be fixed by the court at one-third of the maximum term imposed.

THE NEW YORK CITY DEPARTMENT OF JUVENILE JUSTICE

The Development of the New York City Department of Juvenile Justice

The **New York City Department of Juvenile Justice** (DJJ) was created in 1979, after the passage of the 1978 Juvenile Offender Act by the New York State Legislature. The DJJ was given responsibility for coordinating the care and custody of all juveniles in detention in New York City. Management of the DJJ was divided into three categories. The first was the operation of **Spofford**, a juvenile facility located in the Bronx that provided secure detention for violent juveniles who had been charged with serious offenses. Past problems at Spofford, including frequent escapes, physical attacks, and sexual assaults, had provided much of the impetus for the creation of the DJJ. Because the Department found it impossible to halt the physical deterioration of Spofford or to overcome the negative reputation the facility had acquired over the years, Spofford was eventually closed, refurbished, and reopened as a new facility. The second category was the operation of **Non-Secure Detention**, including the oversight of a number of community based group homes that were run by independent contractors. The third category was the **Administration Division**, which included not only responsibility for budgeting and programmatic planning, but also the operation of community-based juvenile programs.[7]

DJJ provides both secure and non-secure detention facilities for juveniles awaiting adjudication of their court cases. In addition, juveniles who have been adjudicated delinquent and who are awaiting transfer to state institutions after disposition or sentence may be housed in a DJJ facility.

Secure Detention in New York City

The classification of a juvenile detention facility as **secure detention** is similar to an adult maximum-security classification, although the services provided and the staff-to-resident ratio is different. Juveniles in DJJ secure custody facilities have been remanded to the custody of DJJ while awaiting adjudication before the court. Male and female alleged juvenile delinquents and juvenile offenders between the ages of ten and fifteen may be housed in secure detention. Many do not stay very long. Approximately 35 percent are released within five days and 67 percent are released within thirty days.[8]

DJJ has three secure facilities. **Crossroads Juvenile Center** is located in Brooklyn while **Horizon Juvenile Center** and **Bridges Juvenile Center** are located in the Bronx. Bridges is housed in several wings of the old Spofford building that have been renovated.

All juveniles placed in secure detention spend the first ten days in **Intake and Orientation** undergoing education, social service, and medical assessments. The Bridges Juvenile Center serves as the DJJ's intake and admissions facility as well as holding those juveniles and youths awaiting transfer to a state facility. Juveniles who are not released prior to the end of the intake period (generally no more than two weeks) are transferred to a residential unit, either Horizon Juvenile Center or Crossroads Juvenile Center, depending on where their court cases are being heard and where they normally live. In general, juveniles residing in Manhattan or the Bronx are transferred to Horizon Juvenile Center; juveniles residing in Brooklyn, Queens, or Staten Island go to Crossroads Juvenile Center.

Secure facilities restrict the movement of residents by physical methods (e.g., locks) as well as the requirement that residents must be accompanied by a staff member at all times. Residents are regularly searched for contraband. In most secure facilities, residents are awakened at 5:30 a.m., shower and eat breakfast, although if a resident is going to court, he or she wakes up at 5:00 a.m. After breakfast, residents go to school. The New York City Board of Education operates a full-time educational program known as **Passages Academy**, maintaining one site in each of the three DJJ secure facilities, and a fourth site for those juveniles held in non-secure detention facilities.

Students in each Passages Academy are grouped according to their functional levels. Educational programming includes the state-mandated 5.5 hours of instruction each school day during which time the residents study not only traditional academic subjects (e.g., math, science, English) but also individual and community living skills that will help them during their stay in DJJ detention and after their return home. Residents also may receive instruction in subjects such as computers, art, music, health, career skills, and safety education. After school, residents have time to do homework and participate in recreation. Dinner is served at 5:30 p.m. and bedtime is usually 9:30 p.m.

DJJ facilities include a **behavior management system** which is designed to teach juvenile residents that they are responsible for their own behavior, to encourage them to adhere to the institution's rules, and to help them respect the rights and feelings of others. The system includes incentives that reward good behavior with privileges such as extra telephone calls, access to the commissary, and later bedtimes. Negative behavior is discouraged with penalties that place restrictions on the juvenile's privileges and his/her choice of recreational and leisure activities.

Non-Secure Detention in New York City

Non-secure detention (NSD) facilities place fewer physical restrictions on the movement of residents. Residents are supervised by members of staff and may be allowed to leave the facility, if escorted by a staff member, to attend community programs. Alleged juvenile delinquents who are believed to require a less restrictive setting may be housed in NDS facilities while awaiting disposition of their cases before Family Court. These facilities include a network of group homes which are intended to provide a supportive, family-like environment as well as close supervision. Juveniles may be assigned to NSD specifically by a Family Court judge or they may be merely ordered into custody and the DJJ determines whether secure or non-secure detention is appropriate.

Both boys and girls, ranging in age from seven to sixteen years, may be placed in NSD. The average age is fifteen years. In Fiscal Year 2001 there were 485 admissions to NSD in New York City and 1,062 transfers from secure detention facilities to NSD. The average length of stay was 23 days. Approximately 14 percent were released within three days and 34 percent were released within ten days.[9]

Juveniles assigned to NSD undergo an **orientation** procedure at one of two **Intake Houses** which are operated by DJJ. The intake house for girls is located in Manhattan while the house for boys is located in the Bronx. After undergoing medical and mental health evaluations and educational and family assessments, the juvenile is assigned to an appropriate group home facility. NSD has a total of 14 group homes, located throughout the city. Most are operated through contracts with private social service groups. While in NSD, juveniles attend a Passages Academy school facility located in the Bronx, participate in recreational activities, and attend group counseling and tutoring sessions.

Juveniles in Detention in New York City

DJJ facilities house both alleged juvenile delinquents and juvenile offenders. In Fiscal Year 2001, DJJ had 5,313 admissions to detention, of which 485 were to non-secure detention and 4,828 were to secure detention (although some of these were later transferred to NSD). Of these, 90 percent were juvenile delinquents and 10 percent were juvenile offenders. Approximately 82 percent of all admissions were male. Alleged juvenile delinquents spent an average of 18 days in secure detention and 37 days in non-secure detention in FY 2001, while alleged juvenile offenders spend an average of 29 days in secure detention. Brooklyn and the Bronx produced the greatest number of admissions, with almost 31 percent of all admissions in FY 2000 coming from Brooklyn and almost 29 percent from the Bronx.[10]

THE NEW YORK CITY DEPARTMENT OF PROBATION

The **New York City Department of Probation** is responsible for supervising both adults and juveniles placed on probation in New York City. With respect to juveniles, the Department provides a wide range of services to the Family Court.[11]

The Department first becomes involved in a juvenile case during the **Probation Intake** period, after the juvenile has been arrested. As discussed earlier in this chapter, the intake officer interviews all the parties involved, including the juvenile, the complainant, the arresting officer, and the juvenile's parents or guardian. The officer then determines whether the case should be referred to the court for formal proceedings or if it can be diverted from the court. If the case is diverted, or **adjusted**, the case is monitored by the Department for two months.

The Department's **Alternative to Court** (ATC) intake program is designed specifically for first-time juvenile offenders who have been accused of misdemeanors or certain nonviolent felony offenses. The complainant must explicitly consent before the juvenile is eligible for participation in ATC. Admission to the program is also dependent upon the willingness of the parent(s) or guardian(s) to become involved in the program and to attend monthly parent education groups. The goal of the program is to provide early intervention after the first nonviolent arrest and deter the juvenile from any future delinquent or criminal behavior. Juveniles participate in individual and family counseling, law-related education groups, and computerized learning lab services, report regularly to a probation officer, and receive referrals to outside agencies.

The Department's **Alternative to Detention** (ATD) program provides juveniles awaiting disposition with an alternative to placement in a juvenile detention facility. Juveniles participating in ATD generally are chronic truants. They are required to spend the hours of 8:00 a.m through 4:00 p.m. at an assigned ATD center, where they attend school, receive counseling, and participate in recreational programs. The Expanded ATD program provides supervision until 8:00 p.m. and provides participants with tutoring, cognitive skills training, and aggression management training. ATD centers are run by probation officers, social workers, and teachers. As with the ATC program, admission into ATD or Expanded ATD is predicated upon the parent's willingness to work with and participate in the program.

The Department has a special program for PINS and their families. The goal of the program is to divert the child from formal court intervention and to resolve the problem through the use of community-based programs. The majority of children in the PINS program are involved in status offenses such as truancy or refusal to obey a parental curfew. Many parents are referred to the program by the police or school officials.

Juveniles who have been found to be delinquent by Family Court may be placed on **probation** for up to two years. Each juvenile will be assigned a probation officer who provides supervision and is responsible for monitoring the child's behavior at home and at school to ensure the juvenile is complying with the conditions of probation ordered by the court. The probation officer also develops a treatment plan based on the specific needs of the juvenile and his or her family.

The **Juvenile Intensive Supervision Program** (JISP) was developed for juveniles who require additional and more intensive probation supervision in the community but do not need to be placed in a residential facility. Essentially, it provides a community-based alternative to institutional placement. JISP probation officers have small caseloads, generally handling no more than 15 juveniles, and work with the entire family as well as the individual juvenile probationer. Family involvement in the rehabilitation program is emphasized by JISP. JISP probation officers make frequent visits to the juvenile's home and school as well as to any treatment programs in which the juvenile is participating. All juveniles placed in JISP are also assigned to perform 60 hours of mandatory community service. The Department's **Family Court Community Service Unit** works to find locations for juveniles ordered to perform community service as part of their probation. Site providers must provide a high level of supervision as well as providing support and adult guidance to the juveniles.

NOTES

1. Pen.L. §30.00(1)
2. CPL §720.10(2)
3. CPL §720.20(1)
4. Fam.Ct. §123 and §135
5. *Twenty-fourth annual report of the chief administrator of the courts for calendar year 2001.* Available online at (http://www.nycourts.gov/reports/annual/pdfs/2001annualreport.pdf)
6. Pen.L. §70.05
7. The New York City Department of Juvenile Justice home page (http://www.ci.nyc.ny.us/html/djj/home1.html)
8. *Ibid*
9. *Ibid*
10. *Ibid*
11. New York City Department of Probation home page (http://www.nyc.gov/html/prob/home.html)

CHAPTER 10

DRUGS AND CRIME IN NEW YORK

INTRODUCTION

Drug abuse is a serious problem in New York. According to the Division of Criminal Justice Services, in 2002 there were 40,103 adult arrest for felony drug violations and 95,710 adult arrests for misdemeanor drug violations.[1] In New York City, over 77 percent of all adult females and 77 percent of all adult males arrested for any crime tested positive for drug use at the time of arrest.[2] Over 41 percent of high school students in New York State surveyed in 1999 reported that they had used marijuana at least once and over 23 percent were currently using marijuana.[3]

THE AVAILABILITY OF DRUGS IN NEW YORK

Marijuana

Marijuana is the most readily available and commonly used drug in New York.[4] The majority is transported into the state from Florida or states in southwestern portion of the country, although there is a sizable amount brought across the Canadian border and a number of local indoor growing operations.[5] During the first quarter of Fiscal Year 2002, commercial-grade marijuana sold for approximately $100 to $200 per ounce and $200 to $2,000 per pound. Hydroponic produced marijuana and the more potent "purple haze" commanded higher prices.

Cocaine

Cocaine, which is grown in Bolivia, Colombia, and Peru, is easily available in New York. According to the DEA, much of the cocaine brought into New York is supplied by Colombia-based distributers who first smuggle it into the border states (Florida, Texas, California, and Arizona) and then bring it into New York.[6] Cocaine sells for less in New York City than in upstate New York, and the purity levels of both powder and crack cocaine tend to be higher in New York City.[7]

Heroin

The majority of heroin available in New York is imported from South America, although Asian and Mexican heroin are also available. As with cocaine, prices are higher in upstate New York and the purity levels are higher in New York City.[8]

Methamphetamine

According to the DEA, **methamphetamine** abuse is not a serious problem in New York, especially when compared to drugs such as heroin, cocaine, and MDMA. However, the availability, and thus the threat, of methamphetamine is increasing. While much of New York City's supply of the drug comes from the West Coast, methamphetamine is also produced in clandestine laboratories, primarily located in rural areas of the state.[9] Use of the drug among college students and at raves does appear to be increasing.[10]

Club Drugs

Club drugs include a number of illegal drugs that are found at nightclubs and "raves," and on college campuses. Common club drugs in New York include MDMA (Ecstacy) and GHB (gamma hydroxybutyric acid), although the use of Ketamine is increasing.[11] Primary sources of MDMA include Belgium, the Netherlands, and Canada. MDMA is primarily distributed by organized crime groups in New York.[12]

THE DEA IN NEW YORK

The DEA has offices in Albany, Buffalo, Long Island, New York City, Rochester, and Syracuse, and has over 600 employees stationed in the state. During 2002, federal drug seizures in New York seized 3,765.9 kilograms of cocaine, 181.9 kilograms of heroin, 382.8 kilograms of marijuana, and 6.1 kilograms of methamphetamine. In addition, during 2002, the DEA, along with state and local authorities raided 26 clandestine laboratories.[13]

NEW YORK STATE OFFICE OF ALCOHOLISM AND SUBSTANCE ABUSE SERVICES

The **New York State Office of Alcoholism and Substance Abuse Services** (OASAS) is an umbrella organization that administers a large system of programs and services for substance abusers, including both alcohol and drug abusers. The organization directly operates 13 **Addiction Treatment Centers** (ATCs) which are located throughout the state. In addition, OASAS coordinates a network of over 1,200 community-based treatment providers and approximately 400 prevention providers. Each day, over 123,000 individuals receive treatment from OASAS-licensed treatment programs for addiction to alcohol and/or drugs. The majority of these individuals are in outpatient programs, although some are placed in residential settings.[14]

OASAS Services

OASAS administers a wide variety of prevention, intervention, and treatment programs that provide services to individuals with substance abuse problems. **Prevention programs** focus on at risk individuals and use strategies that prevent alcohol, tobacco, and substance abuse by both increasing and maintaining protective factors within the individual and the community and by decreasing the risk factors which affect the likelihood that an individual will become involved in substance abuse. Prevention strategies include education, life skills training, stress management, and support activities. **Intervention programs** focus on individuals who are already involved in substance abuse, and providing them with needed services such as assessment, intervention, placement, referral, and follow-up treatment.

There are a wide range of **treatment programs** offered by OASAS providers. **Crisis services** focus on individuals who are in some way incapacitated by their substance abuse. These services emphasize medically-supervised management and treatment of withdrawal and provide referrals to care and support programs to assist clients with physical problems that are associated with their substance abuse. Withdrawal service programs may be conducted on a residential or outpatient basis.

Outpatient treatment services are designed not only for individuals with substance abuse problems but also any family members who are significantly affected by another person's substance abuse. **Inpatient services** provide full-time intensive medically-supervised care, including both treatment and rehabilitation, for individuals who are addicted to alcohol or drugs. **Residential services** are geared to assist individuals who require a structured residential setting in which to participate in treatment or abstain from substance abuse. Clients are provided with peer group support and assistance in developing independent living skills.

Methadone treatment services focus on those individuals who are addicted to or dependent upon opiates (e.g., heroin, morphine) and include methadone in the range of provided treatment and services. Most methadone programs are outpatient programs, with patients coming in regularly for treatment. However, there are also a number of programs which provide methadone treatment in a residential setting; these programs generally last from one to six months. Finally, there are thirteen **ATCs** spread throughout the state which are operated by OASAS. To be admitted to an ATC, an individual must usually be at least eighteen years of age. ATCs will only admit patients under eighteen if they have written permission of a parent or guardian and undergo an evaluation by the admitting physician. The individual must be addicted to alcohol and primarily require treatment for alcoholism; s/he must not require detoxification or any other acute medical services. Finally, each ATC has a specific "catchment" area, and the individual must reside within the area to be admitted to the ATC.[15]

OASAS Services to the Criminal Justice System

Because alcohol and illegal drugs are involved in a large percentage of crimes, OASAS provides a variety of services to offenders within the criminal justice system. Approximately 70 percent of all juveniles placed in state commitment facilities have problems with drugs and/or alcohol. Because of this, OASAS and the **New York Office of Children and Family Services** (OCFS) implemented a Plan of Cooperation in 1996. Through this plan, community-based agencies licensed by OASAS provide treatment services at 24 OCFS facilities, serving approximately 400 juveniles each year. OASAS also licenses treatment services within jails and prisons to detainees and sentenced offenders.[16]

Approximately 43 percent of all individuals served by community treatment agencies licensed by OASAS also have some criminal justice status. Many are on parole or have been diverted from the criminal justice system into community-based treatment. Over 2,000 treatment places in the state are reserved specifically for these types of individuals.[17]

The **Drug Treatment Alternatives to Prison** (DTAP) program provides residential drug treatment for non-violent drug offenders from jurisdictions in New York City. Offenders are placed in DTAP as an alternative to incarceration in a state prison facility. Currently, approximately 400 beds in a number of licensed provider programs have been reserved for DTAP participants. A study of the Brooklyn DTAP program found that between 1990 and 1996, approximately $5.2 million in state and city corrections costs were saved by diverting felony drug offenders out of prison and into residential programs. DTAP offenders in this program had a re-arrest rate of 11 percent after one year. Non-DTAP offenders had a re-arrest rate of 26 percent. A three-year study of DTAP in several boroughs of New York City found that only 15 percent of participants were re-arrested; none for violent criminal offenses.[18]

NEW YORK CITY BUREAU OF ALCOHOLISM AND SUBSTANCE ABUSE SERVICES

The **New York City Bureau of Alcoholism and Substance Abuse Services (BASAS)**, a division of the **New York City Department of Health and Mental Hygiene**, was created in 1971. BASAS coordinates municipal and community-based services which provide prevention, treatment, and rehabilitation to individuals with substance abuse problems as well as to their families. BASAS works with OASAS to develop ongoing programs and services. OASAS directly funds substance abuse programs in New York City and licenses all treatment services. The Department provides funding for crisis services, outpatient clinics, and community residential programs which provide general services to the public as a whole and provide specialized services to specific client groups such as women, adolescents, older individuals, people with HIV, immigrants, and disabled individuals.

In 1999, there were a total of 164 licensed **treatment service providers** in New York City, operating 466 different programs. These include detoxification and crisis service programs, alcoholism outpatient clinics, drug outpatient services, methadone outpatient services, inpatient rehabilitation programs, and residential services. In addition, there are 100 **prevention service providers**, which operate a total of 1,137 program units. Prevention services are delivered in the workplace, the community, and in public and private schools. BASAS prevention and education activities include sponsoring training sessions for treatment providers and users, providing information about alcohol and drugs, and coordinating programs and events for the annual "April is Alcoholism and Substance Abuse Awareness Month" in New York City (which is actually a state-wide event). To increase community participation, each of the five boroughs of the city has a **Borough Council** which works with BASAS to identify specific community needs and planning priorities and to educate the public about alcohol and substance abuse and about the availability of treatment. Members of the public are encouraged to become involved with their local borough council.[19]

DRUG COURTS IN NEW YORK

During 2001, there were over 17,000 drug-related felony indictments in New York. One approach to breaking the cycle of drugs and crime is the concept of treatment-based drug courts. This approach, which was first developed in Florida in the late 1980s, quickly spread to other states, including New York. By January, 2003, there were 70 drug courts operating in New York with an additional 80 in the planning stages.[20]

The Brooklyn Treatment Court

The **Brooklyn Treatment Court** provides an alternative to incarceration for substance abusing defendants in Brooklyn who are charged with nonviolent felonies. A screening process carried out by the District Attorney's Office identifies eligible cases and refers them to the Treatment Court. Each defendant goes through an orientation and is assigned a case manager who assesses the defendant, determines possible treatment needs, and develops a treatment plan. The plan is based on issues such as the severity of the defendant's addiction, the defendant's criminal history, the severity of the charges against the defendant, and any ties the defendant has with the community. This plan is presented to the judge at the defendant's court appearance

Entry into the program is voluntary. Defendants plead guilty to the charges against them, with the understanding that if they comply with the treatment plan ordered by the court, the plea will be vacated and the court will dismiss the charges. If a defendant fails to complete the program for any reason, the original indictment is reinstated.

Participating dependents are required to appear before the court regularly to report on their progress and to undergo urine tests for drugs. They are also required to perform community service as a form of restitution to the community that was harmed by their addictions. A wide variety of social service providers provide on-site assistance to defendants. The city Department of Health offers health screening, education, and testing for HIV, sexually-transmitted diseases, tuberculous, and pregnancy. A nurse practitioner provided by the New York University School of Nursing provides primary health care at an on-site clinic. At this clinic, defendants have access to physical examinations, mental health care, gynecological examinations, and nutritional counseling. Vocational and rehabilitation counselors provide defendants with assistance in finding employment. The state Human Resources Administration is on hand to offer help with Medicaid, welfare, food stamps, and other entitlements.[21]

Defendants progress through the program based on performance. Rewards for positive performance range from applause from the court to a reduction in the frequency of mandated court appearances. Treatment failures may be punished with writing assignments, more frequent court appearances, or even a period of time in jail.[22]

The Ithaca Drug Treatment Court

The **Ithaca Drug Treatment Court** (IDTC) was organized in 1998 to focus on defendants with substance abuse problems. The court focuses on identifying these defendants as early in the judicial process as possible and making sure they receive the necessary treatment. The program is voluntary and is geared for individuals who are addicted to drugs or alcohol and who are facing criminal charges. The program includes judicial supervision, probation case management, intensive substance abuse treatment, regular drug testing, life skills, and job training. Defendants who successfully complete the treatment and rehabilitation programs receive educational and vocational training and employment assistance, and receive a reduction in charges or mitigation of sentence.[23]

The Drug Court program, which generally lasts between eight and sixteen months, is broken up into four phases. Participants successfully completing all phases receive a conditional discharge from the court and are monitored for one additional year.

The **stabilization phase** is essentially an orientation and is mandatory for all potential IDTC candidates. Before admission into the IDTC program, potential candidates attend a Drug Court session. At the end of the session, they come before the judge, who reviews the program and answers any questions they may have. Defendants who are interested in the program are released to the supervision of the Drug Court Probation Officer. Potential candidates meet with the assigned probation officer daily, appear weekly in Drug Court, undergo random drug screenings, and go through a substance abuse evaluation. After several weeks, when the evaluation is completed, the defendant is given the option of formally entering the Drug Court program. All criminal charges against the defendant must be resolved by a guilty plea through negotiations between the prosecutor and defense counsel. The defendant enters the plea of guilty and signs a formal IDTC contract.

Phase I of the Drug Court program generally lasts between twelve and twenty weeks. During this stage participants report as often as five times a week to their probation officer; eventually this is decreased to three times per week. The participants undergo drug and alcohol screenings, must appear weekly in Drug Court, attend at least three twelve-step meetings each week, undergo physical and dental examinations, complete an educational and employment assessment, and keep a 10:00 p.m. curfew. Participants also undergo any recommended drug and/or alcohol treatment and counseling.

Participants progress to **Phase II** of the program after meeting all requirements of Phase I. Phase II generally lasts between 12 and 14 weeks. During this state of the program, participants meet once or twice a week with probation officers, are required to appear in Drug Court on a weekly basis, and undergo frequent drug screenings. They also participate in group and individual counseling, continue mandatory (verified) attendance at twelve-step meetings, and, if they are not currently employed, participate in educational classes or job skill training programs.

Finally, **Phase III** generally runs between 12 and 24 weeks. During this stage of the program, participants meet weekly with probation officers, as well as undergoing random and unannounced home visits. They appear in Drug Court every three weeks, undergo twice-weekly drug screens, and continue mandatory attendance at twelve-step meetings. They may also participate in other treatment as required. Phase III participants also work with a Family Services Coordinator to develop and complete a community service project; this may be done alone or with other Phase III participants. This project, known as a "Giving Back to the Community" service project, is designed to help participants understand and take responsibility for their actions and assist them in repairing the harm they have caused to individual victims and to the community as a whole. To graduate from the program, participants must complete all three phases, remain drug and alcohol free for a minimum of eight months, and either obtain meaningful employment or be engaged in an educational program. The final decision as to a participant's readiness for graduation is made by the Drug Court Judge.

Supervision of all participants is the responsibility of probation officers who are assigned to the drug court program. Supervision involves regular meetings between participants and probation officers; frequent urine testing; contact between probation officers and other individuals such as treatment counselors, family members, and friends; home visits by probation officers; providing participants with needed referrals; and the preparation of court-required progress reports regarding participants' compliance with program and treatment guidelines and requirements.

If participants fail to comply with any of the program requirements, the court may impose sanctions. Possible sanctions include verbal reprimands, essay assignments, increasing the number of required appearances in court, increasing the number of weekly meetings with the probation officer, community service, or jail time. The program also provides incentives for participants who are attempting to stop their use of alcohol or drugs. These may include applause and/or verbal praise, a handshake from the judge, a decrease in the number of required meetings with the probation officer, a decrease in treatment requirements, and certificates of achievement. For example, after a participant has gone through his or her first week of testing clean for alcohol or drugs, he or she will probably be praised by the judge and may receive applause from other participants. All participants who have reached 100 continuous drug-free days participate in a special ceremony and receive a certificate. Participants moving up to a new phase will receive applause from the court and a handshake from the judge.

Participants may leave the program either through **discharge** or **graduation**. Discharge terminations usually occur when a participant refuses to undergo recommended treatment. If a participant is terminated, a new pre-sentence investigation report is prepared and the offender is sentenced for the original indictment. Offenders who complete the program successfully may go through a formal graduation ceremony, to which their families are also invited. The participants will also receive whatever benefits that were negotiated prior to their entry into the program. Participants generally receive a one-year conditional discharge; during this time they submit to random drug screenings and continue mandatory attendance at twelve-step meetings.[24]

NOTES

1. New York State Division of Criminal Justice Services – Criminal Justice Statistics for New York State (http://criminaljustice.state.ny.us/crimnet/data.htm)
2. Office of National Drug Control Policy (2003). *State of New York: Profile of Drug Indicators*. (http://www.whitehousedrugpolicy.gov/statelocal/ny/ny.pdf)
3. *Ibid*
4. *Ibid*
5. DEA Fact Sheet: *New York* (http://www.usdoj.gov/dea/pubs/states/newyork.html)
6. *Ibid*
7. Office of National Drug Control Policy (2003), *op cit.*
8. *Ibid*
9. DEA Fact Sheet: *New York, op cit.*
10. Office of National Drug Control Policy (2003), *op cit.*
11. *Ibid*
12. DEA Fact Sheet: *New York, op cit.*
13. *Ibid*
14. New York State Office of Alcoholism and Substance Abuse Services home page (http://www.oasas.state.ny.us/index.html)
15. *Ibid*

16. *Ibid*
17. New York State Office of Alcoholism and Substance Abuse Services home page, *op cit*.
18. *Ibid*
19. Bureau of Alcoholism & Substance Abuse Services (http://www.nyc.gov/html/doh/html/bureau/basas.html)
20. Office of National Drug Control Policy (2003), *op cit.*
21. Brooklyn Treatment Court (http://www.courtinnovation.org/demo_02btc.html)
22. *Ibid*
23. Ithaca Drug Treatment Court (http://www.courts.state.ny.us/Ithaca/CITY/DrugCourtWebsiteInfo.html)
24. *Ibid*

APPENDIX

WEB SITES OF INTEREST

There is a large amount of information on New York and the New York criminal justice system available on the worldwide web. Below is a selection of web sites that may be of interest to students.

GENERAL NEW YORK WEB SITES

http://www.state.ny.us/index.html
   This is the official home page for the State of New York. It includes information on New York State government, economy, education, health care, crime and much more. Links to a variety of state government agencies may be found on this site.

http://home.nyc.gov/
   New York City also has a home page with information on city services, agencies, resources, attractions, and events.

http://criminaljustice.state.ny.us/dcjs1.htm
   The New York State Division of Criminal Justice Services provides links to a variety of topics including criminal justice resources, data on crime in New York, and information on missing and exploited children.

http://www.nysl.nysed.gov/ils/
   This is the site of the New York State Government Information Locator Service, hosted by the New York State Library. It provides links to many state and local government agencies.

http://www.cvb.state.ny.us/
   This is the home page of the New York State Crime Victims Board.

http://criminaljustice.state.ny.us/missing/
   This is the home page of the New York State Missing and Exploited Children Clearinghouse.

LEGAL INFORMATION

http://www.findlaw.com/11stategov/ny/laws.html
   The New York State Constitution and all state statutes are available on the worldwide web. Statutes of interest include the Penal Law, Criminal Procedure Law, Correction Law, Judiciary Law, and Family Court Law.

http://www.alllaw.com/state_resources/new_york/
>   This page provides links to various state government web sites, as well as law schools, state bars, and other legal resources.

INFORMATION ON POLICE IN NEW YORK

http://www.troopers.state.ny.us/
>   The home page of the New York State Police Department.

http://www.nyc.gov/html/nypd/home.html
>   The home page of the New York City Police Department.

www.erie.gov/sheriff/index.asp
>   The home page of the Erie County Sheriff's Department.

http://www.co.nassau.ny.us/police/index.html
>   The home page for the Nassau County Police Department.

INFORMATION ON THE COURTS IN NEW YORK

http://www.courts.state.ny.us/home.htm
>   The New York State Courts' web site.

http://www6.law.com/ny/guide/
>   The New York Courts and Law Guide web page contains over 100 links to pages intended to explain the courts and laws of New York to non-lawyers.

http://www.nysba.org/
>   The home page of the New York State Bar Association.

http://www.scjc.state.ny.us/
>   The home page of the New York State Commission on Judicial Conduct.

INFORMATION ON CORRECTIONS IN NEW YORK

http://www.docs.state.ny.us/
>   The New York State Department of Correctional Services home page.

http://www.corcraft.org/index.html
>   The Corcraft home page.

http://www.scoc.state.ny.us/
>   The New York State Commission of Corrections home page.

http://www.ci.nyc.ny.us/html/doc/home.html
>   The New York City Department of Corrections home page.

http://parole.state.ny.us/index.html
>   The New York State Division of Parole home page.

http://dpca.state.ny.us/
>   New York State Division of Probation and Correctional Alternatives home page.

http://www.nyc.gov/html/prob/home.html
>   The home page of the New York City Department of Probation.

http://www.geocities.com/MotorCity/Downs/3548/main.html
>   This web site provides a large amount of information on correctional facilities in New York.

http://www.correctionhistory.org/
>   The New York Correction History Society home page.

INFORMATION ON JUVENILE JUSTICE IN NEW YORK

http://www.ci.nyc.ny.us/html/djj/home.html
>   The home page of the New York City Department of Juvenile Justice.

http://www.ocfs.state.ny.us/main/
>   The New York State Office of Children and Family Services home page.

INFORMATION ON DRUGS IN NEW YORK

http://www.whitehousedrugpolicy.gov/statelocal/ny/
>   The U.S. Office of National Drug Control Policy – New York web site.

http://www.nyc.gov/html/doh/html/bureau/basas.htm
>   The New York City Bureau of Alcoholism and Substance Abuse Services

http://web2k.oasas.state.ny.us/oasas/home.cfm
>   New York State Office of Alcoholism and Substance Abuse Services.

http://www.usdoj.gov/dea/pubs/states/newyork.html
>   DEA fact sheet on drugs in New York.